Lamentations

INTERPRETATION
A Bible Commentary for Teaching and Preaching

INTERPRETATION

A BIBLE COMMENTARY FOR TEACHING AND PREACHING

James Luther Mays, *Series Editor*
Patrick D. Miller, *Old Testament Editor*
Paul J. Achtemeier, *New Testament Editor*

F. W. DOBBS-ALLSOPP

Lamentations

A Bible Commentary
for Teaching and Preaching

John Knox Press
LOUISVILLE

Library of Congress Cataloging-in-Publication Data

Dobbs-Allsopp, F. W., 1962–
    Lamentations / F. W. Dobbs-Allsopp.
        p.   cm. — (Interpretation, a Bible commentary for teaching and preaching)
    Includes bibliographical references.
    ISBN 0-8042-3141-9 (alk. paper)
     1. Bible. O.T. Lamentations—Commentaries.   I. Title.   II. Series.

    BS1535.53 .D63 2002
    224'.307—dc21   2001038294

© copyright F. W. Dobbs-Allsopp 2002
This book is printed on acid-free paper that meets the American National Standards Institute Z39.48 standard. ♾
02 03 04 05 06 07 08 09 10 11— 10 9 8 7 6 5 4 3 2 1
Printed in the United States of America
John Knox Press
Louisville, Kentucky

For
Ginger and Ernest
and
Nan and Charlie

SERIES PREFACE

This series of commentaries offers an interpretation of the books of the Bible. It is designed to meet the need of students, teachers, ministers, and priests for a contemporary expository commentary. These volumes will not replace the historical critical commentary or homiletical aids to preaching. The purpose of this series is rather to provide a third kind of resource, a commentary which presents the integrated result of historical and theological work with the biblical text.

An interpretation in the full sense of the term involves a text, an interpreter, and someone for whom the interpretation is made. Here, the text is what stands written in the Bible in its full identity as literature from the time of "the prophets and apostles," the literature which is read to inform, inspire, and guide the life of faith. The interpreters are scholars who seek to create an interpretation which is both faithful to the text and useful to the church. The series is written for those who teach, preach, and study the Bible in the community of faith.

The comment generally takes the form of expository essays. It is planned and written in the light of the needs and questions which arise in the use of the Bible as Holy Scripture. The insights and results of contemporary scholarly research are used for the sake of the exposition. The commentators write as exegetes and theologians. The task which they undertake is both to deal with what the texts say and to discern their meaning for faith and life. The exposition is the unified work of one interpreter.

The text on which the comment is based is the Revised Standard Version of the Bible and, since its appearance, the New Revised Standard Version. The general availability of these translations makes the printing of a text in the commentary unnecessary. The commentators have also had other current versions in view as they worked and refer to their readings where it is helpful. The text is divided into sections appropriate to the particular book; comment deals with passages as a whole, rather than proceeding word by word, or verse by verse.

Writers have planned their volumes in light of the requirements set by the exposition of the book assigned to them. Biblical books differ in character, content, and arrangement. They also differ in the way they have been and are used in the liturgy, thought, and devotion of the church. The distinctiveness and use of particular books have been taken into account in decisions about the approach, emphasis, and use of space in the commentaries. The goal has been to allow writers to develop the format which provides for the best presentation of their interpretation.

The result, writers and editors hope, is a commentary which both explains and applies, an interpretation which deals with both the meaning and the significance of biblical texts. Each commentary reflects, of course, the writer's own approach and perception of the church and world. It could and should not be otherwise. Every interpretation of any kind is individual in that sense; it is one reading of the text. But all who work at the interpretation of Scripture in the church need the help and stimulation of a colleague's reading and understanding of the text. If these volumes serve and encourage interpretation in that way, their preparation and publication will realize their purpose.

The Editors

PREFACE

The intended audience for the present commentary, as with the other volumes in this series, is preachers and teachers in the church. Yet I write as well with the knowledge (and hope) of being overheard by a Jewish audience and by the public more generally. The Old Testament/Torah is a place of common ground for Jew and Christian, a place to share conversations, to be confronted and claimed by the face of an Other. To be sure, there are substantive differences that distinguish Christianity and Judaism, and I have no doubt that my own Christian stance unavoidably (and happily!) shapes my readings of biblical texts. Still, I have benefited too much from the keen insights of Jewish colleagues and from the love of Jewish friends to write about the Old Testament consciously in an exclusionary or narrowly christocentric way. I share with others the conviction that we Christians come to these texts only belatedly and that we must remain ever mindful of Jewish claims on and construals of our shared scriptural heritage. My ardent hope is that both Jew and Christian will find in this volume much that is of interest confessionally, emotionally, and intellectually.

Similarly, I believe that we in the church today can no longer afford to ignore the larger context in which our ecclesial discourse is always set. The church must engage and interact with the larger world of which it is a part if it is to survive the twenty-first century; our message must implicate itself in the larger arena of public discourse. Consequently, my own interpretive work (and this volume in particular) draws consciously and routinely on the best of critical thinking wherever it may be found, and it seeks to achieve in tone and pitch a discourse open to and engaged with the extraecclesial world. I am convinced that Old Testament literature and the study of that literature has much to contribute to the public discussion of a whole host of issues, including most crucially matters that bear on our notions of human flourishing and well-being.

The present commentary builds on critical work, the sources for which it has not always been possible to credit satisfactorily and sufficiently, given the constraints imposed by the series' guidelines. The list of works cited will provide interested readers with some of the key sources for the kinds of discourse enacted here, while themselves pointing to still other sources. My own ongoing critical work on Lamentations endeavors to fill in whatever gaps still remain.

Many have helped to bring this volume to fruition. It is a pleasure for me to thank them and to acknowledge their contributions here. Above all I am indebted to Patrick Miller and James Mays for inviting me to contribute this volume to the *Interpretation* series in the first place and then for having the patience to wait out my own struggle with authorial voice and with finding an appropriate level of discourse for this work. I also want to thank Jeff Rogers, formerly of Furman University, who encouraged a project that was the original germ for the current volume. One of the late Delbert R. Hillers's chief scholarly bequests to me was the book of Lamentations. Though I am aware that he would not always have arrived at the same readings that I do, nevertheless all of the questions that motivate and inform my readings of these poems ultimately find their origin in his work and thought. This volume, as with all my work, I undertake in homage to a beloved teacher and mentor and a cherished friend, whose passing I mourn a little every day. I have been fortunate to have had many inspiring and energizing conversation partners over the last decade or so, including Adele Berlin, Jill Campbell, Ellen Davis, Ed Greenstein, Lanny Hammer, Lee Humphreys, Avi Hurvitz, Stacy Johnson, Tod Linafelt, Nancy Lee, Carol Newsom, Kathleen O'Connor, Shalom Paul, Kathy Rowe, Robin Salters, Leong Seow, Wentzel van Huyssteen, Neal Walls, Sara Winter, and my teachers and colleagues at Johns Hopkins, Yale, Princeton Seminary, the Hebrew Bible seminar of Columbia University, and the W. F. Albright Institute in Jerusalem. Whatever is good and compelling in this volume emerges out of the work and creative input of these folks. Special thanks go to Philip Bogden and Phil Ihinger for JFMs and for keeping me sane during our Yale years. I heartily recognize the institutional support I received from Yale University and Princeton Theological Seminary while working on this manuscript. I also acknowledge the indispensable financial support of a National Endowment for the Humanities Fellowship and a Special Junior Faculty Leave from Yale University that made possible a sabbatical-year leave (1997–98) at the W. F. Albright Institute in Jerusalem, during which much of the critical and philological work for this volume was completed. I also thank my students at Princeton Seminary for providing me with the opportunity to present and to fine-tune many of the readings that I offer here, with special thanks to Myesha Hamm, Chris Leyda, and Christine Thomas for their acute interest in the project and their help throughout on many different matters.

Leslie, Will, and Henry provide the only context out of which I know how to work and live. Their love and support, too often taken for granted, sustain me always. I am privileged and eternally grateful to be able to travel through this life in their company. Finally, I dedicate this volume to my mother, Ginger Smith, and her husband, Ernest Smith, and to Nan and Charlie Dobbs, my in-laws, in gratitude for the support and love they always have shown me, Leslie, and the boys. These four embody and personify for me the chief audience for which I am here writing, as they are all intelligent, faithful, and devout church people. It is my hope that at last they may be able to glimpse and appreciate some of what I have been doing for these many years.

Lamentations is perhaps known best from its use in the month of Ab services that commemorate Jewish national calamities, including the destruction of the First and Second Temples and the destruction of Jerusalem by the Romans. My own post-Holocaust-inspired reading of these poems is meant to honor and to extend this tradition. But in doing so, especially in my cognizance of these poems' origin in the soil of Palestine, I cannot help but recall still another catastrophe, *Al-Nakba,* the Palestinian Catastrophe of 1948 in which 750,000 Palestinians lost their land and were displaced, a tragic chain of events that continues to rend the Holy Land violently even to this day, some fifty years later. Indeed, today violence between Israelis and Palestinians has reached a level not seen in many years and the hope once inspired by the Oslo Peace accords has all but vanished. It is the echoes of the hurting voices of contemporary Palestinians and Israelis that I hear most prominently and most poignantly as I read these poems. And thus it is my fervent prayer that as these poems are sung and read and prayed today on the soil of their origin, both Israeli and Palestinian may each see in the other an "Other" who commands help and compassion and who ultimately bears the "trace" of YHWH and Allah. In the words of the psalmist, I "pray for the peace of Jerusalem" (Ps. 122:6).

But it would seem that violence, useless suffering, and human inanity know no chronological or geographical borders. On September 11, 2001 (after these pages were already in proof), terrorists in a coordinated attack hijacked four commercial jets and crashed one each into both of the twin towers of the World Trade Center complex in New York City and into one side of the Pentagon in Washington, D.C. The fourth jet crashed in a field in western Pennsylvania, presumably as a result of the efforts of passengers and crew to retake control of the airplane from the hijackers, and thus preventing yet another target from being reached. All passengers and crew on each of the planes were killed.

Hundreds more died in the crash at the Pentagon. And thousands are still missing and presumed dead as a result of the crashes at the World Trade Center—both towers, each more than a hundred stories high, eventually collapsed. The twin pinnacles that once crowned the New York City skyline exist no longer.

> How lonely sits the city
> that once was full of people!

These lines from the opening of Lamentations were the first words read out from one New Jersey pulpit in a service of prayer and mourning on the day after these calamitous events. Sadly, the work of grief that these poems accomplished originally some two thousand years ago still requires attending to. The poet's final plaint before God is no less germane and in need of voicing:

> Why have you forgotten us completely?
> Why have you forsaken us these many days?
> Restore us to yourself, O LORD, that we may be restored;
> renew our days as of old—
> unless you have utterly rejected us,
> and are angry with us beyond measure.

F. W. D.-A.

CONTENTS

INTERPRETATION

Introduction

The destruction of Jerusalem in 586 B.C.E. marks the great watershed in Judean history, and students of the Bible have long recognized the extraordinary impact of this single event upon biblical literature, as survivors sought to counteract the shattered paradigms of old (city, king, temple, land, covenant) imaginatively and rhetorically through an outpouring of literary generativity. Though more complex and multivocal than usually assumed, most of the biblical literature surviving from this period bears the peculiar ideological-theological stamp of the Diaspora communities. So profound, in fact, was the exile experience for the Judaism emerging from this period and for the texts it generated that memories of the population that remained in Palestine and their struggles for survival were all but forgotten. But the continuing presence of people in the land of Palestine throughout the period of Babylonian rule has been made visible once again through archaeological excavations and surveys. While it is clear that Jerusalem and some of the fortress towns and major cities immediately to its south suffered tremendous damage at the hands of the Babylonians—destruction layers exist at Tell el-Duweir (Lachish), Tell Beit Mirsim, and Tel Batash—the rest of the region witnesses a remarkable degree of continuity in material culture down through the Persian period. For example, destruction strata clearly attributable to the Babylonian invasions are lacking in the northern regions (Samaria and Galilee), Transjordan, Philistia, and the Negeb. Cities just north of Jerusalem, such as Gibeon, Mizpah, and Bethel, also appear to have escaped unscathed. And in the south all was not destroyed either, as surveys reveal the ongoing presence of small provincial towns and villages. Even in Jerusalem itself the material remains from burial caves, such as those at Ketef Hinnom and near the Sultan's Pool, support the assumption, also inferred from the biblical text (e.g., Jer. 40:7–12; 41:4–5), that some form of existence continued even among the city's ruins. In short, the notion of Judah's total destruction and depopulation, a notion projected to greater and to lesser degrees in much of the Diaspora literature from this period and later, can finally be laid to rest.

But if the facticity of the Palestinian community's continued existence after 586 is more obvious today than in previous generations, in no way should this lead us to minimize the otherwise catastrophic

1

impact of these events, nor to misread the direness of that community's lived reality. Judah lost its national independence and was forced to live under foreign domination and persecution. Its governing and principal sociocultural institutions were forever changed. Many people died, either in the fighting or through starvation associated with the siege and its aftermath. The cumulative effect of the successive deportations of 598/97, 586, and 582 was severe, even if they were not as all-encompassing or pernicious as earlier Assyrian deportations. The leading citizenry and much of the skilled labor force were cruelly siphoned off the land—not to mention the permanent psychological scars that exile left on those exiled and their loved ones left behind. The economy of Judah was likely reduced to a purely agricultural base, leaving a predominantly rural community to get by as best they could.

And yet, however dark life must have been for the post-destruction community of Jerusalem and its surrounding environs, it is a fitting tribute to this community's resilience that the one literary work that can be attributed to its members most securely, the sequence of five poems collected in the biblical book of Lamentations, is a most profoundly life-embracing work. If Jews historically have been more attentive than Christians as readers of Lamentations, both Jews and Christians alike typically have muted and dulled the unique timbre of the Palestinian voice in these remarkable poems, persistently filtering their readings through the more prominent lenses of the Diaspora literature of the Bible. A chief intent of this commentary is to restore, as it were, something of the distinctiveness of the Palestinian voice found in these poems.

Lamentations may well be the most remarkable and compelling testament to the human spirit's will to live in all of the Old Testament. I hasten to add that these poems constitute some of the Bible's most violent and brutal pieces of writing as well, as they emerge, both literally and figuratively, out of the ashes and ruins of Jerusalem and are filled with horrifyingly dark and grizzly images of raw human pain and suffering. The commentary will endeavor to apprehend and confront the horror and pain of human suffering presented in these poems as a reality in itself, without recourse to romantic or nostalgic notions of the purposiveness or redemptive power of suffering. Readers of these poems who have just witnessed the close of the twentieth century cannot help but read and experience them in light of the Holocaust and the literature of atrocity that our singularly evil epoch in human history has generated. Indeed, Lamentations shares with this body of literature the need to witness to the utterly harmful and irredeemable nature of human suffering. However, Lamentations ultimately arises out of very different historical circumstances. The Holocaust in every way was unique. In it, reality outstripped (and continues to do so to this day)

2

even the most demented and vile contortions of the human mind, and thus the overriding goal of much Holocaust literature is to make such an unsayable and unthinkable reality possible for the imagination. By contrast, the Babylonian destruction of Jerusalem, though singularly important in the history of ancient Judah, was by no means unparalleled in antiquity. Ancient Jerusalemites would likely have had firsthand experience of war and its bloody consequences, and if not, an acquaintance with war would have been mediated through the memories of generations past. This is not meant to devalue in any way the horror and terror that surely accompanied these events, nor to deny that every experience of radical suffering, no matter its cause, is intolerable, but rather to suggest that Lamentations' response to the horrific events that motivated it is shaped as much by familiarity as by horror. That is, Lamentations stubbornly holds onto life and manifests a will to live that comes from knowledge of (or the belief in) tomorrow. Death and suffering are found throughout these remarkable poems, but they stand, for the most part, as "memory's beginning," not life's end (L. Langer, *Holocaust*, 28–29). To be sure, the reader will not find in them, despite many contentions to the contrary, any straightforward and unadulterated statements of hope. Rather, their will to live arises in a more nuanced fashion, almost under the surface of the poetry, through innuendo and implication, in the poems' lyric play, in tone, and in the poet's vibrant intelligence that animates and courses through every line. Literature has always provided people with the metaphors and imagery necessary to enable them to confront and understand the vicissitudes of history, and to help muster the wherewithal to transfigure and survive them. Lamentations stands squarely within such a literary tradition. If these poems do not (because they cannot) imagine, in specific hues and colors, the substance of the tomorrow they want to remember, they do much of the foundation-razing (apropos of their overarching literary genre) necessary to ensure it. The violence and brutality of these lyrics stand as a monument condemning the reality of human suffering. But as they turn over and sift through Judah's literary and religious traditions in order to remember and bend and shape the past so that it serves the poems' present and the community's future, first by articulating the feelings of horror and grief and outrage, and then by measuring them, as they frankly and brutally probe and confront God and God's actions, silence, and absence, and as they seek to realize a new kind of community, these lyrics fashion a linguistic balm capable of salving—if not removing—the scars and wounds of the suffering they so painfully figure. In doing so they create the capacity to be otherwise and the possibility for survival, for remembering the tomorrow that Zion so tragically neglected (1:9a).

3

INTERPRETATION

Date, Place of Composition, and Authorship

Lamentations, like other biblical texts, survives in a mostly decontextualized state. We have no external information about important issues such as date of composition, authorship, general provenance, or setting and nature of performance. So, if we are to know anything at all about these and other issues, it must be deduced almost solely out of the internal evidence of the text itself—aided of course by the kinds of questions posed. The indefinite nature of such deductions, therefore, needs to be stressed at the outset. Nonetheless, the centrality of this kind of information to the interpretive process demands that we articulate just what we think we know about these matters.

These poems probably emerge from a time relatively soon after the 586 B.C.E. destruction of Jerusalem and are likely the product of the community of Judeans who remained in the land. The earliest written traditions about Lamentations (Septuagint, Vulgate, Mishnah, Targums) associate the poems collected here with this historical event. They were believed to commemorate and lament the Babylonian destruction of Jerusalem. Beginning with the Middle Ages, scholars routinely and consistently, though not universally, have continued to read these poems against the general backdrop of the events of 586. The internal evidence provided by the poems themselves is certainly compatible with such a dating and general setting, though there is not much, if anything, in them that requires such a dating. Perhaps the strongest evidence for a sixth-century date is the language of the poems itself, which fits the exilic period, between 586 and 520 B.C.E. (for details, see Dobbs-Allsopp, "Linguistic Evidence").

The question of the poems' original provenance is similarly hard to pin down, the poet's lyric mode of discourse offering little of a concrete nature to go on. Negatively, the poems, individually and collectively, show no "special interest in the plight of exiles in Babylon or Egypt" (Hillers, 15); nor do they exhibit any obvious signs of an official royal or priestly mindset. On the contrary, they seem to evince a primary concern with the fate of the community remaining in Palestine after the destruction, and their general orientation and perspective appears to be distinctly communitarian in nature. Therefore, since we can no longer assume that the Babylonian upheavals left Judah completely depopulated, in light of the basic tenor of the text itself and "in the absence of any strong evidence to the contrary," I presume, with Delbert R. Hillers, that the poems were composed originally in Palestine (15).

Jeremiah was traditionally thought to be the author of Lamentations. This tradition dates back at least to the Septuagint ("When Israel had gone into captivity and Jerusalem had been laid waste, Jeremiah sat

4

weeping and sang this lament over Jerusalem and said . . ."), and is reflected as well in the Vulgate, Targums, Peshitta, and Babylonian Talmud. However, there is no hard evidence to tie the poems in Lamentations to Jeremiah. The strongest evidence for Jeremianic authorship, the sometimes similar phraseology exhibited between Lamentations and the book of Jeremiah, is best explained as resulting from the fact that the two compositions originated in the same general historical period, and thus likely reflect the same dialect of Biblical Hebrew. Moreover, the attribution of Jeremianic authorship itself most likely rests on the ancient custom of attributing works to well-known personages. Jeremiah lived at the right time and was thought to have composed laments (2 Chron. 35:25). A similar practice is witnessed elsewhere in the Bible in the attribution of a large number of psalms to David, and the books of Proverbs and the Song of Songs to Solomon, for example.

Finally, there is also not much in the way of evidence to conclude whether these poems are the work of more than one author. Those who believe in multiple authors also typically either date various poems to different periods, and/or classify poems to different form-critical categories. Given the coherent linguistic profile presented by these poems, date can no longer provide a supportable basis for the suppositions of multiple authorship. The same holds true for the form-critical analysis. Even supposing the validity of the form-critical analysis, there is no reason to assume that a change in form or genre necessitates a change in author. Neither can Iain Provan's nihilistic position—he refuses to take a stand because of the lack of data (15–17)—be embraced. And if there is no clear evidence of multiple authorship, why should one not assume that the poems were written by one poet? Moreover, the widely observed unity of form and point of view, rhythmic dominance of the qinah meter, and general resemblance in linguistic detail throughout the sequence are broadly suggestive of the work of a single author. In the course of this commentary additional arguments are added to these preliminary perceptions of unity, not the least of which is that the sequence of poems may be read as an intelligible whole. There is no reason (either within the poems themselves or within the scholarly discussions about these poems) to suppose that more than one author is responsible for them. Hence I refer to "the poet" throughout. However, in the end, it makes little difference whether one posits a single author or an intelligent editor.

Literary Features

Lamentations is a literary artifact and demands to be read accordingly. Indeed, whatever other agenda one brings to these poems, they must first and foremost be encountered as poems. To this end, questions of a literary nature are posed throughout the commentary. Lamentations' genre and lyrical medium are treated initially and in some detail as a means of orienting contemporary readers to these ancient poems and providing an initial context within which they can be read profitably. An appreciation of Lamentations' lyricism is the key to the structure and dynamics of the individual poems, to the way in which the sequence as a whole coheres and interacts, and even to how the poet articulates theological interests. S. R. Driver eloquently captures the quintessential literariness, and even lyricism, that animates Lamentations when he writes:

> Exquisite as is the pathos which breathes in the poetry of these dirges, they are thus, it appears, constructed with conscious art: they are not the unstudied effusions of natural emotion, they are carefully elaborated poems, in which no aspect of the common grief is unremembered, and in which every trait which might stir a chord of sorrow or regret is brought together, for the purpose of completing the picture of woe. (459)

In what follows, I aim to lay bare something of these poems' "conscious art" and their "carefully elaborated" nature, both as an end in itself and as a means to a greater appreciation of their historical and theological value. And by foregrounding the literary in my analysis, I also mean to assert the transformative capacity of literature, and of poetry in particular. Acts of writing, though ultimately the work of the imagination, have weight and material consequence precisely because they are "imagined within the gravitational pull of the actual," and therefore can hold their own and "balance out against the historical situation" (Heaney, 3–4). Lamentations realizes this capacity in spectacular fashion. Its frequently brutal and black lyrics exhibit such "emotional weight" and "imaginative gravity" that they outstrip the conditions of suffering and pain even as they are describing them. Thus, however momentarily, they succeed in transfiguring these conditions, affirming, in the words of Seamus Heaney, "that poetry is human existence come to life" (cf. 115, 159).

Genre

Knowledge of the relevant generic conventions used in a given literary text is crucial for any act of interpretation. As Alastair Fowler observes, "in literature there is no creation *ex nihilo*" (156). Literary works always draw on previously known works, genres, and literary conventions of one kind or another. It could not be otherwise. Literary communication is impossible without some kind of conventional overlap. The literary interpreter is obliged ethically to honor the material-

6

ity of a past author's product. Thus part of the interpretive project involves being informed in as much detail as possible about a literary work's governing generic conventions. This move pays a handsome aesthetic dividend as well. Awareness of a work's genre typically leads to a more informed, satisfying, and enriched reading experience. Certainly meaning can be extracted from good literary works despite ignorance of their governing generic conventions; however, the more informed the reader, the richer the reading experience.

Lamentations draws on a variety of literary genres, conventions, and traditions. The most important is the city-lament genre (cf. Dobbs-Allsopp, *Weep*), which has greatly influenced the overarching trajectory of the sequence as a whole, as well as many of the individual poems' prominent features, themes, and motifs. The city-lament genre is best known from ancient Mesopotamia, where it undoubtedly originated. It consists of five classic compositions ("Lamentation over the Destruction of Ur," "Lamentation over the Destruction of Sumer and Ur," "Nippur Lament," "Eridu Lament," and "Uruk Lament"), which lament the destruction of Sumer at the end of the Ur III period and more local calamities in the following early Isin period, and their liturgical descendants (*balags* and *eršemmas*) that were employed through the Seleucid period. The five classic compositions depict the destruction of particular cities and their most important shrines. The destruction, brought about as a result of the capricious decision of the divine assembly and the subsequent abandonment of the city by its chief gods, is typically carried out by the chief god Enlil through the agency of an attacking enemy, whose onslaught is sometimes represented mythopoetically as a horrendous storm. The city's chief goddess is usually the other major actor in these poems. She is portrayed as challenging the assembly's decision and then bewailing the destruction of the city. It is generally assumed that these compositions were performed as a part of the cultic ceremonies in which the foundations of the old sanctuaries were razed, just prior to the initiation of any restoration work. The laments were offered, at least in part, to the patron deities in order to appease their anger over the destruction of their temples and in order to ward off future catastrophes. Consequently, the classic city laments typically close by celebrating the return of the gods and depicting the restoration of the city and temples.

The following brief quotations from the "Lamentation over the Destruction of Ur" may serve to illustrate the general style and feel of these laments (quotations are from *ANET*, 455–63). The first poem, in highly repetitive fashion, narrates the abandonment of Sumer by the various gods:

7

> The lord of all the lands has abandoned (his stable),
>   his sheepfold (has been delivered) to the wind;
> Enlil has abandoned . . . Nippur, his sheepfold (has been delivered)
> to the wind.

Next a lament is raised over the city:

> O City, a bitter lament set up as thy lament;
> Thy lament which is bitter—O city, set up thy lament.
> His righteous city which has been destroyed—bitter is its lament.
> His Ur which has been destroyed—bitter is its lament. . . .

In the third poem, Ningal, the wife of the moon-god Nanna and city goddess of Ur, moved by Ur's plight, "herself utters softly the wail of the smitten house":

> . . . Although, because in my land there was bitter [distress],
> I, like a cow for (its) calf, trudge the earth,
> My land was not delivered of fear
> Although, because in my city there was bitter [distress],
> I, like a bird of heaven, flap (my) wings,
> (And) to my city I fly,
> My city on its foundation verily was destroyed;
> Ur where it lay verily perishes. . . .

The governing divine assembly, led by the high god Enlil, decides on destruction despite Ningal's protestations:

> The utter destruction of Ur verily they directed;
> That its people be killed, as its fate verily they decreed.

And then Enlil himself invites in the devastating storm, the storm ordered "in hate, the storm which wears away the land." After a long rehearsal of the destruction, in which walls are breached, gates torn down, and dead bodies piled in the streets, and another prolonged lament by Ningal ("Alas for my city!"), the composition closes in an appeal for the gods to return "like sheep to thy fold" and with a note of rejoicing at the restoration.

The *balag*s and *eršemma*s share many of the generic features of the classic laments, but present them in a mechanical, repetitive, and often unimaginative way. While these latter compositions were performed in sanctuary-razing ceremonies as well, they apparently were also used in numerous other circumstances, including as a part of the fixed monthly liturgy.

8

Outside of Mesopotamia, knowledge of the city-lament genre is reflected in imagery from the Ugaritic Keret epic, in formulaic fragments from classical Greece, and most extensively in the Bible, where it is reflected in literature covering a period of (at least) over two centuries, from the time of Amos (mid-eighth century) to that of Isaiah 55–66 (late sixth century). The genre appears in modulated form in the prophetic literature, especially in the so-called "Oracles against the Nations," and in some of the communal laments of the Psalter. But it is in Lamentations that the genre is most impressively exhibited outside of Mesopotamia. A comparison of the generic repertoire of the Mesopotamian city laments with Lamentations reveals no less than nine important features held in common: subject and mood, structure and poetic technique, divine abandonment, assignment of responsibility, divine agent of destruction, destruction, weeping goddess, lamentation, and restoration of the city and return of the gods. Still, Lamentations is no simple Mesopotamian city lament. Rather, it represents a thorough translation and adaptation of the genre in a Judean environment and is ultimately put to a significantly different use. Indeed, there is very little of the Mesopotamian genre that has been taken up (however mediated) wholly into Lamentations. Lamentations employs structural and rhetorical devices well known to Hebrew poetry. In Lamentations the people are held responsible for the destruction of Jerusalem because of their sin, whereas in the Mesopotamian laments the destruction is attributed to the capricious decision of the divine assembly. Yahweh, the God of Judah, imagined principally in the guise of the divine warrior, is cast as the divine agent of destruction instead of Enlil, who performs this role prototypically in Mesopotamia. In place of a weeping city goddess, whose presence would be anathema in a Yahwistic work like Lamentations, the city of Jerusalem is personified as a woman suffering and mourning the fate of her city and its inhabitants. Finally, Lamentations functions differently than the Mesopotamian city laments, swerving tragically away from the latter's more comic trajectory. For example, the motifs of the return of the gods and the restoration of the temples and city, integral to the Mesopotamian city laments, are completely absent in Lamentations (see below).

Lamentations' divergences from the kinds of city laments otherwise known from Mesopotamia reflect larger differences in the nature of the genre's productivity in Mesopotamia and in Israel and Judah (for details, see Dobbs-Allsopp, "Darwinism"). In Mesopotamia, the city-lament genre exhibits an obvious period of primary productivity during which some or all of the classic city laments stimulated the production of other works, especially the more derivative and secondarily productive *balags* and *eršemmas*. In Israel and Judah, by contrast, the city-lament genre apparently never (at least on present evidence) enjoyed a phase of primary productivity. That is, all of the texts in the Old Testament that may

9

be related plausibly to the genre appear to have been produced according to some fixed formula or exhibit some definite relationship to the major genre tradition. For example, in the prophetic "Oracles against the Nations," the genre is used ironically in modulated form to celebrate rather than mourn the destruction of foreign cities and nations. And Lamentations, as was suggested briefly above, appears to be an adaptation and translation of the Mesopotamian city lament that is ultimately put to a slightly different use. The reason for the secondary nature of the genre's productivity in Israel and Judah can be explained principally in terms of environment. Israel and Judah, unlike Mesopotamia, did not have a long and vibrant tradition of important multiple urban centers. The full flowering of the genre was not called forth until fairly late in the period for which the genre is attested, only when Judah's political and religious capital, Jerusalem, was finally destroyed. All other urban centers paled in comparison with Jerusalem and therefore could not be expected to engender or sustain a similar level of interest and concern. Besides, with Jerusalem's destruction, Judah lost its political independence as well, which would only heighten the significance of the city's destruction and the need for the catastrophe to be memorialized in a poetic composition.

In light of the strong imprint of the city-lament genre on Lamentations, it is very tempting to suggest that these poems, in part or as a whole, served in a similar fashion as the Mesopotamian city laments, namely, as a part of the foundation-razing ceremonies prior to the rebuilding of the Second Temple toward the end of the sixth century (so Gwaltney, 209–10). However, there are a number of features in Lamentations that, when compared with the Mesopotamian city laments, simply do not easily jibe with such a premise. The most striking difference is the complete absence in Lamentations of any mention of God's return to Jerusalem or the restoration of the city and temple. These are not only prominent motifs in the Mesopotamian city laments, they represent these laments' raison d'être, which is, after all, to look forward ultimately to the restoration and rebuilding of city and temples, and the resumption of normalcy for the larger community. The importance of these motifs can be seen by the fact that they comprise over half the "Nippur Lament." The exception proves the rule. These motifs are also absent in the "Curse of Agade," which, instead of looking forward to the city's future restoration, emphasizes the exact opposite, namely, that Agade will not be restored. Lamentations, with the absence of return and restoration motifs, strongly resembles the "Curse of Agade," both swerving tragically away from the more comic trajectory of the other attested Mesopotamian laments. Since these motifs

10

were apparently known in Israelite literature (Isa. 1:21–26; 54:1–17; 62:1–12; Zeph. 3:14–20), one cannot ascribe their absence in Lamentations to mere accident. Indeed, God's abandonment of and return to Jerusalem—themes not restricted to city laments—is spectacularly displayed in Ezekiel (1–3; 8–11; 40–47) and in Second Isaiah (40–55).

In the absence of any return/restoration motifs, there are a number of passages in Lamentations that some would interpret more hopefully, and thus construe as implying the temple's imminent rebuilding. These would include the middle section of Lamentations 3 (vv. 19–24, 25–39), in which the poet draws on wisdom teachings apparently to counsel patience and hope in God; Lamentations 4:22, which, when read straightforwardly, declares that personified Zion's punishment has been completed and that God will no longer continue to exile her; and the concluding section of Lamentations 5 (vv. 19–22), which looks briefly (esp. v. 21) toward the future in a way not uncharacteristic of a foundation-razing ceremony. In each of these three instances, however, where many are inclined to read rather straightforward sentiments of hope and confidence in the future, the poet can be shown as having contextualized the lines in ways clearly intended to frustrate if not totally subvert such inclinations (for details see the commentary). And while this does not constitute absolute proof that Lamentations was not used in a kind of foundation-razing ceremony known from Mesopotamia prior to the rebuilding of the temple in Jerusalem, it does make it unlikely. From what is known of the Mesopotamian laments, the whole tone is wrong, especially after the comic turn is made in these compositions, and restoration and resumption of normalcy are in view. There the tone is much more akin to what we have in Second Isaiah (see below), not the despondency, discouragement, and melancholia in which Lamentations ends.

A final consideration telling against an original association between Lamentations and the building of the Second Temple comes in a series of recent studies that find specific allusions to Lamentations in Isaiah 40–55, or Second Isaiah (Newsom, "Response"; Sommer; Willey). While not all of the allusions brought forward are equally compelling, there does seem to be a sufficient number to warrant the conclusion that the anonymous poet of Second Isaiah was familiar with Lamentations (at least in part). If correct, it would be difficult to maintain that these poems were originally composed for foundation-razing ceremonies of the kind known from Mesopotamia, since Second Isaiah can be dated most securely to the middle of the sixth century. At best, this would have to be a secondary reuse of this material, and even then we would have to posit a significantly different focus for Lamentations than what is normally posited for the Mesopotamian laments. The cumulative weight of each of these considerations (the absence of return and restoration motifs and of straightforwardly hopeful passages and the probability of allusions to Lamentations in Second Isaiah) strongly suggests that, instead of the sanctuary-razing ceremonies posited for the Mesopotamian laments, one should think more in terms of the kinds of public mourning ceremonies that presumably took place at the site of the destroyed city throughout the exilic period to commemorate the catastrophe (Jer. 41:5; Zech. 7:3–5; 8:19). Whether or not these poems were then put to use in some capacity during the rebuilding of the Second Temple (520–515 B.C.E.) must remain an open question.

Other literary genres are drawn upon in Lamentations, especially the funeral dirge and individual and communal laments, all of which are related to a larger lament genre that includes the city lament. These (and others) will be commented on, when appropriate, in the body of the commentary. Like most surpassing literary works, then, Lamentations embodies a good deal of generic mixture. This is not something to be scoffed at or derided, but should be celebrated and enjoyed. In particular, the emotional peak reached in Lamentations 3 and the strong sense of closure effected by Lamentations 5 result chiefly from these poems' employment of forms and motifs drawn from the tradition of individual and communal laments. And the predominantly sad and sorrowful tone that pervades this sequence of poems owes much to the strong accent that the funeral dirge receives in the first poem. Lamentations satisfies to a large degree because it so successfully incorporates a variety of literary genres.

Lamentations as Lyric

Lamentations is written as lyric poetry, and thus a fully satisfying reading of Lamentations can come about only through an understanding and appreciation of its lyricism. Finding a ready-made definition of lyric poetry is no easy task, and here is not the place to undertake an in-depth analysis of the nature of the Hebrew lyric in particular, a subject that remains a desideratum (preliminarily, see Dobbs-Allsopp, "Lamentations as a Lyric Sequence"). It will suffice for our purposes to highlight initially two complementary properties of the lyric: its lack of narrativizing devices, on the one hand, and on the other, its concomitant strong reliance on the naked properties of language as its basic resource for making meaning. That is, without the benefit of narrative devices such as plot, argumentative structure, and fictional characters to help construct meaning and build in coherence and a sense of direction, lyric poems are forced to construct meaning through the manipulation of language alone. As Susanne Langer explains, the lyric "is the literary form that depends most directly on pure verbal resources—the sound and evocative power of words, meter, alliteration, rhyme, and other rhythmic devices, associated images, repetitions, archaisms and grammatical twists" (259). In lyric poetry, character is replaced by voice and persona, and as a result takes on its familiar pronominal form, prototypically realized as an "I" addressing a "You." And without plot or argumentative structure, the continuity and structure of the lyric poem is distinctively paratactic (the placing side by side of words, images, themes, or the like without explicit connectives that coordinate the various parts with one another) and associative in nature. The lyric's centers of "emotionally and sensuously charged awareness" radiate out and relate to one another associatively, through "felt relationship." The resulting play of tonal depths and shadings and shiftings is achieved through "strategic juxtaposition of separate . . . passages without a superimposed logical or fictional continuity" (Rosenthal and Gall, 728). All of this is to say that if we want to get at what lyric poems mean, what they say (to put it crudely), we will need to pay equally careful attention to formal properties and aspects, which are usually glossed over as mere decoration or atmosphere (e.g., sonic elements, meter and rhythm, key words, repetitions, etc.), as we do to semantic content. Moreover, we will need to be prepared to experience the lyric poem holistically, reading both prospectively and retrospectively. It is never a matter of boiling the lyric poem down to its essentials, but rather experiencing it for what it does as it does it. The lyric as a mode of discourse is no better and no worse than other modes of discourse (e.g., narrative, scientific notation, philosophical logic), but it is different and it does have its own unique means of truth-telling.

Some of the telltale signs of Lamentations' lyricism are as follows. First, these poems do not tell a story or mount an elaborate argument. Indeed, plot and argumentative structure are almost wholly lacking, as many commentators have observed. To be sure, the story of the Babylonian destruction of Jerusalem everywhere suffuses the poetry of Lamentations, but nowhere does Lamentations try to tell this particular story. And when any semblance of argumentative logic is deployed (as in 3:25–39), it is always locally contained and subordinated to the poem's greater lyrical ambitions. Neither are there any fully realized and compelling characters in Lamentations to stimulate interest on the part of the audience, but only speaking voices or personae. As Alan Mintz correctly observes, "Lamentations has as its medium dramatized speech" (4). Instead, the poems in Lamentations, to use M. L. Rosenthal's terminology, consist of a series of projections "of specific qualities and intensities of emotionally and sensuously charged awareness" that

13

are achieved or realized chiefly through the manipulation of rhetoric and imagery. Lamentations' emotional and intellectual centers, those tonalities that energize and animate the several poems, are manifold and varied. The catastrophe of 586 would have provoked many conflicting thoughts and emotions among survivors. Grief, guilt, forgiveness, anger, compassion, hope, despair, and shame are only the most obvious set of thoughts and emotions that are evoked and contemplated, voiced and sifted in Lamentations. These erupt as a complex of separate streams like wadis in a desert, each following its own course through the poetry. Some end abruptly, never to be heard from again. Others end in one place but reemerge elsewhere. Two or more may temporarily commingle and then split apart again, and a few may even meander through the whole of the sequence of poems, refusing to be dammed by the boundaries of any one poem. The resulting flood never becomes chaotic, however, because it is contained and controlled by the constraints of the alphabetic acrostic and the other prevalent formal patterns of repetition, for example, the so-called qinah meter.

That each poem is a series of contemplations sifted and strained specifically and intentionally through the sieve of language is nowhere more self-consciously symbolized than in the much maligned acrostic. Here it is clear, in Driver's words already quoted, that Lamentations is "constructed with conscious art" and is not simply "the unstudied effusions of natural emotion." The alphabet is the paradigmatic symbol of language and human cultural achievement. Its persistent and recurring march and its extreme artifactuality beckons readers time and again to attend to the language of these poems. For it is in their language, the images evoked, the play of syntax, the manipulation of rhythm, the alliteration, assonance, and consonance of sound, and the troping in various ways of repetition that meaning is constructed and created. Moreover, these poems, like lyric verse more generally, are dense and highly compressed. Each image or phrase, thought or emotion, requires mapping a complex web of connections. Any one item will resonate both prospectively and retrospectively. Thus, a comprehensive and fully adequate reading of these lyrics will consist in a detailed journey through the multiple and complex streams of emotion and thought that get contemplated and evoked.

It may be helpful, at this point, to offer a few concrete examples of the kind of lyrical means for achieving meaning that I have uppermost in mind.

14   **Metaphor.** No other trope so epitomizes poetry and poetic (nonliteral) meaning than metaphor, saying one thing in terms of another, transferring the connotations of one thing to another. Lamentations, like all poetry, is vitally made of metaphor. Attention to the metaphoric

dimensions of language is announced almost immediately in its personification of the city-temple complex as a suffering and grieving woman (1:1). Even without elaboration this small metaphoric gesture projects sentience and imbues pathos in a way that would be lacking in a more straightforwardly descriptive statement. By simply naming God as "enemy" (2:4–5), the poet invites the reader to consider the divine metaphorically, at a particular angle, such that the notion of the divine held up to the mind's eye is sharply colored. Similarly, to imagine the personified city not as a grieving widow but as a "cruel ostrich" (4:3), or Jerusalem's citizenry as blood-soaked and defiled lepers (4:13–15), distinctly shapes how these are encountered, construed, interpreted. Such entanglements with metaphor richly layer meaning in Lamentations non-literally but significantly.

Diction. The poet's choice of diction often activates connotations over and above a given statement's more narrowly denotative meaning. Lamentations 2:20b provides a good example. In this verse the specter of cannibalism is raised. The language is quite evocative. The NRSV, "should women eat their offspring," sanitizes the imagery in its overtly denotative rendering. The term for "offspring" in Hebrew *(pĕrî)* more literally means "fruit," and while it is true that this term is frequently used figuratively for offspring (cf. Gen. 30:2; Deut. 7:13; Ps. 21:10), as indeed it is here, nevertheless the poet means through his choice of diction to color the mother's act of cannibalism with the lush enjoyment and everyday occurrence of eating fruit: "Should women have to eat their children as if they were eating fruit?" The resulting contrast of images is jarring and very effective. The utterly abhorrent thought that a mother would be compelled to cannibalize her own children as a means of survival is made even more heinous by the sensuality and commonality implicit in the fruit imagery. This tainting of the inhumane, the bestial with sensuous (even erotic) delight continues even through the end of the couplet, as the rare Hebrew word *ṭippūḥîm* "to be reared" (NRSV: "borne") puns on the similar sounding and erotically charged word for "apple" *(tappûaḥ; tappûḥîm;* esp. Song 2:3, 5; 7:8).

Wordplay. The image of "lovers" and "friends" in 1:2 is complex and creatively ambiguous, playing on several of the different nuances attested for these words. Metaphorically and most basically, they conjure the family and friends of the mourning widow who neglect the social obligation of compassion and consolation owed to one in mourning. One of the standard complaints in laments is precisely that the sufferer has been abandoned just when he or she needs companionship most (Pss. 38:11; 88:8, 18). At a somewhat more literal level, they are Judah's erstwhile political allies, who not only have neglected their political obligations owed to Judah, but even turned on her, becoming

15

her enemies. Such terminology was common in the parlance of international relations in the ancient Near East—though in light of the figurative nature of the language in Lamentations, one should resist the temptation to specify in explicitly historical terms precisely who these allies-turned-enemy are. Finally, the reference to "lovers" and "friends" may allude, as in some of the prophets (esp. Hosea, Jeremiah, and Ezekiel), to Zion as a faithless wife (cf. Tgs)—though, if so, this is very much in the background and not emphasized here, and only activated retrospectively in light of references to Zion's sin later on in the poem. Such multivocality is a hallmark of lyric: there is no need to choose between these alternate readings. All are allowed to play out and off one another. The image of Zion's unconsoled suffering and the empathy it evokes in readers dominates the stanza. That Judah's "friends" and "lovers" are understood at some level, albeit somewhat removed, to be her political allies is likely. And though I would not stress the possible allusion to Zion's faithlessness as much as some, neither would I deny its presence. It is there and hovers darkly in the background.

Pun. A different kind of wordplay is exhibited in 1:3c. Hebrew, like English, contains many words that either sound or look alike, creating fertile ground for puns. Puns play with sound and meaning: identical or similar sounds bring together two or more meanings. The pun works when the context gives significance to the variety of meanings. The Hebrew term for "distress" (*měṣarîm*) in 1:3c ironically puns the similar looking and sounding Hebrew name for "Egypt" (*miṣrayim*), a traditional place of refuge in hard times (Joseph story) and the legendary place from which God delivered the children of Israel. The effect of the pun is to heighten noticeably the notion of "distress." Instead of being delivered in/from Egypt, Judah is "overtaken" by "her pursuers" (the same idiom used to relate Pharaoh's pursuit and capture of the Israelites, cf. Exod. 14:9; 15:9) in the midst of "distress." The expectation of deliverance that hovers spectrally in the name "Egypt" is literally, mimetically overwritten in the word "distress."

Euphony. Lyric poetry is frequently marked by the play of sound—rhyme, alliteration, assonance. In many traditions sound is exploited regularly and systematically, such as with end-rhyme in much accentual-syllabic verse written in English. Sonic effects in Lamentations, however, like Hebrew poetry more generally, are nonsystematic, but they appear nonetheless. Unfortunately, this feature is among the hardest for us to gain access to, owing to our imperfect knowledge about how ancient Hebrew sounded, and, in any case, is not usually transparent in translation, even when we are confident of its presence in the original Hebrew. Several examples may be offered, nonetheless, if for no other reason than to remind us of this all too frequently missing dimension of the poetry. Lamentations 1:15 is marked by the chiming of the /ay/ sound throughout (ʾabbîray . . . ʾădōnāy . . . ʿalay . . . baḥûrāy . . . ʾădōnāy). Lamentations 1:10 involves internal rhyme (yādô [noun]/ yābōʾû [verb]; maḥămaddeyhā/ miqdāšāh; rāʾātâ [perf. 3fs]/ ṣawwîtâ [perf. 2ms]; bāʾû [perf. 3mp]/ yābōʾû [imperf. 3mp]—the formal differences among each of these pairs suggest that the rhyming is not accidental!). And occasionally, more functionally focused exploitations of sound effects can be identified, such as the alliteration of the Hebrew letter ṣade in 3:52 (ṣôd ṣādûnî kaṣṣippôr "they have hunted me like a bird"), which functions mimetically, the repeated ṣades trapping and enwrapping the line just as the enemies hunt and entrap the poet.

Alphabetic Acrostic. Each of the poems in Lamentations is shaped in one way or another according to the Hebrew alphabet. All but the last poem are acrostics. Lamentations 1 and 2 are made up of stanzas consisting of three couplets each in which only the initial word of each stanza begins with the appropriate letter of the Hebrew alphabet. The first word of the first stanza begins with *aleph* (the first letter of the Hebrew alphabet), the first word of the second stanza begins with the next letter, *bet*, and so on, proceeding successively letter by letter through the alphabet with each new stanza, until reaching the *taw*, the last letter of the Hebrew alphabet. Lamentations 4 exhibits the same kind of acrostic pattern, except that the stanzas themselves contain only two couplets apiece. In Lamentations 3 the alphabetic scheme is replicated three times over, as the initial word of every couplet within each of the three-couplet stanzas is constrained by the appropriate letter of the alphabet. Even in the final poem, Lamentations 5, where the acrostic is literally absent, the force of the alphabet is nevertheless palpable, as the poem consists of precisely 22 couplets, the number of letters in the Hebrew alphabet. The English reader may gain a feel for the acrostic's presence in Lamentations from Ronald Knox's translation, which attempts (almost uniquely) to imitate the alphabetic pattern of the original in English:

> **A**h, what straits have I not known, under the avenging rod!
> **A**sked I for light, into deeper shadow the Lord's guidance led me;
> **A**lways upon me, none other, falls endlessly the blow.
> **B**roken this frame, under the wrinkled skin, the sunk flesh.
> **B**itterness of despair fills my prospect, walled in on every side;
> **B**uried in darkness, and, like the dead, interminably.
> **C**losely he fenced me in, beyond hope of rescue; loads me with fetters.
> **C**ry out for mercy as I will, prayer of mine wins no audience;
> **C**limb these smooth walls I may not; every way of escape he has undone.
>
> (3:1–9; Knox, 734)

17

As with other linguistic and stylistic elements in lyric verse, form is polyvalent. The alphabetic acrostic in Lamentations offers more than fancy window dressing for the poetry's otherwise separable semantic and propositional content. Literarily, the acrostic functions in several notable ways. First, and most basically, it serves as the literal and very arbitrary container for this poetry. As such, the acrostic is no less and no more significant than other poetic forms better known to us in English canons of poetry (e.g., sonnet, sestina, villanelle, rondeau). To judge from the biblical (and extrabiblical) evidence, the alphabetic acrostic was a common form (Pss. 9, 10, 25, 34, 37, 111, 112, 119, 145; Prov. 31:10–31; Lam. 1–4; Nah. 1; Sir. 51:13–30) and was fairly flexible (i.e., it could frame every line, as in Pss. 111 and 112, every couplet, as in Ps. 119, or even every stanza, as in Lam. 1, 2, and 4). In the absence of plot, form (even in contemporary free verse) plays an extremely important role in lyric verse, as it literally holds the poetry together and guides the reader from beginning to end. Given the fragmentary and paratactic nature of Lamentations' verse, this role is even more pronounced. Second, the acrostic, like other formal features in Lamentations (e.g., the qinah meter, stanzaic form), has a pronounced cohering effect, both on each individual poem and on the sequence of poems as a whole. The patterned repetition of the alphabet helps hold together the otherwise scattered and chaotic lyrics (see below). Third, the acrostic in the variation of its deployment (i.e., the varying of stanzaic length and of alphabetic order—the normative ʿayin-pe order only obtains in the first poem) throughout the sequence gives this poetry a trajectory and a sense of dynamism. Beyond such purely literary uses, the acrostic means symbolically, semantically, even theologically. The poet has chosen language as his means of consolation and there is no better symbol of the power and potential of language than the alphabetic acrostic, modeled most likely on the simple abecedaries that were a commonplace in scribal schools. The alphabet stands, as well, as the paradigm symbol of culture and civilization in the ancient Near East, and thus its prominence in these poems profoundly reasserts the values of civilization and culture even in the face of utterly devastating and dehumanizing suffering. And in its formal completeness and surety of form, in its capacity as that which literally contains and constrains the otherwise chaotic and fragmentary verses of this poetry, the acrostic projects "its formal order as a token, a security—something given in hand—to guarantee the cosmic order" beyond the turbulence of Jerusalem's historical reality (Krieger, 4).

18

Enjambment. Typically in Hebrew poetry, a couplet is composed of two lines that are end-stopped (i.e., line ends are marked by a significant pause) and parallel to one another, and echo or mirror one another in any number of ways—semantically, formally, sonically. Note the following examples of parallel couplets taken from Lamentations 5:

> "Young men are compelled to grind,
> and boys stagger under loads of wood" (5:13)

> "Because of this our hearts are sick,
> because of these things our eyes have grown dim" (5:17)

> "Why have you forgotten us completely?
> Why have you forsaken us these many days?" (5:20)

By contrast, most of the couplets in Lamentations involve varieties of enjambment, a phenomenon in which the syntax and meaning carry over line ends without a significant pause, and either lack parallelism altogether or the sense of parallelism, when present, is not salient. Note the following characteristic examples of enjambed couplets in Lamentations:

> "her pursuers have all overtaken her
> in the midst of her distress" (1:3c)

> "(They) open their mouths against us,
> (that is,) all of our enemies" (3:46; my own over-literal translation)

> "The LORD has destroyed without mercy
> all the dwellings of Jacob" (2:2a)

> "my priests and elders
> perished in the city" (1:19b)

Such a stylistic preference in other poems, once noted, may not occasion much comment. What is classically lyrical about Lamentations, however, is how it harnesses enjambment for meaning. The extensive use of enjambment—affecting over two-thirds of the couplets in these poems—like other formal features in Lamentations, provides a distinctive and unifying texture for these poems, compensating for the lack of more narrativizing devices for constructing coherence. The tug of syntax as it carries over from the first line of a couplet to the second gives these poems energy and a palpable sense of forward movement. The density of enjambed lines per poem moves from its highest mark in the first two poems, to a noticeably decreased use of enjambment in Lamentations 3 and 4, to its near absence in Lamentations 5 (which is predominantly parallelistic in nature). This provides the sequence of poems with a distinct sense of directionality, a curve of movement.

Enjambment is also exploited at more local levels of meaning. For example, the pause at line end frequently frames the initial syntactic unit so as to encourage one interpretation, which is then subsequently

19

given an unexpected twist or turn in light of the continuation of the enjambed unit. These "half" or "provisional" meanings, as they inhere in the orphaned line, are momentary and may counteract or clash with the "whole" meanings that arise once the sentences are completed. For example, consider 2:22a. Unfortunately, NRSV's translation ("You invited my enemies from all around/ as if for a day of festival") is completely transparent and devoid of any tension, obliterating the effect of the enjambment present in the original Hebrew. A more literal translation of the Hebrew looks like this:

> You invited as on a festival
> my enemies from all around

This preserves the momentary tension effected by the enjambment. The first line of the couplet refers to the announcement of a festival, normally a joyous event, involving festivities of all sorts. This day of festivities, however, takes a phantasmagoric turn in the second line. Instead of calling all the tribes of Israel to a celebratory feast, God has called all of Zion's surrounding enemies to make a feast of the city's inhabitants. Thus, the normal expectations associated with a feast day, after being momentarily raised, are dashed with the succession of the second line and the would-be human celebrants metamorphose before the audience's eyes into sacrificial victims. None, we are told in the succeeding couplet, survive (for details, see Dobbs-Allsopp, "Enjambing Line"; "Effects of Enjambment").

These few examples will suffice to illustrate some of the more typical nonsemantic and highly linguistic-dependent means that Lamentations' lyric verse uses to create meaning, and the kind of close reading required to elucidate such meanings. Other lyric tropes (e.g., personification, allusion, rhetoric, and the like) are equally prominent in Lamentations. The exposition offered in the body of the commentary below, while on occasion engaging in this kind of close reading, more often summarizes the results of such close readings. But in either case an appreciation of Lamentations' lyricism is essential to any fully comprehensive and persuasive reading of these poems.

The Unity of Lamentations

Lamentations is capable of being read in a coherent and holistic fashion, as some recent commentators have observed (e.g., Hillers, Provan, O'Connor), but the kind of unity that is enacted is peculiar to the lyric. One of the chief obstacles facing the lyric poet is the limitation of scale that this mode typically imposes. Lyric poems are invariably short because they typically do not organize their discourse by means of cohesion aiding devices (such as plot, argument, or consistency of character). With only language itself as its chief medium of discourse, it is difficult for the lyric poem to sustain itself over long stretches of time and space. Form, such as that exhibited by the villanelle or the sestina in the canonical traditions of English lyric poetry, offers one means by which lyric poems can extend their reach, and Lamentations masterfully exploits the alphabetic acrostic for just this purpose. However, form cannot be stretched indefinitely. It, too, eventually reaches limits beyond which if pushed it self-implodes. Therefore, surpassing encompassment and grandness of scale—both necessary given the enormity of Lamentations' subject matter—can only be truly managed in the lyric mode by successively linking individual lyric poems and molding them into a greater, organic unity. What gets enacted in such a process, then, is a sequence of lyric poems whose nature and dynamic, holistically considered, is essentially that of a lyric poem writ large.

Beyond being written in a predominantly lyric mode, lyric sequences have two counterposing characteristics: on the one hand, they are composite works, consisting of multiple discrete and autonomous poems, and thus project a strong sense of fragmentation; on the other hand, they exhibit to greater and to lesser degrees perceivable manifestations of coherence, whether through large-scale repetition, such as calendrical or numerological patterns, or through smaller scale and less formal means, such as lexical and key word repetition and the like. Yet however fragmented or coherent, the sequence's overarching structure(s) is explicitly lyrical in nature and design, marked by a conspicuous sense of organicism that ultimately defies reduction to thematic, narratological, or logical explication or paraphrase.

Daniel Grossberg has tried to get at the sense of fragmentation projected in Lamentations by specifying some of the elements that effect it, what he calls Lamentations' "centrifugal" tendencies (83–104). Among the aspects that contribute to the centrifugal (fragmented) experience of Lamentations, Grossberg identifies the presence of five distinct and autonomous poems, the "loose juxtaposition of heterogeneous parts" within each poem, the multiple shifts in voice which occur in these poems, and the intentional suppression of "place, time, and order of events" (84–96). Additions to this list include the variable realizations of the acrostic and other formal patterns, the dependence on multiple and disparate genres and traditions, and the dynamics and instability of the lyric mode of discourse itself (as evidenced in such practices as wordplay, for example, which forestall readerly certainty and assurance). Among other things, these fragmented or centrifugal aspects of Lamentations resonate mimetically, gesturing effectively toward the fragmented reality of post-destruction Jerusalem. The poet's whole attempt to render this chaos into language, to contain his fragmented lyrics within the frame of the alphabetic acrostic, thus becomes an attempt to control and contain and encompass the suffering that has engulfed Jerusalem and its inhabitants.

If Lamentations, true to its enabling technology, is marked throughout by fragmentation, it is nevertheless the case, as Grossberg also maintains, that this sense of fragmentation is more than compensated for by other, integrating or "centripetal" tendencies within the sequence. That is, Lamentations finds ways to "accommodate discontinuity" and to overcome the junctures between and within the poems "without brutally closing them" (Greene, 20), one net effect of which is to achieve a delicate and pleasing balance between centrifugal and centripetal pressures. Lamentations' accommodating practices are multiple and varied and of a kind incumbent with its explicitly lyric mode of discourse. Formally, coherence is built into the sequence of poems through various patterns of systematic repetition, chief among which are the alphabetic acrostic, the uniformity of the stanzas within each of the poems themselves (each stanza, with some minor exceptions, containing a fixed number of lines), the extremely high prominence of closed couplets throughout, and the rhythmic dominance of unbalanced and enjambed lines (the so-called qinah meter; cf. Grossberg, 84–86). As Barbara Herrnstein Smith explains, "To the extent that stimuli possess similar features they form groups and are perceived as unified, coherent, and stable structures" (41). Thus, as a pattern of repetition—whatever the pattern may consist of—becomes more apparent, each succeeding repetition of the pattern becomes more secure and stable, and in this way, systematic repetition strengthens the formal coherence of a work. In Lamentations, as one proceeds through the first poem, the alphabetic pattern, for example, becomes readily apparent: the first word of each stanza is constrained by the appropriate letter of the Hebrew alphabet. As the reader approaches the *taw* (last) stanza, there is an obvious sense of closure that is to be affirmed and enjoyed, but also must ultimately be overcome as the whole continues. In Lamentations 2 the acrostic starts over again and a new pattern is perceptible. Not only do the stanzas succeed according to the order of the alphabet, once the end of the alphabet is reached the pattern starts all over again. This experience of starting the alphabet over again noticeably diminishes the closural force experienced at the conclusions of Lamentations 2, 3, and 4, and consequently, further strengthens the feeling of cohesion, the expectation of continuation. Lamentations' other formal patterns of repetition (e.g., qinah meter, enjambment) nicely mirror the patterned progression of the alphabet, essentially redoubling, time and again, the cohering effect on the reader.

The unity of Lamentations is suggested in a variety of less formal ways as well. The similarity of situation, subject matter, mood, and general perspective assumed or shared by each of the individual poems bind the whole together (Grossberg, 83–84, 95–96; Dobbs-Allsopp, *Weep*, 31–32). The predominant use of traditional imagery, as Grossberg suggests, anchors the work within an inherited literary tradition, which exerts a strong centripetal force (96–97). The fact that the language of each of the poems can be dated typologically to the same period, the exilic period, is consistent as well with the thesis of the poems' larger unity. And lastly, there is a web of verbal, thematic, and vocal links to connect the poems in a complex, chainlike unity, wherein each poem is joined to some subset of the other poems in a multiplicity of overlapping ways (for details, see Dobbs-Allsopp, "Lamentations as a Lyric Sequence").

But no matter how pronounced this sense of coherence, at its most fundamental level, Lamentations, like other lyric sequences, is composed of a succession and interaction of varied and multiple affects, which steadfastly resist all attempts to map, paraphrase, or otherwise reduce to logical or thematic content. They can only be experienced successively, progressively as they are evoked. Their effects are generally momentary and local: the haunting if hopeful emergence of personified Zion out of the ruins of Jerusalem (1:1); confessions of sin that must come to terms with the exile of innocent children and the real hurt and suffering of a woman raped (1:5, 8–9); the absence of compassion (1:2, 9, 16, 21); God's merciless and violent attack against God's own people (1:13–15; 2:1–8); the satisfying if ugly calls for retribution against the enemy (1:21–22; 3:64–66; 4:21–22); the damning accusation against a God who would cause women to eat their own children (2:20); the heartfelt desire of a man to find comfort and solace in his religious heritage (3:19–24, 25–39); the multiple and brutal images of suffering that are the staple of these poems; and God's figured absence and silence that, by the end of the sequence, become oppressive and deafening. There is no ordering or scripting of such moments. The poetry simply builds in intensity until a certain kind of emotional or cognitive intensity or awareness is reached and then lets go, releasing the built-up tension before starting over anew. Only the acrostic and the other formal patterns of repetition keep this multitude of affects from turning into a chaotic and uncontrollable flood.

Theology   23

Apropos of the lyric medium in which it is embodied, the theology of Lamentations is occasional, pluralistic, equivocating, and fragmentary. Nowhere are there specific themes systematically developed or theological arguments set out in detail, and the poems steadfastly resist all attempts to superpose on them a single unifying theological perspective. As such, these poems' theology is hard to outline and summarize without giving a false impression. Nevertheless, as a means of providing an initial orientation to this peculiarly lyric theology and in order to relieve the ensuing exposition in the body of the commentary of some of its burden, I set down here in preliminary fashion some of the more conspicuous centers of theological sensibility found in Lamentations. The ensuing inventory of topics, ideas, and sentiments, while appropriately comprehensive, is by no means exhaustive, nor have I attempted to systematize or integrate the poet's thought beyond what seems justified by the poetry itself. Indeed, if anything, it is the distinctly particular and fragmentary nature of the theology of Lamentations that is so congenial to our postmodern moment. Lyric poetry's capacity to give free expression to one compelling mood or idea at a time, no matter how partial the result in light of larger worldviews, provides an important corrective to the systematic bent of mind traditionally associated with much theological inquiry. There are times when it is appropriate to yield utterly to a single compelling feeling or attitude (cf. Kinzie, 200). For the most part, the topics discussed below constitute aspects of what Walter Brueggemann has recently characterized as "Israel's countertestimony." Arising out of a context that is stridently incongruous with Judah's past experiences of God's beneficent sovereignty, these poems confront God with the hurt and pain of this lived reality, remind God of God's past promises of care and nurture, express grief, anger, and a sense of abandonment, question the rightness of God's actions, and even witness, candidly, to the harmful nature of both God's presence and absence, all as a means of mobilizing God, reactivating the Yahweh of old, and converting God's present fury into future favor. While these are not stances for all times and places, they do resonate powerfully and carry more normative weight today than in previous generations, given the realities of our post-Holocaust world where, sadly, more and more of human life is centered around experiences of negativity and radical suffering.

Consequences of Style

One of the first things to notice is that the theological stances taken in Lamentations are as much shaped by the lyrical nature of the poems' discourse as by their propositional content. As Alan Shapiro observes, "the formal and stylistic choices a writer makes are fraught with extraliterary judgments, biases, commitments that have moral as well as aesthetic implications" (1). The mode of discourse chosen for reflection, whatever its nature, is not value-neutral. Rather, it already expresses a view on the nature of understanding. For example, emotion and feeling are integral to Lamentations. Some emotions are simply voiced, such as grief for the dead or for those who have suffered greatly (1:2a, 16a; 2:11, 13) or anger at those who have caused the suffering (1:20–22; 3:64–66; 4:21–22). Other emotions are intended to evoke a response from the poems' readership. Compassion is one such emotion. Lamentations insists that compassion is the only appropriate response to radical suffering (cf. Dobbs-Allsopp, "Tragedy," 56–58). This insistence, however, is never argued literally or developed thematically, but rather is embroidered rhetorically, lyrically into the very fabric of the poetry itself. These poems construct compassion in their readers, positioning them so that they care intensely about the sufferings of Zion and her inhabitants (see the comment on Lamentations 1 below). But whether voiced or evoked, emotions are clearly valorized in Lamentations, as indeed they routinely are in lyric poetry more generally. This prizing of emotion has theological import. It asserts that a well-lived life is one that is entangled deeply with human emotion. Human beings are passionate creatures whose natures are constituted as much by emotions as by physical and cognitive needs and desires. Therefore, part of any adequate response to radical suffering, these poems remind us, must involve "not only intellectual appreciation" but also "emotional reaction" (Nussbaum, 69).

As another example, take the strongly paratactic nature of the poetry in Lamentations. Ideas and images are routinely juxtaposed to each other without being explicitly linked. This forces the reader to consider each idea on its own and then in relation to those that are most contiguous to it. Individual truths are allowed to surface and be experienced on their own, but are also ultimately required to be considered as a part of a larger whole, which acts as a strong deterrent to the domination of any single perspective. In 1:5 we read that "the LORD has made her (= Jerusalem) suffer." The line break after "suffer" ensures that the reader contemplates this startling statement. God did not "punish" or otherwise "reprimand" Jerusalem, but God "made her suffer," God intentionally caused her pain. The second line of the couplet then shifts the perspective slightly: "for the multitude of her transgressions." In other words, Jerusalem's "transgressions" precipitated God's actions, and thus, our original aversion to God's behavior is mollified somewhat, but only somewhat, as we are still haunted by the nature and intentionality of God's suffering-causing activity. The final couplet exploits this slippage one final time: "her children have gone away,/ captives before the foe." God's infliction of suffering on Jerusalem ultimately results—though the link is only implicit in the concatenation of lines—

25

in the exile of the city's children. The image of children being forcefully taken into captivity can only evoke feelings of sympathy, compassion, and ultimately anger. Whatever guilt there is on Jerusalem's part cannot, ever, rationalize the suffering of innocent children. Here, then, is a wonderful example of how the poet's paratactic style impinges on his theological outlook. The attribution of sin and the reality of suffering each have their own claims to make, but neither can be considered in isolation from the other. Human responsibility must be owned and the consequences of past actions assumed, but sin, no matter how severe, can never justify human suffering.

Parataxis operates similarly above the level of the line in Lamentations, as in Lamentations 3. The counsel advocated in the middle section of the poem (vv. 19–24, 25–39), to persevere in the belief that if God "causes grief, he will have compassion" (3:32), is juxtaposed paratactically with sections (3:1–18, 43–66) attesting to the persistence of distress and despair (Dobbs-Allsopp. "Tragedy," 47–49). That we must ultimately read the counter claims of these sections together is shown by the acrostic that binds all of them together. The hope of God's compassion must come to terms with the obviousness of its current lack (for details, see the commentary below).

These are but two examples of how the poet through his predominantly paratactic style refuses to grant dominance to any one perspective or proposition. Individual truths are allowed to be experienced on their own, but they are also ultimately forced to compete with other, no less substantial truths. Tensions between contrasting positions are intentionally created, and the poet routinely fails to grant closure to these tensions. Thus, the search carried out by some for a dominant theological perspective, whether it be reflective of the Deuteronomy or royal Zion traditions, is antithetical to the poet's lyric way of thinking and writing. His style engenders in readers a process of reflection and thinking that demands constant attention to and interpretation and reinterpretation of individual details, words, images, propositions; it stresses responsiveness and attention to complexity, and discourages the search for single and all-encompassing answers. Moreover, the density and terseness of the poetry, full of all kinds of wordplay and allowing the excessiveness of language to flood in from the margins, only adds to the effect of the parataxis. Complexity is stressed, difficulty engendered, reductionism eschewed. The poet's time and circumstances likely did not permit the formulation of simple and singular solutions, and his paratactic habit of thought is generally reflective of and isomorphic to this.

26

Other aspects of the poet's style bear on the poems' theological outlook as well. One further illustration will have to suffice. As noted above, lyric discourse is characterized generally by a lack of plot or argumentative structure. That there is an obvious absence of logical development in Lamentations has been observed repeatedly by commentators. One implication of this lyric style is that the poems never really appear to go anywhere, either individually or as a collection. To be sure, there is a strong sense of formal closure in Lamentations, but otherwise the poetry seems to be transitional or processual in nature, always moving but never getting anywhere. The poetry reaches periodic heights of responsiveness, points at which the reader assents, "Yes, I too feel something like that!" or "Yes, I know this to be true!" But these are only "momentary stays against confusion," as Frost would say. No sooner are they reached than the poetry moves on again, pulled by the tug of the enjambing syntax or by the ever onward march of the alphabet. This inculcates a habit of continuous reflection and thinking. Power is located in the transitional, and not what results from the transition. This would certainly be a powerfully liberating perspective in a period when absolutes seem illusory or ungraspable, the past is gone and the future uncertain. Liminality is here embraced and made into a potent force of empowerment. Though the poet knows not where he is leading his community—he never offers a vision for the future such as that found, for example, in Ezekiel 40–48—he does know that he must get them through the pain of the past and on the way toward a new tomorrow, regardless of whatever that tomorrow may ultimately entail. And if the final character of that future society is not clear, there are nonetheless certain qualities we may infer that he would instill in it—for example, respect for human dignity and human suffering, an equal prizing of community and of the individuals who make up that community, a deep desire for continued relationship with God, and the like. These, of course, are qualities that by their very nature can never be perfected or fully realized, but require constant attention and nurturing. And thus, the lack of thematic closure in these poems provides an apt fit to the time in which they were written and the poet's vision.

Each of these brief examples shows that insofar as elements of style and form matter and mean literarily they are also open to extraliterary —even theological—construals. In the case of Lamentations, whether it be in the poetry's prizing of emotion, paratactic play, or lack of teleology, such construals play an important part in these poems' overall theology.

Anti/Theodicy 27

Central to Christian and biblical faith alike is the affirmation of God's providential care for the world. But such an affirmation is most severely tested by the reality of evil and radical suffering, a reality all too plainly familiar in a world so recently riddled by the atrocities of two world wars, the Holocaust, Stalinist gulags, Hiroshima and Nagasaki, Mao's purges, the Catastrophe, the killing fields of Cambodia, the specter of nuclear annihilation, Nicaraguan death squads, and ethnic cleansing. And if this litany of atrocity from the twentieth century were thought to be only a ghastly nightmare from a bygone age, the events of September 11, 2001, in the United States stunningly—horrifically— remind us of evil's omnipresence even here in the postmodern, post- Holocaust world of the twenty-first century. The Babylonian destruction of Jerusalem and the terrible suffering that accompanied it prompted the same kinds of theodicy questions for sixth-century Judeans as those raised for their twentieth and twenty-first century counterparts: How can the lordship of God continue to be affirmed in the face of such hor- rendous evil? If God is omnipotent and good, why is human suffering so endemic in this world? The overwhelming response in the exilic litera- ture of the Bible is theodic (or theodicean), explaining in various guises Jerusalem's destruction and the extreme suffering of the city's inhabi- tants as just punishment for human sin. The importance and success of the Bible's dominant theodic interpretations of the exile should not be undervalued. The ongoing vitality of the Judeo-Christian religious tra- ditions owes much to this literature's tenacious affirmation of God and of God's goodness, power, and active providential care of the world even in the face of such adversity.

Lamentations, too, unquestionably contains identifiable theodic strains of thought. The depth of these poems' piety, their unabashed fidelity to and intentional alignment with God, is articulated most spec- tacularly in the very nature of their form of discourse, speech (prayers, laments) addressed to God. Recent scholarship on the lament literature of the Bible has rightly accented the profundity of the faith commit- ment implicit in these writings, as they stake all on God, even in times of deepest despair, when all evidence speaks against God's continuing relevance (Brueggemann, *Old Testament Theology*, 53–54; Miller, 98, 101; Dobbs-Allsopp, "Tragedy," 53). Lamentations, amid expressions of honest grief and hurt, hard questions, and angry protests, insists on addressing God, on bringing the reality of human hurt before the throne of the Lord (1:9c, 11c, 20a, 21–22; 2:20–22; 3:43–45, 55–66; 5:1, 19–22). Moreover, by foregrounding the metaphor of God as warrior (esp. 1:13–15; 2:1–8), the poetry affirms God's ongoing and vigorous potency. The destruction of Jerusalem was no accident, nor was it the result of the superiority of other gods or foreign powers. Rather, it came about as a consequence of God's deliberate and planned (esp. 2:8, 17) actions. And the periodic calls for vengeance (1:21–22; 3:64–66; 4:21–22), though ugly, manifest a sure confidence in God's future vitality. Thus, if life can go on without a rebuilt Jerusalem or temple and without the Davidic monarch, it cannot even be contemplated without God at its center, without the possibility of transcendence and the capacity for novelty and innovation that it inscribes: "Restore us to yourself, O LORD, that we may be restored;/ renew our days as of old" (5:21). Finally, Lamentations shares the general cultural assumption, attested throughout the ancient Near East, that national disasters were necessarily a consequence of human sin. The acknowledgment of human sin and guilt, while not as pervasive as much of the critical literature supposes, is explicit in Lamentations (1:5b, 8a, 18a, 22b; 2:14b; 3:39, 42; 4:6, 13; 5:7, 16). Indeed, the intentionality of this assignment of sin is dramatically underscored through a comparison with the Mesopotamian city laments, in which the destruction of the city comes about through no fault of the city's, but by the capricious decision of the gods. As Enlil explains in the "Lamentation over the Destruction of Sumer and Ur," "Ur was granted kingship, it was not granted an eternal reign. . . . Who has (ever) seen a reign of kingship that is everlasting!/ Its kingship, its reign has been cut off!" (*ANET,* 617). That Lamentations assigns any responsibility to the people for the city's destruction, therefore, is very significant. Lamentations' sixth-century poet knew well both that human existence takes place within a larger cosmic setting, and that people must bear responsibility for the actions they take within the created world known to them. There is no attempt here to dodge the reality of transcendence or the ethical sense of responsibility inculcated in ancient Judean culture (and ultimately inherited by Judaism and Christianity) by the concept of sin.

Given the presence of such prominent theodic impulses in Lamentations, it is no wonder that the dominant interpretive pose assumed by most critical interpreters of these poems has been overwhelmingly theodic in orientation. But to read Lamentations as theodicy is finally to misread Lamentations. Alongside the theodic there appear decidedly more tragic or antitheodic sensibilities (Dobbs-Allsopp, "Tragedy"; Braiterman). Zachary Braiterman calls antitheodic all refusals "to justify, explain, or accept as somehow meaningful the relationship between God and suffering" (31; cf. 4, 35–59; see Farley for a comparable understanding of "tragedy"). The appeal of antitheodic sentiments, as with literary tragedies, is increased at precisely those moments when social and symbolic orders seem most vulnerable, when a community's very survival is at stake. At such times, "the need to uphold an endangered community may deflect religious actors from defending God or explaining evil" from within the normative frameworks of meaning already in place (Braiterman, 20). Though potentially blasphemous, the bite of antitheodicy's sting depends fundamentally on a persistent and stubborn love for God: "Faith because it is trust in God demands justice of God" (Berkovits, 68). The poet of Lamentations, with the future existence of the post-destruction community in Palestine at issue, searches out a middle way through to survival that continuously insists on the need to negotiate between theodic and antitheodic impulses.

For example, these poems' steadfast adherence to the God of Abraham and Sarah, Isaac and Rebekah, and Jacob and Rachel, and their attestation to God's ongoing potency must vie with distinctly antitheodic postures as well. The metaphor of God as warrior ultimately proves double-edged. Of all the biblical metaphors for God this is the most problematic, because it showcases violence at the center of Judah's speech about God and because it is open to nonpartisan construals. The poet exploits both. This time Judah bears the brunt of God's violent behavior. The multitude of dead bodies, fractured bones, and broken spirits that fill the lines of this poetry attest to the horrific outcome of God's attack. Much of the hurt is attributed directly to God, and the poems forthrightly confront God with this harmful reality, for example, "Is there any pain like my pain/ which [the LORD] inflicts on me?" (1:12b); "Look, O LORD, and see/ to whom you have done this:/ Should women eat their offspring,/ the children they have born?" (2:20a–b); "I am the man who has seen affliction/ under the rod of [the LORD's] wrath!" (3:1; all the author's very literal translations). The language in these passages, and throughout the sequence (1:5b, 12c, 13–15, 17b, 21b; 2:1–8, 17, 20–22; 3:1–18, 40–45; 4:11, 16a; 5:20, 22), highlights God's "suffering"-causing acts, not God's punishment or righteous judgment. Indeed, God is even metaphorized as "enemy" (2:4a, b; 5a), the ultimate manifestation of raw and malevolent power that aims only to maim, murder, and break. Therefore, the metaphor of God as warrior is not monolithic. It contains both theodic and antitheodic dimensions, and the poetry taps into both, even though they are at cross purposes.

Other antitheodic sentiments inform the presentation of God's presence in Lamentations as well. Negatively, metaphors for God other than the warrior metaphor are almost completely lacking, effectively denying readers access to more comforting images of God. And when such images do appear, they never signify straightforwardly. The image of God as king, the central biblical metaphor symbolizing divine providence, only occurs obliquely in reference to God's eternal enthronement in heaven (5:19; cf. 2:1), where, however, even the metaphor's overt theodic buoyancy is undercut by disjunctive phrasing and an implicit contrast with the destroyed temple, God's earthly throne. And the beneficent and nurturing images of God in 3:19–39 serve principally to remind God of God's fidelity to and providential care of Judah in the past, and to provoke the reactivation of that fidelity and care in present circumstances, and not so much as a resounding affirmation of God's overriding goodness. Even God's absence and silence are figured oppressively in Lamentations. Specific allusions to God's abandonment of Jerusalem appear throughout (1:1; 2:1, 3, 6, 7, 8; 5:20, 22) and, conspicuously, only God's voice is lacking from this otherwise highly "dialogic" poetry. Both motifs underscore God's present inaccessibility and imply God's refusal to comfort or give aid.

Such antitheodic construals of God provide eloquent if troubling testimony that God is not always experienced as a beneficent force, and sometimes honest expression of God's felt oppressiveness is necessary and even healthy. But ultimately it is Lamentations' peculiarly aggregate portrayal of God, encompassing assertions of allegiance to God and protestations against God's harmful actions, that sets this poetry apart from other exilic writings and resonates so powerfully for contemporary peoples of faith. This capacity to imagine God variously and even paradoxically, resisting the pressure to smooth out the rough edges in its resulting portrait, suggests a potentially fruitful strategy for Christians and Jews living in a post-Holocaust world and trying to navigate the nettlesome questions surrounding the issue of theodicy. Instead of staking out an extreme position and insisting on a fully congruent theory, Lamentations charts a middle course, which, however theoretically incongruent, gives pragmatic warrant to love God and to protest the aversiveness of evil.

Lamentations' treatment of human sin exhibits a similarly stubborn insistence on mixing theodic and antitheodic perspectives. As noted above, the acknowledgment of human sin in Lamentations is explicit, genuine, and significant. This acknowledgment serves to remind us that human existence—even amidst the worst imaginable atrocities—takes place within a reality of being and life that ultimately transcends the limitations of individual human concerns and desires, what the later New Testament writers would call the "kingdom of God"; and second, that the historical reality through which men and women necessarily understand, shape, and create their lives, both individually and collectively, requires human accountability and responsibility for what transpires in history. However, the poems ultimately resist the temptation to view the destruction of Jerusalem and its catastrophic suffering one-dimensionally in terms of human sin alone or "to absorb the problem

31

of suffering into guilt and sin" (Farley, 52). Such resistance is never argued explicitly, literally. Instead, Lamentations mimetically shows sin's inability to absorb the community's suffering. This is accomplished in several ways. First, in comparison to the multiple and finely detailed portraiture of suffering found in the poetry, references to sin are infrequent and always non-specific. That is, if anything, suffering is shown to absorb sin and not the other way around. Moreover, the flattened nature of the portrayal of sin does not seize the reader with the same intensity of the images of suffering, and thus sin is effectively denied much of its purchase power in the poems (Dobbs-Allsopp, "Tragedy," 34–37). Second, one senses in places an intention to stress both the utter meaninglessness of suffering, accented most effectively in the multiple depictions of children starving and dying (2:11c, 12, 19c–d; 4:3–4), orphaned and exiled (1:5c; 5:3), and murdered (1:16c; 2:22c; 4:2) and cannibalized (2:20b; 4:10), and suffering's gratuitous excess, portrayed most impressively in the images of excessive violence, such as God's continual beating ("again and again, all day long") of the "man" in 3:3 or the blackened and skin-shriveled visage of parched and starved people (4:8–9; 5:10). Both seem to imply the presence of a qualitative disconnect between Judah's sin and the superfluity of the punishment she received, a sentiment that perhaps underlies the aphorism in 4:6: "For the chastisement of my people has been greater/ than the punishment of Sodom,/ which was overthrown in a moment,/ though no hand was laid on it" (NRSV). Or as Norman K. Gottwald maintains, there appears in Lamentations the idea "that Judah has both sinned and been sinned against" ("Lamentations," 650). Finally, when sin is mentioned, its force is frequently softened, blunted, and even undercut contextually by being linked to specific instances of suffering, as illustrated above with reference to 1:5 (cf. 1:18; 3:42; Dobbs-Allsopp, "Tragedy," 37). In this way, the poetry is able to give credence to both realities, the reality of sin and the reality of suffering, while at the same time insisting that these realities must be considered and weighed together. The resulting tension, though never resolved explicitly in the poetry itself, effectively frustrates any attempt to explain Jerusalem's suffering too superficially solely in terms of sin. Therefore, though responsibility for suffering that is unleashed by human cruelty and perversity must have its say and finally be owned, the suffering itself, in its pure aversiveness and utter meaninglessness, remains and can never be justified. And thus, as with its depiction of God, so also Lamentations' treatment of sin is creatively heterogeneous, giving both theodic and antitheodic notions their due, without attempting, prematurely, to resolve the paradoxes that emerge. This poet's ancient faith, then, as initially discerned

32

from his portrayal of God and his treatment of sin, in its honest struggle to balance fidelity to God and attention to felt human needs, in its dynamism, openness to change, and willingness to live with paradox and uncertainty, has much to commend to those of us who live in these early hours of the twenty-first century.

Suffering and Language

Among the cruelest phenomenal qualities of suffering is its purely aversive capacity to strip away a person's mental abilities and to destroy language, "bringing about an immediate reversion to a state anterior to language, to the sounds and cries a human being makes before language is learned" (Scarry, 4; cf. Soelle, 69, 70; Levinas, 91, 92). Lamentations retards and inverts this corrosion of language through a recovery of language itself and by giving voice to Jerusalem's experience of suffering. Encasing the poetry in an alphabetic frame (four times over!) visibly displays and enacts this recovery of language, as words and phrases literally materialize out of the very letters of the alphabet by which they are themselves composed. The movement from the sequence's opening primordial scream of "Eikhaaah!" (which is as much a token of glossolalia or pure sound—the kind of prereferential ejaculation to which language is so often reduced by extreme suffering—as a semantically weighted word [NRSV's "How"]) to the articulate speech of the rest of the poetry ("lonely sits the city . . .") similarly well symbolizes these poems' reclamation of language from the wordless garble of anguished speech (cf. 2:1; 4:1). And the regaining of voice is fictively and spectacularly enacted in the figure of personified Zion, whom readers literally witness coming to voice over the course of the first two poems, at first slowly and fitfully in abrupt eruptions of entreaty (1:9c, 11c), but eventually with more assurance and fortitude emblematic of her reemergent vitality (1:12–22; 2:20–22).

Perhaps Lamentations' most ambitious and pervasive means for giving voice lies in the distinctively ritualistic quality of its lyric. Beyond the more fictive capacities of the lyric noted in our earlier discussion, Lamentations' lyricism is enabled by and shot through with ritual or performative elements as well. As Hillers observes, "Both the poetic forms found in the book and the organization of the poems fit Lamentations for 'ritual' in the broad sense, in which many a poem is an abstraction from experience that invites contemplation, repetition, and the participation of others besides the author" (6). Lyric poetry, generally, is discourse that is meant to be uttered again. Through its ritual properties the lyric poem becomes accessible, open, in a way analogous to liturgies and other structures of devotion, and achieves a kind of transitivity, a quality of transferable experience, whereby the reader, enchanted and entranced, entertains the statements made by the poem's speakers, tries them on, and reexperiences them from the inside, as it were (Greene, 9). In this way, the poetry itself through rituality becomes a coercive force for giving voice.

This rituality works mostly under the surface of the poetry in Lamentations, manifested in and activated through the poems' recurring rhythms, forms, and sonic features, breaking in on readers' consciousness only at those moments when they find themselves persuaded to and indeed identifying with the sentiments expressed (as, for example, by personified Zion in the first two poems). Rituality is also explicitly scripted into the sequence on a larger scale as the ritual giving of voice provides Lamentations with its basic curve of movement, its overarching trajectory. Through the first three poems the reader is allowed, for the most part, to remain a passive observer. However effective the personalizing of suffering in the figures of personified Zion and the man of Lamentations 3, they nevertheless remain at some level "others" to readers. Their experiences and hurts, empathy causing as they are, remain theirs and not ours. We the readers may be moved and angered, but only as a collective third party. This begins to change midway through the third poem, where for the first time the voice of the audience ("we") is inscribed explicitly within the poetry (3:40–47). Here there is a brief joining of identities, as the man's experience becomes also our experience. We briefly taste and voice for ourselves the bitterness of his suffering, but after seven short couplets the "I" is reasserted and we the audience are allowed to resume our onlooker status.

The ritual inscribing begun in Lamentations 3 is picked up again in Lamentations 4. This time instead of focusing on a particular figure, as in the earlier poems, the poet presents a series of vignettes featuring representative groups of individuals. Here there is a distinctive widening of the poetry's reach and perspective. No longer is the dominant voice that of an individual, but of a group of individuals. Then in 4:17 the poet shifts into the first-person plural voice again ("we"). The transition is so smooth it is almost imperceptible. This is because we the readers have been prepared for this, not only by our experience from Lamentations 3, but by the group—communal!—orientation of the first part of Lamentations 4. By the end of this poem the reader's inscription is complete. Lamentations 5 is voiced completely by "we" the reader. And thus Lamentations works its ritual magic slowly but determinedly over the course of the sequence as a whole, and by the end the poetry's readership becomes Lamentations' third embodiment of suffering. This final rendition of suffering again travels over the same geography of pain as was traversed earlier. The difference is that this time it is explicitly the reader's pain and the reader's suffering, which makes all the difference. The screams and atrocities and protests that these poems figure are thus coercively superimposed on the reader so that they are felt and understood and experienced and finally voiced as the reader's own. For those who come to Lamentations hurting and struck dumb by suffering's cruel ravages, not only do they find comfort in the knowledge that they do not suffer alone, but they also find, unbidden, a language for their suffering. To come across language in which one finds one's own hurts and grief so precisely and accurately named and expressed can be a wonderfully consoling and forever transformative experience.

The potential significance of Lamentations' voicing of pain may be measured in any number of different ways. Medically, the binding up of the mental wounds caused by suffering is every bit as important as healing the sufferer's physical wounds. In particular, as Dorothee Soelle well stresses, the "phase of expression" in which sufferers find a language for voicing their fears and pain is all important and cannot be skipped (71–72). Language and the "powers of conception" that language enable are decisive for human "creatural viability"—humans are fundamentally biocultural beings whose existence and flourishing depends on the physical wellness of a biological organism and of that organism's enduring capacity to create culture. Robbed of linguistic capabilities, a person becomes "a kind of formless monster with neither sense of direction nor power of self-control, a chaos of spasmodic impulses and vague emotions" (Geertz, 99). Therapeutically, the poet's act of linguistic creation and the subsequent acts of recreation by the poems' readership, like all material acts of making, project aliveness and sentience outward, while at the same time forcing pain itself into an objectified state and thereby alleviating and, when most successful, even eliminating pain's aversiveness (cf. Scarry, 5–6, 164, 288). Ethically, pain brought to speech, as it is in Lamentations, is an act of protest, an assertion of pain's uselessness and malignancy that is unforgivable wherever and whenever encountered, and that always calls for active consolation and medication (Levinas, esp. 90–101; Brueggemann, *Old Testament Theology,* chaps. 2–3).

Lastly, even imaginatively, the weight of Lamentations' fictive language is such that it is able to render suffering endurable, or "sufferable," as Clifford Geertz says (104). The imagination is a person's "last resource for the generation of objects" that the world fails to provide, and as such it potentially wields tremendous power. For example, if there is no actual food available for a hungry person, imagining berries and grain, at least

35

temporarily, can transform the aversive sensations of hunger into potentially positive feelings and in so doing perhaps motivate action that will eventually alleviate the hunger itself (Scarry, 166–67). Or in conditions of political and juridical oppression, poetic images of a just and incorruptible dream court can alleviate some of the sting of injustice, allow tyranny's oppression to be endured a little longer, and inspire work toward justice and fairness for all (Heaney, 38–62). Similarly, in Lamentations, suffering's survivability is above all implicated fictively, imaginatively through language in the personae of Daughter Zion and the man of Lamentations 3. Both are depicted as having suffered severe trauma (at the hands of God) and, most important, as having survived. In each instance the reader is left with the enduring image of speech recovered, as both Zion and the man recede from the poetry literally speaking—a gesture that symbolizes language's rebirth and suffering's ultimate medication.

In sketching the various kinds of work that poetry of grief and suffering routinely accomplishes, I do not mean to determine in an *a priori* fashion Lamentations' meaning and function for all situations. It is surely the case that readers will come to these poems (collectively and individually) and remain unmoved by them, or will not find in them thoughts and feelings that mirror their own experiences. Rather, it is the prizing itself of the language event (e.g., poem, novel, short story, sermon) as work that I wish to highlight. Work is most often conceptualized as a physical action, something we do, something we can accomplish tactilely with our hands. But linguistic acts, as they open up and forge "paths on which language gets a voice," to borrow a phrase from Paul Celan (as cited in Felstiner, 140), are every bit as crucial and theologically significant in times of great suffering as anything we can physically do, and it is this that the above survey is meant to stress. Lamentations' giving of voice to suffering is absolutely necessary if we are to survive lamentations (cf. Linafelt).

Grief, Complaint, Anger, Fidelity

What gets voiced in Lamentations is as important as the fact of voicing itself. Four aspects of Lamentations' voiced content may be highlighted initially: grief, complaint, anger, and fidelity. These poems show and voice grief throughout (1:2, 11, 16, 17, 20–21; 2:9–13, 18–19; 3:48–51; 5:15, 17). This liturgy of grief functions in multiple ways. Practically, through the example of its speech, Lamentations both gives permission to grieve and provides a vocabulary for grief. Indeed, by including expressions of grief in speech to God, Lamentations, like the Gospels' portrayal of a grieved and grieving Jesus, witnesses grief and the work of grief as integral parts of biblical faith and piety. More therapeutically, as Hillers well notes, Lamentations originally "was meant to serve the survivors of the catastrophe simply as an *expression* of the horror and grief they felt. People live on best after calamity, not by utterly repressing their grief and shock, but by facing it, and by measuring its dimensions" (4). The poetry continues to function in a therapeutic vein even for those of us who come to and read these poems many centuries later. As we read and willingly enter into the world of discourse that Lamentations creates, we submit ourselves to Lamentations' consoling ministry of language whereby grief is ritualized and thus made bearable. In naming grief, grief itself becomes owned, valorized, and thus ultimately consolable and healable. As Geertz notes, one of the most important things that liturgies and poetries of grief can do is to teach us how to grieve (103–5). Grief itself cannot be avoided, but it can be made endurable, sufferable. In fact, one of Lamentations' most hopeful facets is the multitude of images of grief-stricken people—Zion, the man, the poet-narrator, assorted members of the larger community—who nevertheless are portrayed as surviving. The implicit message is that grief, no matter how debilitating, is finally survivable. Grief need not do us in, but rather can deepen and enlarge us, both by "our refusal to vanish" because of it and by our refusal "to let others vanish." In turning wordless grief into articulate speech, Lamentations transforms loss into remembrance and bequeaths to its readership of all ages an inheritance of projected aliveness (cf. Hirsch, 80–87).

Finally, by locating grief at the center of its discourse, Lamentations valorizes grief's epistemological capacities. Western culture, in particular, oftentimes appears impatient with or embarrassed by acute grief and deep sorrow and thus rushes to medicate it away. But grief and the need to grieve is a part of our creaturely makeup, and like other human emotions embodies in holistic fashion (kinetically and cognitively) a powerful way of knowing. In particular, grief identifies through the objects it takes those people and things deemed most important to us, and acknowledges our fundamental neediness and lack of self-sufficiency, our vulnerability to external forces beyond our control. The latter, in particular, as James Gustafson might say, provides the kind of empirical occasion in which the reality of transcendence that marks the divine is most readily apprehendable. Therefore, by creating space for grief and teaching how to grieve, Lamentations models a way of knowing that is essential to our well-being and health. Indeed, as the psychiatric and medical professions know all too well, grief ignored or too quickly bypassed potentially can fester and grow into harmful pathologies that ultimately distort and deform our creaturely makeup.

Grievance stands alongside grief as a featured part of Lamentations' voiced content. As Claus Westermann reminds us, the overwhelming majority of lines in Lamentations are dedicated to complaint (222). Indeed, each of the sequence's major voices features prolonged stretches of accusation-filled complaint addressed to God (1:12–22; 2:20–22; 3:1–18; 5:1–18). We have already noted the church's recent (re)discovery of the importance of lament and complaint to biblical faith. Here I want to sketch more precisely just what is at stake theologically for the church in appropriating complaint as a mode of address to God. In particular, one notes what the valorization of complaint implies about the nature of God, humanity, and the divine-human relationship. To voice complaint in the midst of suffering is a bold and heroic feat of self-actualization, as Brueggemann describes:

> The moment when Israel found the nerve and the faith to risk an assault on the throne of God with complaint was a decisive moment against legitimation. The lament is a dramatic, rhetorical, liturgical act of speech that is irreversible. When spoken, it is done and cannot be recalled. It makes clear that Israel will no longer be a submissive, subservient recipient of decrees from the throne. There is a bold movement from Israel's side—a voice that does not silently and docilely accept but means to have its dangerous say, even in the face of God. In risking this form of speech, the conventional distribution of power is called into question. It is no longer placidly assumed that God has all the power and the covenant partner must simply submit. Pain speaks against legitimacy, which now for the first time is questioned as perhaps illegitimate. (*Old Testament Theology*, p. 27)

In complaint, suffering's aversiveness is resisted and its affront to human dignity is named as unnatural, abhorrent, and unacceptable. Complaint boldly reasserts the goodness for which we were created as the only authentic mode of existence for humanity.

Second, complaint also reaffirms the radically relational nature of the divine-human relationship that undergirds biblical faith. There is, of course, no question as to God's ultimate sovereignty in this relationship. But the prominent role of lament and complaint in the psalmic laments, Job, and Lamentations reminds us that God's sovereignty is exercised to the benefit of God's covenant partner, and therefore not only does it tolerate human input, it requires it. It is our responsibility to bring our concerns—pain and suffering foremost among them— before the throne of God and to insist on God's renewed action on our behalf. In one respect, complaint is the lifeblood of the biblical notion of covenant: it ensures that the relationship is alive, dynamic, and open. Here faith is real, contested, actively negotiated. As Brueggemann observes, "The voiced hurt of Israel is the material base from which the holy power of God is activated to transform, destabilize, and reorder the world" (*Old Testament Theology*, 48; cf. Levenson, esp. 149–56). Similarly, complaint recharacterizes God. Scripture confesses God as a "living God" and complaint stakes all on the accuracy of this belief. God as sovereign is free to act as God chooses, but complaint asserts concomitantly that God's choices must take account of human trouble: "God is no longer a trouble-free God, and the trouble is recharacterized as something that now is the proper agenda of Yahweh" (Brueggemann, *Old Testament Theology*, 29). Omnipotence when recharacterized through complaint ceases to be a static attribute and becomes instead "a dramatic enactment: the absolute power of God realizing itself in achievement and relationship" (Levenson, xvi). Thus, biblical complaints attest to God's willingness to be impinged upon by human concerns—nothing falls outside of God's responsibility. And if God as God must retain unlimited freedom to act, even potentially to the perceived detriment of humanity, God's inmost will, as revealed most prototypically in the election of Abraham (for Jews) and in the incarnation in one Jesus of Nazareth (for Christians), is for interactive and vulnerable community with the world, even at the cost of death.

In these poems one hears not only complaint but occasionally even anger directed toward God. Lamentations 2:20–22 is an especially good example, where, as O'Connor notes, we are confronted by Zion's "unbridled anger at God" (1043). Such modeling of anger in prayer to God is critical, for it shows that even our most damning and hurtful thoughts and feelings may be brought before God. To have permission and an outlet for the expression of rage has important cathartic value, as many biblical scholars and theologians are now recognizing. This is especially true for those who have experienced the helplessness of victimization. Expressing anger can often serve as "an alternative to living in the realm of inner deadness" caused by victimization (Billman and Migliore, 120). Moreover, 2:20–22 also shows how extremely valuable our emotions can be as guides to and motivators of right action. As noted above, finding "a language that leads out of the uncomprehended suffering that makes one mute" (Soelle, 70) is an incredibly significant and salvific act in and of itself. In Lamentations 2 it is Zion's anger and nothing else, boiling under the surface for most of the poem, that ultimately leads her to speak, to articulate, and to name her hurt and pain. And what is more, this is not only speech for speech's sake, however therapeutic that may be, but it is speech addressed to God. God's silence is pervasive, even deafening, in Lamentations. It is in and through and by means of her anger that Zion refuses to accept God's muteness as the status quo. Angry Zion "transcends the mute God" of Lamentations and insists on "the speaking God of a reality experienced with feeling in pain and happiness" (Soelle, 78).

This of course is not to say that all forms of anger are necessarily justified or always appropriate. Beyond their kinetic surge of affect and the quality of their felt experience, emotions like anger also have a cognitive content that is open to criticism and discussion. Very simply—indeed too simply—anger consists of a painful feeling component and the belief that one (or someone held dear) has been slighted, wronged, injured in a very serious way (cf. Nussbaum, 383). At the level of the text in Lamentations, Zion's pain is explicitly represented in terms of her own personal victimization (especially in the first poem) and in terms of the hurt caused to her metaphorical children, the men, women, and children of Jerusalem. Moreover, it is made equally clear that God is the chief cause of this hurt and this pain (see esp. 2:1–8), thus confirming Zion's belief that God has indeed killed and butchered her citizenry. Thus, it is fair to conclude that Zion's expression of anger in this instance is more than justified. But what is crucial is that this is an opinion that can be sustained critically, and therefore the valorization of specific instances of an emotion need not necessarily justify all forms of that emotion. Nor should anger be our sole stance before God. The poem's lyric mode of discourse actively frustrates proclivities toward such universalization. Lyric's capacity to express compellingly felt moods and ideas freely, no matter how partial or limited in perspective, does not *ipso facto* require that these moods or ideas be always and everywhere appropriate or that other, even potentially conflicting, moods cannot also be appropriate. Zion's anger at God in 2:20–22 need not *necessarily* impinge one way or another on the other stances she takes before God.

Lastly, fidelity to God is central to what is voiced in Lamentations. Though this aspect of Lamentations' voiced content also has been previously noted, its importance and manner of articulation justify further commentary. Fidelity to God is nowhere explicitly named in Lamentations, rather, it is articulated rhetorically and generically. That is, the poems on occasion specifically address Yahweh, the God of Judah (1:9c, 11c, 20a; 2:20a; 3:42, 55–66; 5:1, 19). But even were such explicit invocations completely absent, we still would know from genre considerations that it is God who is the poems' primary intended audience. In our tendency to privilege propositional content over more formal aspects of literary art, we are in danger of overlooking the underlying allegiance pledged by these poems to Yahweh. Recalling Lamentations' overriding lyricism, a mode of discourse that by necessity can mean as much

40

through form as through content, will perhaps help us to recognize the implications of faithfulness that inhere in these poems' address to God.

Still, it is hard for us today to appreciate fully the radicality of these poems' tenacious allegiance to the God of the ancestors, Yahweh Sabaoth, even when conscious of the meaningfulness of rhetoric and genre. As a means for gaining some perspective, consider that in antiquity, when civilizations suffered the kind of overwhelming defeat and collapse experienced by Judah at the beginning of the sixth century, they routinely became relegated to the dustbin of history. Witness, for example, the fate of the various superpowers of the ancient Near East—Assyria, Babylon, Hatti, Egypt, which, once expunged from history, were never heard from again. Ironically and by contrast, the kingdom of Judah, always only a marginal political player in its day and perennially a cultural backwater, survived, primarily through its religious heritage, to shape much of Western culture. This state of affairs owes much to the exilic and post-exilic writers, like the poet of Lamentations, who refused to concede victory to the deities of their conquerors and instead continued steadfastly to engage Yahweh, prayerfully, liturgically, even if not always in unabashed adulation. Fidelity to God, though never topicalized, remains the driving force behind these poems, and it does so fully aware of the terrible nature of God's violence and the pain of God's abandonment.

The Face of Suffering

From the very beginning Lamentations *visually* confronts the reader with the hurtful reality of human suffering in extremity (cf. Moore). Images of the human body mangled through violence, contorted by hunger, or bent in grief appear in almost every line. On the one hand, suffering is rendered mostly in piecemeal fashion through a succession of abrupt and fragmented images. These focus attention at the level of individual and particular experiences: a woman raped, a child starving, a man attacked by a lion or hunted like a bird, young boys compelled into slavery and old men abused and no longer respected, a people spurned by their God. Yet that these very concrete and specific instances of suffering have been intentionally gathered together, each strung, as it were, like individual pearls on a necklace formed by the alphabetic acrostic, ensures that they mean cumulatively as well as individually. That is, this profusion of images constructs a richly and finely contoured topography of pain and suffering, eerily mirroring the shattered and fractured reality of post-destruction Jerusalem. The sheer number and diversity of these evocations—they overwhelm and suffuse every aspect of the poetry—gestures effectively toward the vastness and incomparability of a suffering in which no one is left untouched. On the

41

other hand, recognizing, as Wendy Farley notes, that suffering "arises out of the particularity of a situation and is experienced through personal immediacy" (56), a significant number of these fractured images are gathered and unified through a common voice or persona— Jerusalem personified as a suffering woman (chiefly in Lamentations 1 and 2), the male voice in Lamentations 3 ("I am the *man* who has seen affliction," 3:1), and the communal "we" of the final three poems (3:40–47; 4:17–20; 5:1–22). Each perspective views the reality of pain and hurt but in different embodiments and using different language. If the great multiplicity of images of suffering in Lamentations foregrounds the depth and breadth of these horrific events, then the extended encounter with these specific personae focuses most sharply the personal and individual embodiments of the victimization, as the hurt and humiliation of particular and identifiable figures are shown repeatedly.

The portrait of suffering that emerges in Lamentations stands poignantly as a monument to the many who suffered and died in the Babylonian destruction of Jerusalem. Yet in gathering these fragmented images of human suffering, the poet wants to do more than only ensure the enduring memory of this terrible event, though that in itself is a praiseworthy accomplishment. He also means to set them beside his more directly voiced utterances (see above) as a means for winning God's regard and for commanding compassion. That is, one finds no prolonged discussion, for example, probing the many unsettling questions raised by the reality of human suffering in this world, but only the insistence, voiced time and again, that God "look" and "see" the human face of suffering: "O LORD, look at my affliction" (1:9c), "Look, O LORD, and see/ how I am being distressed" (1:11c, au. trans.), "See, O LORD how distressed I am" (1:20a), "Look, O LORD, and see/ to whom you have harmed thusly" (2:20a, au. trans.), "My eyes will flow without ceasing,/ without respite,/ until the LORD from heaven/ looks down and sees" (3:49–50), "See, O LORD, the wrong done to me" (3:59, au. trans.), and "[O LORD,] look, and see our disgrace!" (5:1). These poems stake all, it would seem, on the conviction that the mere sight of Jerusalem's bruised and battered population is sufficient to reawaken God from God's silence and inactivity and move God to responsibility, forgiveness, and compassion. A similar conviction about the mysterious and primordial ethical power revealed in the "face to face" encounter with the "Other" informs the thought of the philosopher Emmanuel Levinas. For Levinas, the "face" is "that which thus in another concerns the *I*— concerns me—reminding me, from behind the countenance he puts on in his portrait, of his abandonment, his defenselessness and his mortal-

42

ity, and his appeal to my ancient responsibility, as if he were unique in the world—beloved. An appeal of the face of my fellowman, which, in its ethical urgency, postpones or cancels the obligations the 'summoned *I*' has toward itself and in which the concern for the death of the other can be more important to the *I* than its concern as an *I* for itself" (227). Thus, in good Levinasian fashion, the multiple and variegated "faces" of hurting humanity that are represented and evoked in these poems mean to provoke in God an ethical response of empathy for the countless numbers of abandoned, defenseless, and mortal people who, as it were, stand behind the poems' "plastic forms."

Implicit, as well, in Lamentations' imaginistic discourse is a strong valorization of embodied life and trust in God's final nonindifference to human hurt. The many graphic representations of exposed nakedness (1:8b), burned and broken bones (1:13a; 3:4), bloodied visages (1:15c; 4:14), expiring infants (2:12), slain bodies (2:21a), and the searing physical ache of profound grief (1:20; 2:11) all serve "to remind us that we are embodied creatures, that our bodies and the bodies of others need attention and care" and to protest all harmful abuse of our bodies and of the bodies of our neighbors (Billman and Migliore, 108). Moreover, in presenting these images of violated and mutilated bodies before God, these poems dare to believe that Judah's collective bodily integrity and well-being still matters to the God who created an embodied humanity in God's own image, and who elected the seed of Abraham in a thoroughly carnal way, through body and blood (cf. Wyschogrod, 58–65, 175–77)—a belief that for Christians is symbolized paradigmatically in God's own embodiment in Jesus Christ and in the cross event, where God through the suffering of the embodied Christ responds unequivocally to this world's suffering with a suffering for the suffering of others (cf. Levinas, 94).

Furthermore, insofar as lyric poetry is quintessentially discourse that is intended to be overheard, the ethical appeal incarnated in Lamentations' imagery is directed no less urgently to those of us who overhear this poetry. We, too, like those "passersby" in 1:12, are implored to "look" and "see" Zion's unparalleled pain and are meant to be lured away from neutrality and toward the concerns of those who have suffered. The move is crucial because, as Levinas so well understood, suffering that is "intrinsically senseless" and excessive and totally overwhelming, like the suffering represented in Lamentations, has no way out except through the "beyond" that "appears in the form of the interhuman" (94). We who read these poems, even belatedly, no less than the God who is addressed overtly, stand as the "beyond" that constitutes suffering's only promise of consolation, amelioration, and salvation. By

43

helping us to imagine ourselves in the other person's skin, to see things as if we were, even momentarily, that other person, suffering and hurting, this poetry empowers us to imagine a world "as it could be otherwise," a world where the other's suffering is consoled and comforted and then resisted and protested (Kearney, 368–71). So the claim that this poetry makes on us through its images of a wounded humanity is finally nothing less than Jesus' own embodied example of a selfless love for our neighbor.

Finally, it is in the "face to face" encounter with the other who confronts us from without that the epiphany of God is primordially mediated to us and for us, or as Levinas says, that God falls "into meaning" (Baird, 81; cf. Levinas, 57). God is encountered in the face of the suffering other and our relationship to God, then, is to be worked out through our engagement with the other, through our care for the other. From the point of view of biblical faith, the God of Israel, however mediated (e.g., whether through the covenant with Abraham or the incarnation in Christ), is made known and always encountered through the fragmentation and brokenness of created historical existence. And thus, Lamentations, as it facilitates encounters with the suffering other through its imagery, literarily and linguistically creates space for God's eruption into our lives, for revelation.

Divine Violence

For people of faith, one of the most disturbing aspects of Lamentations is its threefold depiction of divine violence (1:13–15; 2:1–8; 3:1–18). It is ultimately easier to come to terms with God's absence and silence, even if willed, than to imagine God as actively violent and hurtful. To our human way of thinking, the latter represents a difference in degree of a whole order of magnitude. And yet it is precisely the abusive and harmful presence of God that we meet unmistakably and repeatedly in the lines of this poetry. Therefore, however loath we may be to take up the topic of divine violence, it is a topic that cannot be evaded if we are to encounter this part of scripture with the integrity it so richly deserves. If the ultimate why of God's violence (as we perceive it) must necessarily remain beyond our ken, shrouded in mystery, there are, nevertheless, a number of things that may be said constructively with respect to the presence of divine violence in Lamentations. First, that violence is a part of the scriptural witness to God cannot be gainsaid. Its thematic appearance in the Old Testament is by no means limited to Lamentations alone (cf. Job 16:1–17:16; Ps. 88; Jer. 20:7–13), nor can Christians sidestep the unpleasantry of this aspect of the divine by moving to the New Testament (Heb. 12:5–11). Indeed, it is above all an event of violence, the death of Jesus of Nazareth, crucified on a cross, that stands at the center of the Gospel stories about Christ. Second, divine violence cannot be treated in isolation from other language about God. If God is violent, God is also loving, benevolent, compassionate, all powerful, and wise. And for Christians the violence of the cross itself represents, preeminently, the revelation of the nonviolent love of God, God's solidarity through Christ with us as victims of violence, and the promise of God that the violence and counterviolence of this world will not win out in the end. Here it is helpful once again to recall Lamentations' overriding lyric sensibility, which, while giving expression to one compelling thought (such as God's capacity for violence), does so without insisting that this thought is always and universally appropriate and while acknowledging the always ever larger world of discourse in which all discourse necessarily takes place. Third, by locating violence in the divine, Lamentations compels us to confront the topic of violence more generally. Our world no less than the world of our ancient forebears is a world of violence. Whether it is at home, in the schoolyard, on city streets, or on the shores of another country, violence would appear to be sewn into the very fabric of our domestic, social, and political lives. We all, in one form or another, are caught up in violence's vicious play, either as victims or victimizers, or more likely, a bit of both. This is true even despite our best and most ethically responsible intentions to the contrary: to have regard for an "Other" means de facto to disregard some other "Other," even to condemn that "Other" to death (Derrida, 85–86). Violence in modern-day America and throughout the world is a topic we ignore at the peril of ours and our children's lives. Fourth, Lamentations' attribution of violence to God, especially as that violence finds its mark in God's faithful servants, gives honest expression to the felt experience of God's hostile presence; it acknowledges that we do not always experience God as comforting, loving, familiar, that sometimes our lived reality gives every impression of being radically out of alignment with the beneficence and weal of God's promises. For the faithful language of God—God-talk—is that language by, with, and through which we construe those aspects of our creaturely existence that we deem to be most vital, crucial, of ultimate concern. By linguistically inscribing God into the violence of human suffering and physical pain, our poet in a very real way is attempting to lend his discourse of human hurt the heft and weight it requires, and to say what is not only destructive of language itself but what is ultimately unsayable in language and saying it in a way that is compelling and that communicates and is respectful of suffering's ultimate quiddity. The suffered experience of post-destruction Jerusalem was so severe and so nonsensical and aversive that the only means

45

by which this poet can even begin to approach measuring such hurt is by attributing it directly to God. Finally, the descriptions of God's violence, especially as they are voiced in the complaints of Zion (1:13–15, 20–22) and the man (3:1–18), are leveled as accusations, protests against the reality of such violation of human bodily integrity, and therefore ultimately serve to delegitimize the violence that so routinely seems to afflict human lives. In the end, as Brueggemann observes, believers "cannot answer for or justify [such] violence, but must concede that it belongs to the very fabric" of biblical faith (381).

Fragments of Hope

Hope, like much else in Lamentations, is multidimensional, fragmentary, and uneven, and if it is never boastful or celebratory and if at times one has to strain to hear even its loudest notes, its presence in these poems, nevertheless, is unmistakable. Hope is implicated above all in the fact of survival, for these poems are pitched toward survival. Each poem is voiced from the perspective of survivors—personified Zion, the man of Lamentations 3, the communal voice heard sporadically throughout the sequence, though chiefly and most emphatically in the final poem, are survivors all. And it is the variegated voice of survival that each persona leaves in bequest to Lamentations' readership: Zion hurting, very much in pain though able to articulate that pain (1:20–22) and even to rage at her God (2:20–22); the man, his suffering unabated, summoning God's help (3:55–63) and inveighing against his enemies (3:64–66); and the community able to address God, even if only with hard questions and unhappy avowals (5:19–22). The title of Tod Linafelt's recent monograph, *Surviving Lamentations,* captures precisely the guiding tilt of these poems. And when read against the backdrop of tragic literature more generally, these voices take on a heroic hue, though in a distinctly un-tragic way. Unlike classic tragedies, where the hero is some individual of rank or status who wins heroic stature through action, the voices in Lamentations are plainly common and predominantly communal and their chief heroic quality lies in the accident of their survival—"I am the man who has known affliction" (3:1, as in NJPS)—a feat not achieved necessarily by noble means (note the reference to cannibalization of children in 2:20b). The hope that inheres in such survival is not principally inspirational or celebratory in nature, but more closely akin to the faintest sense of relief that accompanies the realization that one is still not dead, that life itself stubbornly persists (cf. Linafelt, 20–25).

Indeed, it is the hope of projected life that is felt most strongly in

Lamentations. As noted above, aliveness and sentience are projected in Lamentations' recovery of language and bestowal of voice. And there is a liveliness in the kind of lyric play (illustrated above) that belies the poetry's otherwise gloomy subject matter and sad tonal shadings. As Heaney writes:

> [W]hen a poem rhymes, when a form generates itself, when a metre provokes consciousness into new postures, it is already on the side of life. When a rhyme surprises and extends the fixed relations between words, that in itself protests against necessity. When language does more than enough, as it does in all achieved poetry, it opts for the conditions of overlife, and rebels at limit. (158)

Lamentations stimulates hope as much through its lyric effects as it does through any of its overtly thematized subject matter. Suffering is resisted and defied and despair is held in check by the energy and robustness of the poem's lyric play. This is typical of tragic lyric poetry. As Ronald P. Draper observes,

> The form of the poem, by creating a pressure against which language exerts itself, . . . and all the modifications of tone and attitude that are effected by diction, rhythm, syntax and rhetorical and figurative devices are likewise the means by which an equivalent of the tragic protagonist's resistance rather than capitulation to suffering may be created within the lyric. (4)

This kind of lyric play in and of itself cannot bring about a change in the material conditions of suffering envisioned in the poems, but it can "break the dominion of suffering over the spirit" and mediate through the moments of pleasure and delight and aliveness which it effects a "taste of love" and the "power of courage" that are themselves at least the beginnings of hope (Farley, 117, 132–33).

Hope inheres as well in the poetry's many small gestures that embody human dignity and advocate human rights: the protests against suffering's aversiveness; the voiced resistance to the reality of divine violence; the embryonic sense of justice and fairness that hides in otherwise cold and ugly invectives; the calls for compassion; the prizing of emotions; the respect shown for embodied life; the foregrounding of community; and the faith placed in the life-giving powers of the human imagination. None of these are ever elaborated upon, nor are they ever woven together into a whole. Rather, they are simply allowed to pulse, mostly individually but clearly heroically, through the lines of these poems. Each in its own way, however small and seemingly insignificant, reasserts the goodness for which God created human beings.

47

The lone thematic treatment of hope appears in the middle section of the third poem (3:19–24, 25–39). There the speaker distinctly articulates a resolve to hope, locates that hope in God, and seems genuinely buoyed (at least momentarily) by traditional admonitions to trust God and accept suffering. Owing to its thematic embodiment, its more or less central location within the larger sequence, and its pronounced theodic proclivities, scholars have shown a tendency to highlight the theological significance of this version of hope, some even proclaiming the section Lamentations' high point and theological center. What is potentially disturbing about the privileging of this theodic construal of hope is that when left unqualified it risks transfiguring the pain and suffering so prominently displayed in Lamentations in a way that can endow them with a false and hurtful sense of meaning and purpose. In an age after Auschwitz such a risk, even if unwitting, cannot be tolerated. As Irving Greenberg pointedly reminds us, "No statement, theological or otherwise, should be made that would not be credible in the presence of the burning children" (23). Moreover, it ultimately distorts and simplifies the overall complexity of the poetry in Lamentations, which actively resists explanations or justifications of human suffering, first, within Lamentations 3 itself, where the theodicy of hope that gets played out at the poem's surface is localized, countered, questioned, and generally complicated in important ways (as I try to show in detail in the commentary below), and second, within the larger sequence of poems, where, as we have discovered, there exists a variety of different inflections of hope, some of which clearly ground their acts of expectation in resistance to suffering's aversiveness. Like other aspects of Lamentations' theology, then, its hope has both theodic and antitheodic poles that readers are encouraged to engage tensively and holistically. But whether theodic or antitheodic, hope in Lamentations has but one object, God, and one desire, to see suffering relieved. As Jon D. Levenson astutely observes, "the overwhelming tendency of biblical writers as they confront undeserved evil is not to *explain* it away but to call upon God to *blast* it away" (xvii). It is this very sentiment that stands as the ground of Lamentations' variously expressed and fragmented hope.

No Comfort

LAMENTATIONS 1

In the opening poem of Lamentations, readers are confronted at once with the hurt and pain of physical suffering in the lived immediacy of a single woman ravished, abandoned, and uncomforted. That woman, the personified, destroyed city of Jerusalem, is the central figure through and in which Lamentations 1 is shaped and unified. Otherwise, it is only the poem's formal patterns of repetition that hold the whole together. The alphabetic acrostic constrains the first line of every stanza and the stanzas themselves consist of six lines or three couplets (1:7 is the only exception). Along with Lamentations 2, this poem exhibits the highest proportion of enjambed lines within the couplet. The first half of the poem (1:1–11) shows the suffering as it is refracted through personified Jerusalem herself. She is the grammatical and semantic topic throughout, the chief antecedent of most of the verbs and pronominal forms in this section. Third-person feminine pronominal forms dominate. This serial repetition of like independent pronouns and pronominal affixes on nouns and verbs serves as an important organizing device throughout Lamentations, helping to secure intersectional unity (e.g., first-person singular forms [I/me/my] in 1:12–22, third-person masculine forms [he/him/his] in 2:1–8, and first-person plural forms [we/us/our] in 5:1–22). The suffering itself is related through a series of images that are drawn chiefly from female experiences: Jerusalem is imagined as a widow (1:1b), a princess who has become enslaved (1:1c), a woman exiled and homeless (1:3a–b), a refugee relentlessly pursued by her captors (1:3c), a mother forced to watch her children taken into captivity (1:5c), and a woman subjected to sexual assault and rape (1:8–10). Throughout this half of the poem the reader is positioned principally as a third party who is only hearing of Jerusalem's horrid experience from someone else. The reader is not totally disinterested. Presumably members of the poem's original audience would have experienced the events refracted in the poem and, besides, the figure of Zion is at one level a personification of the people

49

themselves. Therefore, while space is created initially between Jerusalem's experience and that of the reader through the poem's positioning of the reader, allowing him or her to remain detached (aesthetically) from the events described in the poem, there is nevertheless a close connection between the two that lies dormant, just under the surface of the poem, to be exploited later. That is, this poem, and indeed Lamentations as a whole, exhibits strong sympathies for the plight of the personified city and those whom she represents.

A dramatic shift occurs in the second half of the poem (1:12–22). The suffering in this section is voiced instead of shown, as the personified city becomes the poem's principal speaker. Now first-person singular verbs and pronouns dominate. Jerusalem names her suffering (e.g., "Is there any pain like my pain" [au. trans.], 1:12b); identifies, in especially dark language, her chief tormentor, God (e.g., "From on high he sends fire,/ and causes it to descend deep in my bones," 1:13a); and calls for vengeance against the enemies (1:21–22) who surrounded (1:17b) and prevailed over her (1:16c). The reader is now confronted by the actual presence of the sufferer whom he or she only heard about in the first half of the poem. The result is that the aesthetic distance between the discourse of the poem and the reader's experience of that discourse is suddenly collapsed. The use of the first-person voice draws readers into the poem, makes them identify with the speaker, and invites them to experience vicariously the suffering and affliction that the poem figures. And in an effort to ensure the success of the poet's rhetoric, the reader's sympathies are elicited more or less explicitly from the outset of Jerusalem's speech, as the personified figure asks the passersby, who function as stand-ins for the poem's readers, whether there is any pain like the pain God has inflicted upon her (1:12). Thus, this poem's placement at the outset of the sequence is crucial for the success of Lamentations' larger rhetorical ambitions.

Excursus: **Personified Zion**

The figure of the personified city in this poem and the next is undoubtedly the most compellingly drawn figure in the whole of Lamentations. One of the consequences of the city-lament genre having been transplanted to Israelite/Judean soil was the metamorphosis of the city goddess into the personified city (presumably because of the theological pressures associated with ancient Israel and Judah's monolatrous culture). The personified city-temple complex in Lamentations functions analogously to the sorrowful, tender, and compassionate weeping goddess in the Mesopotamian laments, who so vividly and graphically realizes the agony and torment and distress that so assaulted

50

the Sumerian psyche through the experience of the catastrophic close of the Ur III period. Like these weeping goddesses, the personified city in Lamentations mourns the destruction of her city and temple and the suffering of her people (1:2a, 4c, 8c, 16a, 17a, 21a; 2:19c), confronts God in his capacity as the divine agent of destruction (1:9c, 20–22; 2:20–22), and is portrayed as a mother (1:4b, 5c, 11a, 15, 16c; 2:9b, c, 10a, 14, 19c, 21b, 22c; 4:13; cf. 5:3) who has become homeless and unable to find rest (1:1c, 3a–b, 7a). Moreover, she is even imbued with a series of epithets that all have good divine parallels: "daughter [of] Zion" (1:6a; cf. 2:1a, 2b [MT], 4c, 5c, 8a, 10a, 13a, 15b, 18a; 4:21a, 22a), "maiden Judah" (2:2a [Vg]), "maiden (= "virgin" in NRSV) daughter [of] Judah" (1:15c; cf. 2:13b), and "daughter of my people" (= "my people" in NRSV; 2:11b; 3:48; 4:3b, 6a, 10b). Indeed, the phrases translated by the NRSV as "she that was great among the nations" (1:1b) and "she that was princess among the provinces" (1:1c) cannot be so construed syntactically, but instead must name the city who is imagined as widow and slave in these couplets: "Lady/Mistress over the Nations" and "Princess over the Provinces." Good parallels to the latter are again found among divine (and royal) epithets in West Semitic, and especially in Akkadian and Sumerian in the Mesopotamian city laments, where the weeping goddesses bear comparable epithets. In addition to further elaborating the poet's portrait of the personified city and revealing her divine lineage, these epithets, given their divine associations, enhance the status and authority of the figure so entitled. She is no mere woman, but a woman infused with the aura of divinity and royalty, and thus a woman whose testimony cannot be lightly dismissed. Furthermore, several of the epithets—those involving terms for "daughter" and "maiden"— effect undertones of affection, sympathy, and vulnerability that, among other things, help draw readers to Zion's side.

The use of personification to render the figure of Jerusalem in this poem has a number of felicitous consequences that move beyond its original theological motivation and that bear directly on the poem's achievements. By imbuing the city with personality and individuality, the poet gives his portrait of suffering the humanity and concreteness required to ring true to and to grip his audience. That is, it is one thing to look at a city in ruins, even if it is your own city, and quite another to imagine that city as a person who has suffered enormously. A city however beloved remains an inanimate object. Once destroyed it can always be rebuilt, even, at least potentially, better than before. But a person can never fully erase the scars of radical suffering. Moreover, as Farley notes, suffering "arises out of the particularity of a situation and is experienced through personal immediacy." However it is occasioned, she continues,

51

"it is always and irreducibly my own. Even if my suffering is explicitly as a member of a community, the experience of it remains uniquely mine and cannot be absorbed into the larger whole" (56). Therefore, the poet's use of personification both skillfully ups the emotional ante—Jerusalem, as city is something more than the sum of all of its walls, buildings, gates, and roads, and the full gravity of its destruction can only begin to be fathomed if we envision the city as a person—and gives authenticity and sharpness to the city's plight by individuating the experience. And yet as personified Jerusalem's communal identity is so obvious—she is the people personified as well as the city's leading citizen—the particularity of the pain and anguish that she refracts is made so as to resonate more broadly.

The use of personification in these poems also adds a depth and complexity of character to the figure of the city-temple complex that is missing in the weeping goddess motif in Mesopotamian laments. Personification may be likened to a sentence that has a literal subject and a metaphorical predicate. The subject, the object personified, is always to be taken literally and is always present at some level. The metaphorical predicate provides the persona and any second-order referents, and it is that which engages the reader. In the case of the personified city in Lamentations, the city constitutes the literal subject, whether referring to the actual physical entity of walls, gates, roads, and buildings or by metonymic extension to the city's human inhabitants. A variety of feminine imagery forms the metaphorical predicate, the persona that enlivens the figure of Zion in these poems. Any or all of these aspects of the personified figure may be foregrounded at any one time. Moreover, an additional layer of complexity is added by the fluidity of geographical references associated with the personified figure in Lamentations, for example, Zion, Jerusalem, Judah, and even Jacob and Israel. While there may well be an intended narrowing or enlarging of focus depending on the specific geographical term used in any one instance, we should not insist on distinguishing these figures too sharply. This kind of fluidity of reference is traceable within the biblical traditions themselves. For example, within the Zion tradition, talk of Zion moves to talk of Jerusalem and even to the whole land of Israel and Judah quite easily, with no apparent distinction intended. The name Zion itself, which occurs fifteen times in Lamentations and is by far the most common geographical designation used in these poems, exhibits especially fluid associations. Originally, it probably was a designation for Jebusite Jerusalem, which David is said to have conquered (2 Sam. 5:7; 1 Kgs. 8:1). It then becomes a specific designation for the Temple Mount (Pss. 48:2, 11; 78:68–69; Isa. 31:4; Joel 3:17, 21)—which likely is its prototypical resonance throughout Lamentations. And eventually, through synecdoche, Zion becomes a designation for the whole of Jerusalem (2 Kgs. 19:31; Isa. 2:3; 30:19) and, in Lamentations, through the cohering force of the personification and genre associations, even Judah. Such fluidity allows the poet to manipulate the breadth and depth of focus as he deems appropriate without destroying the coherence imposed by the use of the female persona.

Finally, if personified Jerusalem finds her literary roots in Mesopotamia, she gains an afterlife in the Hellenistic *tychē poleōs*—the deified personification of fortune or fate, the *mater dolorosa*, the Shekhinah and the personified "Community of Israel" known from the Talmud, and the Gospels' portrayal of Jesus' lament over Jerusalem. Regarding the latter, both Matthew (23:37–39) and Luke (13:34–35) portray Jesus uttering a lament over Jerusalem ("Jerusalem, Jerusalem . . .") in which he likens himself to a mother hen and remarks on the abandonment of the temple. And in a passage unique to Luke (19:41–44), Jesus weeps over Jerusalem and utters a second lament. This time he predicts that in the "coming days" Jerusalem will be besieged and destroyed and she and her children dashed to pieces (see also Matt. 23:38). That the Gospel writers' dependence on the city-lament tradition in these passages is not mere happenstance is further suggested by our poet's determination to show Zion as taking on her children's sins and suffering in ways that prefigure the Jesus of the Gospel accounts (see below). For Christians, then, the hurt, grief, and love refracted in and through personified Jerusalem gains special significance as it reverberates and echoes in the similar portrayal of Jesus in the New Testament.

Lamentations 1:1–11

A Lament over Zion

The poem itself opens ominously at night (1:2a) and amid the aftermath of the catastrophe, portraying in its first couplet the image of ruined Jerusalem and the death, suffering, and cultural upheaval which a broken and deserted city so powerfully symbolizes. Many of the Bible's destruction narratives (e.g., Gen. 19; Josh. 2; Judg. 19–21) are set at night to evoke the sense of malevolence and foreboding associated with darkness. Indeed, words for "night," "darkness," and "blackness" always have negative and disastrous associations in Lamentations (see 2:1a, 19a; 3:2; 4:8; 5:10). Superimposed over this image of dark destruction are the sights, sounds, and feelings associated with a funeral. Key elements of the funeral dirge are liberally deployed in this initial stanza. The poem's opening particle ("How," esp. Isa. 1:21; Jer. 48:17); the use of the contrast motif—here contrasting a populated, secure, and queenly Jerusalem before the destruction with a deserted, widowed, and enslaved Jerusalem after the destruction; the imagining of Jerusalem as a widow; and the rhythmic frame of the qinah meter, which begins in earnest in the second stanza and continues prominently throughout the rest of the poem, all are elements found in or associated with Israelite funeral dirges. This strong evocation of the funeral dirge effects a predominantly sad and somber tone that matches the eerie darkness in which the poem is enshrouded. More immediately, it provides the context in which personified Jerusalem is first encountered. The poet, drawing on the personified city's divine lineage, skillfully brings the metaphor to life right before the reader's eyes. The poem's opening couplet is rich and complex, full of the kind of wordplay illustrated above in the Introduction. The first double entendre plays on the phrase "lonely sits" which, when considered initially and in isolation from the sentence's conclusion in the second line of the couplet, suggests the image of a city set apart and secure (Num. 23:9; Deut. 33:28; Jer. 49:31), an image of Israel in fact foretold by Balaam in Num. 23:9. The placement of the line terminus after "lonely" in the Hebrew ensures that this initial image of a city set apart and secure will resonate with the reader. Unfortunately, the rendering of NRSV obscures the effect of the Hebrew lineation, which is better captured in the following translation:

> How she sits alone,
> the city that once was full of people!

In this translation the comma and the line break force the reader to consider, at least initially, the significance of the phrase "How she sits alone" without reference to the second line. The subject-noun phrase, which follows only in the succeeding line, remains compatible with this positive notion. Only the introductory "How!" (and its mournful associations) and the immediately following image of Jerusalem as "widow" intimate that the phrase can take on another meaning as well, that of a city alone and abandoned (cf. Isa. 27:10). The image, then, must be radically reenvisioned. The city does not sit alone, apart from other nations, because it is secure and privileged, but because it has been deserted. Thus, two images are presented and allowed to play off one another. The net effect is to contrast Jerusalem's glorious past, when she sat

54

securely, filled with many people, and her desolate present, when she sits alone, abandoned, and demolished.

This first double entendre sets the stage for the second, out of which the persona of the city emerges. In the immediately succeeding couplets the city of Jerusalem is said to have become "like a widow" and enslaved in a labor gang (i.e., "a vassal"). That is, the city is anthropomorphized and, as was noted earlier, named using the epithets "Lady/Mistress over the Nations" and "Princess over the Provinces." Therefore, by stanza's end the opening couplet takes on an additional resonance as "the city that once was full of people," which may be construed appositionally as well as adjectivally, consisting of yet another epithet of the personified city: "Lady/Mistress of the People." The key word in the Hebrew *(rabbātî)* is contextualized so as to allow for two competing interpretations, either as the adjective "full, many, great" or as the substantive "lady, great one" (as commonly in titles). The image on the appositional reading, then, is that of the persona of the city sitting alone at the site of ruined Jerusalem—an image comparable to that of the city goddess in the Mesopotamian laments sitting and lamenting at the site of her ruined city. Thus, the personified figure of Jerusalem comes to life in the words and phrases which constitute the poetry itself, as if the stone and mudbrick of the destroyed city suddenly by poetic magic metamorphose into the flesh and bones of a woman with blood coursing through her veins.

This act of linguistic creation, all the more striking as it is accomplished amid the sorrowful sounds and images of a funeral, strongly symbolizes the poem's embrace of life. While the personified city is evoked intentionally as the subject of the dirge in these opening lines, which allows access to the complex range of emotions and thoughts that death and loss elicit in human beings, that she also is imagined (contradictorily!) as widow and slave shows that she is not quite dead. That is, unlike Amos' image of Maiden Israel (Amos 5:2), who has fallen dead and will not rise again, personified Jerusalem in Lamentations 1 is shown weeping in 1:2, going into exile in 1:3, and speaking throughout the second half of the poem. By bringing the personified city to life out of the dying husk of the ruined material city, the poet effectively tropes the acts of human and cultural creation contained in the Genesis stories, albeit in a transposed mode and with more sorrowful accents, and fashions a metaphorical substitute for the material act of rebuilding (the raison d'être of the city-lament genre as known from Mesopotamia) that cannot yet be envisioned. Each time we, the readers, return to these words, reading or hearing them afresh, we breathe new life back into Jerusalem, we match the poet's originary feat of creation with one of

55

our own, thus enabling Jerusalem to shimmer again with imaginative and life-enhancing presence. It is in the fact of the personified city's continued existence (now and then, literally and figuratively in our imagination), in her ability to cry and articulate pain and outrage, and even in her continued suffering where this poem's strong grip on life is to be found. The city, like the people whom she embodies and is a part, is alive and exhibits a will to live. This is not life celebrated, but it is life embraced, and it is such an embrace which, according to Geertz (104), ultimately leads people to find the wherewithal to endure prolonged and intense suffering, and in enduring, ultimately to survive.

The second stanza (1:2) builds on the personification introduced in the first and continues to evoke the funeral scene. Jerusalem, perhaps as widow, is envisioned as mourning the death that surrounds her. The imperfective verb form in the Hebrew ("she weeps") makes one of its rare appearances here, viewing Jerusalem's crying as dynamic, ongoing, and thus decidedly emphasizing the sense of immediacy and the need for prompt action. The latter is instantly frustrated in the stanza's second couplet, as the funeral scene becomes strange and twisted. It was customary for the friends and relations of the bereaved to offer comfort and consolation. However, in the opening line of 1:2b we are informed that there is "no one to comfort" the grieving Jerusalem. None of Jerusalem's metaphorical "loved ones" or "friends" (who in the idiom of ancient Near Eastern diplomacy may also represent Judah's more literal erstwhile political allies—see above) will console her. Indeed, not only is the personified city bereft of comfort, but her friends and loved ones turn on her, becoming her enemies. The lack of a comforter or helper is mentioned again four more times in the poem (1:7c, 9b,17a, 21a; cf. 16b). The theme is never developed logically or fully, but is simply allowed to surface here and there. Its force is nevertheless felt, especially as it is repeated, lending a certain pathos to the description of Jerusalem's plight. It evokes (without explicit comment) sympathy and anger in the reader who is made to feel that the city deserves comfort in such a situation. The intensity builds with every repetition. It also functions as an incantation to call forth or conjure the sought after comforter, first, from among the poet's compatriots (esp. 1:2a), but ultimately from God (1:9b, 17a, 21a; see the portrayal of God as the divine comforter more generally, e.g., Pss. 71:21; 86:17; Isa. 12:1; 49:13; Jer. 31:13). In this way the poem not only poignantly depicts the suffering of broken Jerusalem, but it also means to compel its readers to respond compassionately to this suffering.

As suggested above (see the Introduction), compassion is one of those emotions that Lamentations more generally seeks to evoke in its readership. Phenomenologically, compassion is predicated upon the ability to recognize the other person as human and as suffering (Farley, 37; Nussbaum, 383–84). Beyond the incantatory "no comforter" theme just noted, Lamentations 1 facilitates a compassionate disposition in its readers most spectacularly through the figure of personified Jerusalem. Not only is the reader shown Jerusalem's suffering in human form, but she or he sees and hears her reacting to this suffering. In other words, the reader is unmistakably confronted by suffering in a most particular and personal form, which, as already suggested, is all important for the veracity and allure of the image. The myriad of vignettes that picture representative segments of the population suffering and in pain supplement and complement the portrait of suffering realized in personified Zion. That is, the multiple images of others suffering (mothers and children, men and women, young and old, priests and prophets, kings and princes), though not elaborated on in detail, serve both to individuate and particularize further the experience of suffering by focusing on specific groups or individuals, and to democratize and pluralize this same experience by insisting (through the contrivance of the alphabetic acrostic) that these individual vignettes be viewed cumulatively as well. Therefore, the portrait of pain registered in Lamentations 1 effectively achieves a communal scope without sacrificing the requisite individual particularity, and thus compassion's response can be no less encompassing and particularly focused. In fact, many of the images that make up the mosaic of suffering in Lamentations 1 are such that they can only be responded to by compassion. That is, compassion is one of the responses that the poet seeks to elicit from his divine and human audience.

Compassion insists, as well, that human suffering must ultimately and always be resisted (Farley, 37). This is accomplished at two levels in Lamentations 1. At the divine level, the poem insists that God's redemptive love is to be made manifest in the pain and cruelty of the present suffering. In addition to the "no comforter" theme, God is routinely beckoned to "look" and "see" Jerusalem suffering (1:9c, 11c, 20a) and to "hear" the city's groans (1:21a). In 1:18 God is specifically imagined as the just judge who is expected to act compassionately on behalf of his subjects (see the discussion below). The this-worldly focus of divine redemption offers an important counterbalance to some of the more dominant eschatological perspectives exhibited elsewhere in the Bible. At the human level, the poem resists suffering first by identifying the conditions that cause suffering. As we will see, the second half of the poem is preoccupied with just such an effort, as it clearly identifies God and the enemy as the immediate causes of the destruction of Jerusalem and the resultant suffering (see below). The poem also seeks

57

through some of its more aesthetic qualities (e.g., its lyric mode of discourse) to nourish and salve the human spirit and keep it from falling into despair. Finally, insofar as God is a "model for" human activity, to expect God to exercise compassion is also to expect God's earthly subjects to do the same. And in fact, the call for God to take notice of Jerusalem's (corporate and individual) suffering is extended to the human realm more generally (including the poem's readers!) in 1:12: ". . . all you who pass by!/ See and look!/ Is there any pain like my pain?" (au. trans.). The passersby function here as a kind of dramatic stand-in for the reader, and thus the solicitation of sympathetic onlookers is meant to involve the reader in Zion's pain directly.

With friends and loved ones turned into enemies, the scene in 1:3 metamorphoses again, this time from funeral at the site of the ruined city to exile among the nations and no rest. The transition from 1:2 to 1:3 exhibits no obvious logical development, only the progression of the alphabet from *bet* to *gimel*, and perhaps an associative link between the "enemies" at the end of 1:2c, and exile among the nations and being pursued and overtaken in 1:3. The sense of metamorphosis is a consequence of juxtaposition and parataxis; it literally emerges in the space between the stanzas. Indeed, it is at this point in the opening section of the poem that the centrifugal tendency of the poetry begins to be felt most keenly, the sense of fragmentation to become most apparent. Individual stanzas succeed one another paratactically with only the cadenced progression of the alphabet and the patterned repetition of third feminine pronominal forms to hold them together, strong threads that sew together otherwise disparate and disjointed stanzas. The exile imagery in 1:3 picks up on the enslavement imagery raised at the end of the first stanza. The personified city in her dual capacity as lamented corpse and bereaved widow taps into two of the most obvious experiential realities associated with a city's destruction in antiquity: death and loss. Of course, the other chief experience of a such a catastrophe was exile and enslavement. In the ancient Near East, those among the vanquished who were lucky enough to survive the actual fighting were frequently subjected to exile and enslavement, especially the skilled laborers and members of the ruling elite. Slavery was an economic boon in the ancient Near East, depended upon by all monarchs, great and small alike. Here the poet aims to give expression to the reality of slavery for those who are actually enslaved: "suffering" and "hard servitude." The yoke imagery in 1:14b similarly symbolizes the reality of the enslaved. In 1:5c and 18c the perspective is slightly different. These two couplets represent the emotional distress of those who are forced to watch loved ones taken into exile. This is especially clear in 1:5c, where

58

Jerusalem's children are imagined as being taken into exile by the enemy. Now even if we stipulate that the children are intended here chiefly as a metaphor for the city's adult population, we are not simply to ignore the vehicle of the metaphor, namely, the children. The image of a child being physically separated from his or her parents and forced into a separated existence resonates no matter the obviousness of its ultimate referent and is meant to ratchet up the emotional quotient. It effectively captures, even if in an overdetermined way, the agony and heartbreak of watching a loved one forcibly taken against his or her will.

"Suffering" (Exod. 3:7, 17; 4:31) and "hard servitude" (Exod. 1:14; 2:23; 5:11; 6:6) comprise two of the dozen or so allusions to the Egyptian captivity in this poem (see below). Here, however, instead of being delivered out of the affliction and hard servitude in Egypt and ultimately given rest in the promised land (Exod. 33:14), Judah is "exiled" from the affliction and hardship associated with the siege and destruction of Jerusalem (e.g., 1:12–22; 2:1–8) only to be denied a "resting place." She moves from one horror to another. The reference to Judah's inability to find a "resting place" has many resonances: it mirrors the plight of the weeping goddess in the Mesopotamian laments and the personified city elsewhere in the Old Testament (e.g., Isa. 23:12); it is one of the treaty-curses threatened should Israel fail to live up to her covenant obligations (cf. Deut. 28:65); it is that which is denied to those who are suffering (e.g., Jer. 45:3; Job 3:26); it comes to women through marriage (cf. Ruth 1:9); and it was one of the chief promises made by God to Israel (e.g., Exod. 33:14; Deut. 3:20; Josh. 1:13, 15; 22:4). The lack of rest, in each of these dimensions, signifies negatively, turning upside down the positive sentiments normally associated with the rest motif in Judah's literary tradition and thus emphatically pointing up Jerusalem's reversal of fortunes. The Hebrew term "distress" in 1:3c is similarly multivocal. Beyond its more literal connotations and its pun on the name "Egypt" (see the Introduction), the term, as in derivatively related words in Jeremiah (4:31; 48:41; 49:22, 24), intentionally evokes the pain and suffering experienced by women in childbirth.

The reference to "Judah" in this stanza is not to be construed as signifying a persona distinct from that of Zion. Rather, as noted above, the frequent changing of names for the personified figure in Lamentations mostly seems to shift the geographical focus projected by the figure itself. Here the focus enlarges to include the entire nation of Judah, the significance of which lies in registering the national scope of the calamity. The political featured prominently in Judah's cultural and religious self-understanding. Yahweh's relationship with Judah was established as much through the national polity as through individuals. As

59

Michael Wyschogrod observes, "the relationship that started with Abraham, the individual, soon becomes a relationship with a nation that becomes the elect nation. The promise of salvation is thus not held out to man as an individual but as a member of his nation" (68). Therefore, the need to counteract the loss of national independence would be a central concern for any fully comprehensive response to the events of 586 (cf. Isa. 40–55; Ezek. 40–48). Lamentations, however, offers no such tonic. Rather, the evocation of the nation here chiefly serves to heighten the sense and depth of loss refracted in the personified figure, to point out a dimension of hurt that someday would require mending.

The scene shifts back to the site of the destroyed Jerusalem in 1:4. Again, the stanza is not explicitly situated into its surrounding context except through the acrostic (the letter *dalet*) and the repetition of pronouns (e.g., "her gates," "her priests," "her young women," and "she"). It begins in reverse of our expectations: the city roads mourn the absence of the festival goers. What is striking, however, is the fantastic or surrealistic quality of this image. Instead of the literal deathly silence that surely prevailed, the poet, by endowing the roads with life and voice, accentuates the lack of gaiety and celebration that usually accompanied such festival processions (Pss. 42:5; 68:25–26; 84:4, 6, 7; 149: 1–5) and registers, quite appallingly, the complete absence of people (who do not come, presumably, because they are dead—an implication of the verb "mourn"). Then in the second couplet a more normative image appears as the priests lament the destruction of Jerusalem's city gates. In the final couplet the structuring device of cause and effect, lament and reason for lament, is abandoned. Instead, the maidens and personified city are shown responding alike to the destruction and suffering. The distinction between animate (festival goers, priests) and inanimate (roads, gates) that is played on and contrasted in the first two couplets is totally collapsed in this final couplet. The image evoked is that of total suffering, a suffering that encompasses people and city alike; indeed, a suffering so great that people and city architecture are completely entangled and defy separation.

The topic of sin is encountered for the first time in 1:5. As was noted in the Introduction (see above), in exilic writings the dominant theological response to Jerusalem's destruction and the peoples' suffering was to rationalize them in terms of God's just punishment for sin. Lamentations unmistakably voices such theodic strains of thought, especially here in the first poem. Sin is attributed to Jerusalem by the poet-narrator twice in the first half of the poem (1:5b, 8a) and the personified city herself confesses sin on at least two occasions in the second half of the poem (1:18a, 22b)—there are possibly two other confessions of sin (1:14a, 20b), though both texts are suspect. Thus, sin is referred to in this poem perhaps as many as six times, far more frequently than anywhere else in Lamentations. This strong emphasis on sin shows clearly that the poet is interested in acknowledging the reality of communal sin and guilt. Yet despite such seemingly straightforward representations of Judah's sin, the poem also actively resists the temptation to collapse too facilely the reality of sin and guilt with the reality of radical suffering. Such resistance, as in 1:5, is typically subtle and oblique. The "multitude" of Zion's "transgressions" are acknowledged but never specified. We are never informed as to the precise nature of Zion's infractions. Moreover, their portrayal here is flattened, spare, and does not readily seize the reader's imagination, especially in comparison to the many and finely painted pictures of suffering that appear elsewhere in the poem. And the brutality of God's actions—God "made her suffer"—combined with their harsh consequences—children going into exile as "captives before the foe"—serve to soften, blunt, and even undercut the force of the acknowledged "transgressions." In this way, then, the poem is able to give credence to both realities, the reality of sin and the reality of suffering, while at the same time insisting that these realities must be considered and weighed together.

The principal motivation behind this strategy of counterpointing sin with suffering is to elicit a response from God, to make God look down from heaven and put an end to the community's suffering (cf. 3:49–50). In antiquity, the cultural assumption that sin triggers divine anger and punishment was matched by an equally strong assumption that repentance should bring about divine compassion and forgiveness. Such an expectation is clearly expressed in 3:42: "We have rebelled and transgressed,/ *but* you have not forgiven!" (au. trans.). The God to whom loyalty and obedience are owed on pain of punishment is also the God who undertakes to care responsibly for his (or her) human subjects. Thus, it is in the poet's interest to point out, as compellingly as possible, God's lack of care, in this case as manifested in the excessive and dire nature of God's human subjects' suffering, as a means of winning the deity's attention. This may feel manipulative, yet as Thorkild Jacobsen reminds us, it also reflects a healthy sense of human self-importance, a belief that the individual, and in this case the community as a whole, matters deeply to the deity (150). So the poet's strategy of counterpointing and undercutting sin with multiple and arresting images of suffering can serve both to curry God's favor and to articulate a belief that human hurt and pain cannot, finally, be accounted for solely in terms of sin and guilt.

Note further that by the nature of the poem's presentation of the community's sin, either having it always attributed to or confessed by the personified city—no individuals or groups are otherwise identified as a being sinful or guilty in this poem—the community is, at least symbolically, relieved from the burden of its sin through a kind of literary displacement. That this is the poet's intended effect is suggested by the fact that the images of suffering in the poem are also always filtered through the persona of the city. Never is human suffering portrayed in the poem without being explicitly connected to personified Jerusalem. Even when the suffering of others is portrayed, they are always explicitly connected to the personified city: "*her* priests are sighing" (1:4b), "*her* maidens are suffering" (1:4c), "*her* children go into captivity" (1:5c), "*her* princes . . . cannot find pasturage" (1:6b), "*her* people fall into the hand of the enemy" (1:7c), "all of *her* people are groaning" (1:11a), "he sacrificed *my* mighty men" (1:15a), "to destroy *my* young men" (1:15b), "*my* children are being destroyed" (1:16c), "*my* young women and men go into captivity" (1:18c), and "*my* priests and elders die in the city" (1:19b; all au. trans.). The effect of incorporating so completely the pain and distress of the people into the figure of the personified city is to project, if only momentarily, the redemptive image of a mother who is only too willing to bear the suffering of her children, an image that strongly resembles that of the city taking upon herself the burden of her children's wrongdoing (cf. the image of the "suffering servant" in Isa. 52:13–53:12 and Ezekiel's symbolic act in Ezek. 4:4–8). The point here is not that a fictional literary metaphor can in reality absolve the community of its guilt or relieve it of its suffering, but that through such imaginative envisioning readers (and writers!) are liberated from the burdens of their everyday hurt and guilt and enabled to contemplate afresh the openendedness of life, to glimpse with renewed vigor and grandeur the possibilities for survival and new life.

The next two stanzas (1:6–7) foreground the city's catastrophic reversal of fortunes. Zion's past "majesty" is now "departed" (1:6a) and her princes are now prey ("stags" in 1:6b–c). The imagining of the "princes" as "stags" plays on and eventually overturns the Old Testament's practice of using animal names metaphorically as designations for community leaders. By evoking the image of the stag hunt (for the sense of "pursuer" here, see 1 Sam. 26:20), the princes metamorphose into very pathetic beings, which contrasts rather dramatically with the usual practice of using animal names to convey admirable qualities, such as strength and leadership. In the days of her current "affliction and wandering" (1:7a; cf. 1:3; 3:19; Isa. 58:7), Jerusalem remembers the "precious things" from earlier times (1:7b), while her foes mock this turn of events (1:7d). Lamentations 1:7 is remarkable as well for its extra couplet (cf. 2:19), which, even if not original, fits contextually and helps explode any saturating effects that might accompany the poem's otherwise rigid stanzaic structure.

Verses 1:8–10 are unified by the image of Jerusalem as a sexually assaulted woman. These stanzas also provide an especially good illustration of how the poet is able to manipulate successfully the gender of his principal vehicle as a means of sharpening the "raw reality of suffering" (Farley, 52). In the prophetic literature, one finds with some frequency besieged cities and countries metamorphized as sexually assaulted women. The motif, presumably inspired by the cruel punishment sometimes meted out to a woman in ancient Near Eastern societies for sexual misconduct, includes a complex of images:

Crimes or sins are attributed (Isa. 47:6–7, 10; Jer. 13:22, 27; Ezek. 16:15–34; 23:1–22; Nah. 3:1–4).

As punishment the personified city's skirts are lifted up over her face (Jer. 13:22, 26; Nah. 3:5) or her nakedness is revealed (Isa. 47:3; Ezek. 16:37; 23:29).

Others see the city's nakedness, shame, or reproach (Isa. 47:3; Jer. 13:26; Ezek. 16:37; Nah. 3:5).

The city is derided (Ezek. 16:44–58; 23:3; Nah. 3:6–7).

The perspective presented in these prophetic passages has been labeled "pornographic" by some and characterized as reflecting a specifically "male gaze" (Gordon and Washington, 310–13, 320). Such contemporary characterizations have merit insofar as they accentuate the fact of the violence done to the personified city and underscore that those who literally "see" the city's "nakedness" are typically male (Ezek. 16:37; Mic. 4:11; Nah. 3:5)—in fact, these passages are all shown from the perspective of the attacker(s): the city is cast explicitly (and usually grammatically) as object.

Lamentations 1:8–9 would appear to be drawing rather intentionally on this prophetic motif, as evidenced by the presence of the motif's component images: sin is attributed to Jerusalem (1:8a), her past admirers see her nakedness and revile her for it (1:8b), and her bloodied skirts are referred to (1:9a). Thus, it may be assumed, insofar as the poem is culturally situated in a context where adultery is defined asymmetrically in terms of the rights of the husband as head of the household, that the poet means to tap into the motif's cultural symbolism, including the idea that the assault results from and is (partially) justified by Jerusalem's sin. Yet there are subtle but significant differences in how the

63

motif is realized in this poem as compared with the prophetic literature that ultimately cast the imagery in a different light, creating tensions that shift the focus away from the issues of sin and guilt and toward the experience of pain and suffering.

Among the most notable differences between 1:8–9 and the prophetic motif on which these stanzas draw is how in the former the logic of the prophetic deployment is exploded. For example, sin is attributed to Jerusalem (1:8a), but it is nonspecific (she is never accused of "adultery" or "whoring," for example) and does not result in her skirts being pulled up over her face. Jerusalem is reviled because her "nakedness" is seen. But this "nakedness" is nowhere connected directly to the punishment of the adulteress as presented in the prophetic motif (or assumed by Israelite legal custom). That is, all the details surrounding the exposure of the city's "nakedness" have been suppressed, and as a result, the image swells with potential connotations, perhaps referring to the prophetic motif, but maybe calling attention to the shame or disgrace that the exposure of the naked body triggers in many cultures, including that of ancient Judah (Gen. 9:20–27; Provan, 44; Hillers, 86), or to the plain fact that Jerusalem has been raped or sexually abused (Kaiser, 175; Mintz, 4). Or perhaps all three are meant to resonate. The mention of Jerusalem's "skirts" is similarly ambiguous, again intentionally giving rise to a multiplicity of possible resonances. Is this a reference to menstruation (so Provan, 45; Hillers, 86), or does the blood on Jerusalem's skirts (and the "uncleanness" this causes) evidence bleeding from an attack? "The biblical poet's use of the metaphor here," as observed by Pamela Gordon and Harold Washington, "has the ghastly capacity to sustain both images" (321). And if menstruation is uppermost in mind here, what is the ultimate significance of this image (cf. Hillers, 86)? Perhaps it is intended as a metaphor for impurity "that stems from moral rather than physical causes," as was common in sources other than the Priestly source (Milgrom, 38; cf. Isa. 64:5; 2 Chron. 29:5; Ezra 9:11). And yet, even if such a sense is present, its force is significantly lessened because menstruation can and does pertain to Jerusalem most literally as she is imagined as a woman. That is, "it is unclear," as O'Connor observes, how the personified city "could be held responsible for the natural discharges of her body" (1030).

The complexity and ambiguity of the poetry here should clue us in to the fact that this poet is up to something very different from his prophetic predecessors. This is confirmed when we pay explicit attention to the grammar of Lamentations 1. Personified Zion is the object of this poem's reminiscence. However, she is consistently presented as the grammatical subject of feminine verb forms in the first half of the poem. In the second half of the poem, the same humanizing effect is achieved through a combination of direct discourse and first-person verb forms and nominal, object, and possessive suffixes. That is, the personified city is not objectified in quite the same way as she is in the prophetic literature. Thus, I suggest that the poet, while consciously evoking the complex of associations raised by the prophetic motif of the besieged city as assaulted woman, ultimately shows the motif from a significantly different perspective, namely, that of the victim herself.

Here the poem's "feminine positioning" of its audience is not intended principally to shame or degrade (although this it does) but to communicate horror at the violence that was committed against this one woman. As long as the city can be objectified as a someone other than ourselves, as she is in the prophetic literature, we as readers are not forced to engage her emotionally as a person. But as soon as we view her experience from her perspective, then we are forced to engage her as a fellow being. It is here that 1:8c and 1:9b–c become especially significant. They show Jerusalem reacting to the sexual assault she is forced to endure: she screams "aloud" (an additional nuance of the Hebrew particle missed in NRSV's "she herself groans") in agony and turns away in horror and shame (1:8c); she falls down in shock (1:9b) and beseeches God to "see" her suffering. And those who might (stubbornly) read past these few verses cannot ignore Zion for long, as she will speak for herself throughout the second half of the poem. The personified city in Lamentations is no passive object that can be easily ignored. As a woman raped and defiled, who survives and speaks, Zion provides a powerful witness to pain and suffering, and thus the reader is forced to reckon with the human consequences of the punishment (however legally justified) that was inflicted on Jerusalem, and this radically alters how the prophetic motif of the besieged city as sexually assaulted woman is treated and received in Lamentations 1. The poet ultimately refuses to reduce everything to what is legally justified, and thus presents a much more complex but ultimately more humane and compassionate view of the personified city and her plight. If wrongdoing is admitted and condemned and the harshness of God's judgment is spectacularly figured, the dehumanizing nature of the punishment itself, as judged most tellingly by Jerusalem's own response, is also prominently displayed.

Lamentations 1:10, like 1:8–9, portrays Zion being sexually violated, though in 1:10 the rape imagery is evoked metaphorically and is viewed from a different perspective. Here the enemies are portrayed as stretching their hands over Zion's "precious things" and as "entering" her sanctuary. Both of the terms for "precious things" (Song 5:16) and "entering" (Gen. 16:2; 19:31; 38:9; Ezek. 23:44) are used elsewhere to connote sexual intercourse. As Mintz explains, the metaphorical image of sexual violation here is "founded on the correspondence body//Temple and genitals//Inner Sanctuary. So far have things gone that even in the secret place of intimacy to which only the single sacred partner may be admitted, the enemy has thrust himself and 'spread his hands over everything dear to her' (1:10)" (4). As confirmation of this general line of interpretation, note the striking parallel found in one of the Mesopotamian *balag*s:

> The treasure was . . . in the prow of the boat
> I, the queen, was riding in the stern of the boat
> That enemy entered my dwelling-place wearing his shoes
> That enemy laid his unwashed hands on me
> He laid his hands on me, he frightened me
> That enemy laid his hands on me, he killed me with fright
> I was terrified, he was not afraid of me
> He tore my garments off me, he dressed his wife in them
> That enemy cut off my lapis lazuli, he hung it on his daughter.
> (Cf. Dobbs-Allsopp, *Weep*, 48)

What is allowed to resonate metaphorically in 1:10 is made explicit in this *balag*. In particular, both passages portray the looting of the temple and its treasures and represent this defilement as an attack on a woman. In the *balag* the city's patron goddess is represented by the embodied and enlivened cult image, forming the counterpart to personified Zion in 1:10. The city goddess, as the cult image come to life, relates her terror as the enemies lay their hands on her and violently tear off her clothing.

Both the *balag* and 1:10 would have signified according to the patriarchal ideology of their day. In war the rape and abuse of women traditionally symbolized the power of one group of men to exert its authority over another group. A man's ability to protect his women was central to his male identity, and by contrast an inability to exercise such protection was the ultimate male humiliation. This, of course, neatly corresponds to the literal imagery portrayed in 1:10 (and what stands behind the metaphorical imagery of the *balag*!), the looting of the temple treasures (Hillers, 87), which, like the spoliation of divine images more generally in the ancient Near East, symbolizes (from the victor's perspective) the superior might of the victor's god(s) and the humiliation of the loser's god(s). What is most remarkable, however, is how the common subject matter and their immediate juxtaposition of 1:8–9 and 1:10 compel the reader to identify the two incidents, the net effect of which is to further problematize the already blurred relationship

66

between assault imagery and guilt. The reader cannot help but notice that what is partially evoked as right judgment in 1:8–9 (Mintz [3]: "the text here implies that in her glory Fair Zion conducted herself with easy virtue and 'gave no thought to her end' [1:8]") is viewed far more negatively in 1:10, where the intent would appear to be to arouse God's vengeance for the violation of Zion. Here, again, the poem's elusiveness, its refusal to come down solidly on one side of an issue, is used to great effect.

In 1:11 the people "groan," in reaction both to the assault on Zion in 1:10 (mirroring the personified city's own reaction, 1:8c) and to their "search for food" (1:11a). NRSV's "treasures" (rendered as "precious things" in 1:7a and 10a) captures only one sense of the Hebrew word. In a more horrific vein, the Hebrew is surely intended to signify "children" as well, as in Hos. 9:16, resulting in the grotesque proposition that life is preserved only at the expense of the lives of children, who were themselves to ensure survival into the next generation. The first half of the poem closes with a plea voiced by the city: "Look, O LORD, and see" (1:11c). These words form a chiastic hinge with the second line of the opening couplet of 1:12 ("Look and see," lit. in the Hebrew, "see and look"), joining the two halves of the poem. The final line, "how worthless I have become," may also be rendered as "how I am being distressed," which better emphasizes, commensurate with the line's syntax, the ongoing and persistent nature of Zion's suffering. Indeed, it is the persistence of Zion's suffering that finally motivates her sustained speech that comprises the second half of the poem.

Lamentations 1:12–22
Zion's Complaint

Having significantly problematized the simplistic equation of "sin equals suffering," the poet goes on to explore the broader complexities surrounding the question of responsibility. In particular, he shows that the actions of God and the enemy are the active and immediate causes of the suffering. God is the other dominating presence in the poem. The first part of the poem is notable for its scant references to God. God is only referred to four times: in 1:5b we are told that God caused the city's grief and then personified Jerusalem addresses God on three other occasions (1:9c, 10c, 11c). The absence of God is figured thematically through the divine abandonment theme (as in 1:1a) and imaginatively

67

as a part of the metaphorical surplus of the widow imagery in 1:1b, i.e., God is implicitly understood as the unmentioned dead husband (as made clear in Tgs and 4QapLam 2:8—one of the manuscripts found at Qumran and related to the biblical book of Lamentations; cf. Isa. 54:4–5; 62:4–5; Jer. 51:5). These spare mentions of God and God's figured absence gesture toward the larger sequence in which God is never heard from, though constantly addressed and beseeched. By contrast, God factors prominently in the second half of the poem. God is introduced from the start in 1:12b–c and is the subject of a string of masculine finite verbs in 1:12–19. In 1:20–22 God is either addressed by imperatives or is the subject of second-person finite verbs. Fittingly, this section of the poem is framed by an inclusio relating to God's violent activity: in 1:12b the personified city calls attention to how God "dealt" (au. trans.; MT's passive verb is likely not original, see some Greek manuscripts, Syr, Vg) with her violently and in 1:22 she implores God, using the same language, to "deal with" her enemies as "you have dealt with me."

The second half of the poem opens with Jerusalem's entreaty to the passersby to notice her pain and suffering, which she says God has caused. The language here, "that which the LORD inflicted," intentionally echoes the only finite clause in the first half of the poem of which God is the subject: "because the LORD inflicted [suffering] on her" (1:5b, au. trans.). The stanza-closing mention of the "day of his fierce anger" ultimately prefigures the stormy "day of the LORD" passage that opens Lamentations 2. But more immediately it introduces a succession of stanzas (1:13–15) in which God's suffering-causing activity is more specifically figured. Here, the poet, following his prophetic forebears (beginning with Amos 5:18), evokes the transformed "day of the LORD" motif to symbolize God's battle against Jerusalem. God is imagined as the enemy, a name God is given explicitly in Lamentations 2 (vv. 4a, b, 5a). In 1:13 Jerusalem relates how God trained his arsenal of divine weaponry—here consisting of fire and a hunting net—against her. The personal nature of the attack is stressed throughout. The net that is thrown at personified Jerusalem's feet can only be predicated of an animate figure. And in the first and third couplets, the poet bends language typically used to describe the physical destruction of cities and countries so as to give it a more personal and biting color. While the "sending of fire" is a common military tactic (Judg. 1:8; 2 Kgs. 8:12; Ps. 74:7), and the image of bones burning signifies pain and decay (Job 30:30; Ps. 22:14; Jer. 20:9)—bones were conceived of as the seat of vigor (Job 20:11; Prov. 16:24), nowhere else does God attack someone personally in such a manner. The pathos is thus effectively heightened by the twist given the image in the second line. A similar effect is achieved in the third couplet. Verbs and nouns meaning "to ravage, be desolate" (from the Hebrew root *šmm;* NRSV "left me stunned") frequently describe a deserted and devastated land, country, and especially city (Lev. 26:33; Isa. 54:3; Jer. 12:11; Amos 9:14). However, the appearance of the verb translated "faint" in the second line, which carries the general meaning of "physical infirmity" and is always predicated of a person—referring to menstruation (Lev. 12:2; 15:33; 20:18), general sickness (Deut. 7:15; Ps. 41:4; Isa. 1:5), sickness as a treaty curse (Deut. 28:60), and the weariness that accompanies sorrow and distress (Jer. 1:22c; 5:17; 8:18)—shows that the poet has something more personal in mind as well. And we do find that the Hebrew word translated here as "left me stunned" can be predicated of individuals as well. Of special note is 2 Samuel 13:20, in which the same verb describes Tamar's physical state after she has been raped by Amnon. Thus, the verb, here applied to the city imagined as a woman, may well carry overtones of rape and physical abuse, in addition to its more straightforward denotation of a destroyed and devastated city.

Though the Hebrew text of 1:14 is corrupt, it is clear that the assault imagery continues, but this time the emphasis is on the intentionality of God's actions. According to the NRSV, God places a yoke on Jerusalem, symbolizing her enslavement—and referring back to the enslavement language found in the first half of the poem (1:1c, 3a). Once sapped of her strength, God hands the city over to her enemies (lit. "those whom I cannot withstand"). In 1:15, with the guardian presence of the personified city out of the way, God turns God's attention to the human defenders of the city. This stanza is characterized by a confounding of the expectations raised by the imagery used. An assembly is called (1:15b), not for a festal celebration, but for the slaughter of the city's young men. God's treading of personified Judah as in a winepress evokes the blood-spattered image of the Divine Warrior (Isa. 63:1–6 and Joel 4:13) who otherwise wreaks havoc on Judah's enemies. The most interesting image in the stanza, however, is that of the sacrificial feast suggested in the first couplet. Here the poet plays on the double association of the noun translated by NRSV as "warriors," which literally refers to "bulls" but which may also function as a metaphorical designation for leaders (cf. Isa. 10:13; Pss. 22:12–13; 68:30). When the noun is read literally as "bulls," the sacrifice imagery evinces no reaction. However, when it is realized that "bulls" also stands in as a designation for Jerusalem's warriors, the scene is given a horrific twist. The feast metamorphoses into a grisly spectacle in which Jerusalem's mighty warriors become sacrificial victims instead of joyful celebrants.

69

In 1:16 the personified city's tears, as earlier in 1:2, are surely provoked by her people's suffering—a sense reinforced by the repetition of the "no comforter" theme here as well. However, given the personal attack she has sustained, her crying is as much for her own suffering. In 1:17 Zion raises her hands in a gesture of entreaty to God that God might comfort her. But the only answer (which in fact is not to answer *her* at all!) is to command the enemy to surround her, thereby ostracizing her as a "menstruant."

This extended portrayal of God has multiple effects. First, it shows God as a vibrant and powerful force, a deity who remains fundamentally in control of historical events, and therefore a deity who is to be reckoned with and who merits the survivors' veneration. God intentionally orchestrated and personally carried out the attack. God was in charge of the attacking forces. It was he who commanded the enemy and handed the city over to them. Here, then, the poet is seen making a strong case for continuing Judah's Yahwistic tradition. Indeed, God is always in focus in Lamentations, as God is implicitly or explicitly always one of the poems' intended addressees. God is directly addressed throughout the poem (1:9c, 10c, 20–22) and is one of the targets of the poem's "no comforter" refrain. Indeed, one may conclude that as in the Mesopotamian city laments, which were ultimately offered to the appropriate deity as a means for appeasing that god's anger, the poems in Lamentations are finally addressed to God in the hopes of coaxing God's return and eliciting from God some kind word. Thus, the deity continues to provide the chief matrix through which life is to be pursued. If the post-destruction community can carry on without a temple or without a rebuilt city, it cannot go on without God.

However, if God's divine omnipotence is effectively salvaged through this kind of portrayal, it just as clearly shows that God must bear a share of the responsibility for the suffering Judah had to endure. It is unmistakable that God was its immediate and mediated cause. If God is grammatically topicalized throughout this section of the poem, it is nevertheless suffused, like the rest of the poem, with images of Judah's suffering. The section opens by calling attention to the city's suffering, which is immediately shown to have been caused by God. And the poem ends by underscoring the city's suffering: "for my groans are many/ and my heart is faint." And it is the specific intention of 1:20 to confront God with the personified city's suffering. Here the poet has adapted the "reception of bad news" motif found elsewhere in biblical literature (Isa. 13:7–8; 21:3–4; Jer. 6:22–23; Ezek. 21:11–12). This time it is not a reaction to bad news, but a reaction to the personal assault of the deity: "See, O LORD, how distressed am I!/ My stomach churns./ My heart turns over within me./ How very bitter am I" (au. trans.). The effect of filtering God's actions through a sieve of human suffering is to show that they have human consequences and that these consequences must be faced. If God remains for the poet the fundamental power controlling human history, then it is God who must ultimately be held responsible for the pain and suffering experienced in that history.

Lamentations 1:18 is emblematic of this dual perspective on God. As phrased, the stanza's opening line is ambiguous (cf. Provan, 53). On the one hand, it may be construed as a legal declaration of innocence, "The LORD is in the right!" (so NRSV; see Exod. 9:27; 2 Kgs. 10:9; Job 32:1). On the other hand, the statement may be read as "The LORD is just!", which reflects the common ancient Near Eastern standard of divine and royal behavior (Deut. 32:4; Ps. 119:137; Jer. 12:1; Zeph. 3:5). The ambiguity between these two distinct semantic fields is creatively and uniquely exploited here. The declaration of God's innocence is plainly evoked, though its force is nonetheless significantly softened: it is not accompanied by the other half of the verdict formula ("and I am in the wrong"), as in, for example, Exodus 9:27 and Nehemiah 9:33; it is cast in the third person instead of the second person (as in 4QLam^a 3.8; Ezra 9:15; Ps. 119:137; Jer. 12:1), thus robbing it stylistically of much of its pathos, vigor, and directness; and the references to pain (1:18b) and exile (1:18c) are immediately juxtaposed, thereby forcibly reminding the audience that no matter the ultimate rightness of God's act, one cannot ignore the human pain and hurt it caused.

Still, however softened, the rightness of God's action is declared and the charge of rebellion owned. But instead of continuing with a statement of Zion's guilt, the next line beckons all the peoples to hear in a fashion reminiscent of similar addresses found in covenant lawsuits (e.g., Deut. 32:1; 1 Kgs. 22:28; Isa. 1:2; Mic. 6:2). Thus, the declaration of God's innocence is transformed retrospectively into an appeal to God in God's capacity as the "just" judge (esp. Ps. 7:9, 11; Jer. 20:12; Zeph. 3:5). Only here the witnesses invoked are not the mountains or the earth called on God's behalf to testify to the covenantal bond joining the deity to his people, but are "the peoples" called by Zion to witness her pain and suffering. The closest parallel on this reading is Jeremiah 12:1, where Jeremiah in his own lawsuit *(rîb)* demands to have his day in court before God (similar to the general situation of Job): "Just are you, O God! For I will make a claim against you. Surely, I will speak charges against you" (au. trans.). The images of suffering that come here and in the succeeding stanzas are intended, as in similar passages (cf. Ezra 9:15; Neh. 9:8, 33; Dan. 9:14), to move the just judge, regardless of the offence, to compassion. Here, then, through careful attention to

71

phraseology the poet is able to recognize God's rightness while at the same time making a strong claim for the need to respect human suffering and to effect divine compassion.

Finally, the presentation of God's actions in the latter half of the poem are unusually dark—perhaps not as dark as in the first part of Lamentations 2, but dark all the same. God "inflicts pain on me" (1:12b), "God causes my suffering" (1:12c), "he sends fire/ into my bones" (1:13a), "he casts a net at my feet/ he turns me away" (1:13b), "he ravages me" (1:13c), "my feet/ are entangled by his hand" (1:14a), "his yoke is placed upon my neck;/ he saps my strength" (1:14c), "my Lord gives me/ into the hand of those whom I cannot withstand" (1:14c), "he sacrifices my warriors" (1:15a), "he called a festival against me/ to shatter my young men" (1:15b), and "as in a press the Lord has trodden/ Fair Maiden Judah" (1:15c, NJPS). This depiction, with its hyperbolic reaches, compellingly renders the experience of suffering from the inside out, as it were, from the perspective of one currently undergoing the suffering, in which extremes are magnified. The strategy is effective and the hard edge of the presentation is sharpened all the more by being placed in the mouth of the metaphorical victim herself. By endowing Jerusalem with speech in the second half of the poem, the reader, who throughout the first half of the poem is allowed to observe Jerusalem's plight passively and remotely, is engaged directly as a "thou" ("O, all you passersby,/ see and look!" 1:12a, au. trans.) and thereby forced to encounter the reality of suffering in the "lived immediacy" of a human life (Mintz, 5). These dark images of God as voiced by the personified city herself, then, help refine the picture of the suffering as suffered, and as a consequence make it all the more difficult for the reader and for God to ignore or justify the suffering.

The poem's final section (1:20–22) is marked most prominently by the imprecation it levels against the enemy, and thus the poem once again invokes a key element of the funeral dirge. Funeral dirges, especially those for individuals who were murdered, frequently contain curses aimed at the murderer (2 Sam. 2:21; 3:39). In Lamentations 1 the enemy stands in as those who are most immediately responsible for the destruction of Jerusalem, and therefore the target of the survivors' outrage. The enemy's culpability, though abundantly indicated throughout the poem (1:5a, c, 7d, 9c, 10a,14c, 16c, 17b), is inscribed one last time through a pun involving similar looking and sounding words for "distress" and "enemy." The implication is that it is "my foe" (sar-lî; cf. Ps. 27:2) who is responsible for the city's "distress" (sar). The thought here and in the other parts of the poem, as rightly noted by Gottwald, is that the enemy has inflicted far greater damage than war-

ranted ("Reconsidered," 169). The invective, though ugly and repug-
nant, like that of the rape imagery encountered earlier in the poem,
nevertheless provides a convenient and necessary outlet for the anger
and rage that the catastrophe and its attendant suffering ignite. Anger,
like sorrow, at the horror of suffering is a necessary prerequisite to being
able to resist suffering. Here, too, is where the poem best expresses "the
sharp edge of anger at the unfairness and destructiveness of suffering"
(Farley, 12–13). The curse serves as a proxy for the community's inability to resist the enemy actively, and as such the poet once again effectively inculcates a compassionate disposition within his readers. As
Farley writes, "In the midst of hopeless or intolerable suffering,
redemption cannot lie only in the expectation that suffering will cease.
It will lie instead in the capacity of the sufferer to still taste the presence of divine love even through the torment" (117). The invective in
such a situation, however chauvinistic, becomes a potent and necessary
form of empowerment, a means for invoking the belief in God's power
of redemption.

And yet the poet is very careful with his language here. Though the
enemy has overplayed its role, the poet only desires that God mete out
a punishment that fits the crime. He wants God to treat the enemies
exactly as they have treated Jerusalem. The poet's phrasing exhibits an
intentional correspondence between the wrong perpetrated by the
enemy against Jerusalem and the desired judgment, as so often especially in the prophetic literature of the Bible. The personified city
implores God to bring against her enemies the day that God had called
against her—namely, the "day of his fierce anger" (1:12c) and do to
them what God did to her. Of course, there is one significant difference
between the phrasing here and in the other places in the Bible where
the punishment is made to mirror the crime. Here Jerusalem is inveighing against the enemy literally for that which "you, God, have done to
me." This way of phrasing things suggests something of the imprecation's larger purview. The enemy is only the most obvious and immediate target of the poem's anger. For to utter imprecations at the enemy
is to implicate God implicitly as well. In city laments the divine agent
of destruction and the enemy are two sides of the same coin (Dobbs-
Allsopp, *Weep*, 55–65). That is, mythopoetically, the enemy are merely
a tool to be wielded by God (1:14c, 15b, 17b). But our poet is not content to leave the issue here. Rather, in 1:12–15 he clearly portrays God
as enemy, even if he does not name God as such (cf. Westermann, 133).
And the city's personal and political friends and loved ones, insofar as
they have failed to comfort the city, have also been written into the
imprecation against the enemy. All of which is to say that if the poem's

73

anger takes special aim at the enemy, it intentionally overshoots this target and pointedly finds its mark in other equally deserving targets as well.

The poem's final couplet, "for my groans are many/ and my heart is faint," through its imagery and the strong realization of the qinah meter, closes the poem in a way very reminiscent of how it started, at the site of a funeral amid much suffering and distress. This impression is strongly reinforced by the inclusio that is formed between "for my groans are many *(rabbôt)*" and "the city that once was full of *(rabbātî)* people" (1:1a), effecting one last rendition of the contrast motif: the material city's many people in the past are poignantly contrasted with and replaced by the personified city's many sighs in the present. The transformation of the physical and material Jerusalem into the personified Jerusalem, already accomplished in the poem's initial stanza and integral to the poem as a whole, is brought into prominence one last time here at the poem's conclusion. The gesture's symbolic value is highly significant. Unlike the Mesopotamian city laments, which ultimately look forward to a return to normalcy (i.e., temples and cities rebuilt, gods returned, social order restored), Lamentations 1 (like the sequence as a whole) entertains no such restoration. The material rebuilding of the temple or the city of Jerusalem itself is nowhere in view. This is metaphorically symbolized by Zion's faint heart, the poem's final image, which stands in contrast to a "restful heart" that characterizes the sense of well-being and security that accompanies the rebuilding of a city or temple, as, for example, in Azitiwada's famous Phoenecian building inscription (*ANET*, 653–54). But this is not to deny that the poem is ultimately about rebuilding and restoration. It is. As Gottwald well notes, Lamentations as a whole "struggles toward a new ethical and spiritual foundation for community" ("Reconsidered," 169). The poem in and through its deeply figured lyrics offers speech as its principal restorative act, an act that by its very nature is never finally completed but always remains poised for continuation and renewal, much like the march of the alphabet in Lamentations, which, once having run its course, can only begin over again. The alphabet at last has run its course in this first poem and the personified city is clearly spent by the effort. And though still groaning her many sighs, symbolizing her ongoing agony, she nevertheless *is* groaning, and that is the poem's poignant closing gesture. Her groaning, however agonized, evidences "a human presence that refuses to be silenced" (Poirier, 164) and it is with such a refusal that the poem leaves its readers poised for new (if still hard) life, strongly implying that there is transformative significance in the movement from silence to speech,

74

however agonized is the latter. If we can only name our pain and hurt and find a language that can figure it, then we may ultimately dare to hope and to endure. Though Lamentations 1, as merely a specimen of language, cannot lay claim to having literally or physically altered the world, past or present, it nevertheless is the case that for those readers who surrender themselves to the twistings and turnings of the poem's lyric discourse the world is a different place, at least to the imagination, and that is not only not an insignificant accomplishment in its own right, but is fundamental to our ability to flourish as human beings in this world.

In the silence that follows the final *taw* of the alphabet, however, despite the life-sustaining force of the poem's linguistic play, the powerful and haunting presence of Jerusalem ultimately remains unrelieved and unvanquished, as if immune to all forms of incantation. As the very embodiment of suffering, the image of personified Jerusalem conjured by the poet, that of a woman for whom pain and hurt are her only knowable reality, stands as a forceful if horrific reminder of the incommensurability and nonredemptive nature of suffering. Suffering is always personal and always harmful, and the scars that it leaves are never completely erasable. Jerusalem, then, as she haunts our memories in the poem's aftermath, both compels our desire for survival and acts as a disturbing memorial to the reality of human suffering in this world, and the need to combat such suffering wherever it occurs.

Excursus: Allusions to the Egyptian Captivity

A part of this poem's overall success is its ability to find a vocabulary that is able to figure the immensity and intensity of the community's suffering in a way that remains respectful of those who have suffered. That is, it is able to mediate dignity effectively to the sufferer and to preserve the strong intuition of the "unassailable dignity of human beings," and thereby to resist suffering's dehumanizing effects (Farley, 79, 82). The problem is articulated rather explicitly by the poet-narrator in the second poem:

> What can I say for you, to what compare you,
> > O daughter Jerusalem?
> To what can I liken you, that I may comfort you,
> > O virgin daughter Zion?
>
> > (2:13a–b)

In 4:6 Sodom is offered as a negative standard by which to measure Jerusalem's devastation. In Lamentations 1 the standard of measurement hit upon is the captivity in Egypt, encapsulated in Israel and

Judah's chief founding myth. There are possibly as many as twelve separate allusions, with varying degrees of specificity, to the Egyptian captivity in this poem. Two examples may be given to illustrate the kind of allusions I have in mind. In 1:3a both the words translated "suffering" and "hard servitude" allude quite specifically to the Egyptian captivity. It is the Israelites' "suffering" at the hand of the Egyptians that God "sees" (Exod. 3:7; 4:31) and from which God promises to deliver them (Exod. 3:17). With one exception (Isa. 14:3), the word translated here "hard servitude," when it has the specific meaning "servitude, labor of captives," always refers to the Egyptian captivity (Exod. 1:14; 2:23; 5:11; 6:6; Deut. 26:6). Here, however, instead of being delivered out of the affliction and hard servitude in Egypt and ultimately given rest in the promised land (Exod. 33:14), Judah is "exiled" from the affliction and hardship associated with the siege and destruction of Jerusalem (e.g., 1:12–22; 2:1–8) only to be denied a "resting place" (1:3). She moves from one horror to another.

A second example involves the Hebrew root translated "to sigh, groan" (*ʾnḥ*), which occurs five times in this poem (1:4b, 8c, 11a, 21a, 22b). In 1:4c the priests groan as much because of their own suffering as because of the sight of the ruined gates. The people groan in 1:11a because they are hungry. The other three times (1:11a, 21a, 22c) the groaning is Zion's own. The root appears chiefly in late texts in the Bible. The only genuine early occurrence of this root is in Exodus 2:23, where the Israelites "groan" because of their "hard servitude" under the Egyptians. They "cry" to Elohim, and Elohim "hears" their cries and "remembers" them. In Lamentations, Zion "cries out" (2:11a) to God, and God is constantly beckoned to "hear" the groans of Zion and her inhabitants (1:21a; 3:61) and to "remember" Jerusalem (3:19–20; 5:1). The expectation, raised specifically by this allusion to the Egyptian captivity, is that God will hear the groans of God's people and will remember them and act for their salvation as in the past. But in Lamentations these expectations are shattered. The only evidence of God's presence is in the guise of the Divine Warrior who battles against Jerusalem (1:13–15; 2:1–8) instead of on her behalf, showing that God in fact has not "remembered his footstool" (2:1c). And there is no evidence in the poems that God either "hears," "sees," or otherwise recognizes the people's suffering.

These are but two of the dozen allusions to the Egyptian captivity found in Lamentations 1 (see 1:1c, 3c, 4c, 9b, c, 12a, b, c, 15b, 18b, 22a, b). All require spelling out in considerable detail and all have disparate and multiple functions, depending on the individual contexts in which they appear. However, each implicitly or explicitly, as evidenced in the two examples cited here, compares the Babylonian destruction of Jerusalem with the Egyptian captivity, and each time the point of the comparison is to note the various ways in which the present crisis surpasses that of the mythical paradigm. This is striking. Elsewhere in biblical tradition the Exodus motif is typically used as a "guarantee for salvation of the people in a current crisis" (Paul, 101; cf. Num. 24:8; Judg. 6:13; 1 Kgs. 8:51–53). Here, by contrast, the repeated allusions to the Egyptian captivity serve only to underscore the severity of the present experience, especially given that salvation is nowhere in sight (cf. Amos 3:1–2). Indeed, God's present silence and absence are thrown starkly into relief against the backdrop of God's salvific response to the Egyptian captivity. By identifying the present post-destruction community with those mythopoetic "children of Israel" under the leadership of Moses, the poem is able to honor and to dignify associatively the present experience of suffering, and perhaps even to inculcate a small sliver of hope. That is, the Egyptian captivity is one of those "dangerous memories" which ultimately testifies to the nonfinality of the powers of destruction and domination (Farley, 128). The liberation and redemption of the Hebrew slaves from Egypt as remembered in the story of the exodus manifests the compassionate power of God in history, and thereby holds out the prospect that God's compassion may yet be realized in the present as it was in the past, God's current silence and absence notwithstanding.

A Day of Anger

LAMENTATIONS 2

The second poem's strong formal resemblance to the first—the acrostic affects only the first line of every stanza, the individual stanzas (except for 2:19) contain six lines (or three couplets), and enjambment within the couplet remains prominent—secures a definite sense of continuity, which is underscored by the general similarity of subject matter, the prominence of the personified city, and even the occasional recurrence of lexical or phrasal items, such as the opening ejaculation, "How," that carries the sad tonal shadings of the first poem over into the second. Indeed, so similar are the form and feel of the first two poems that they may have been created originally as a pair, twined compositions. But amid all of the formal sameness there is much that is different. This difference is announced most conspicuously in the poem's framing inclusio ("on the day of his anger" [2:1c]/ "on the day of the anger of the LORD" [2:22b]) which signals a shift in perspective. The day that gets thematized in the poem's opening section (2:1–8) is the day that Jerusalem was destroyed and it is God who is mainly in focus here—God is the grammatical subject of almost every clause in these initial stanzas. Zion, by contrast, is reduced essentially to a place, nothing much more than the material city and temple, though the frequent use of Zion's epithets reminds the reader of the personification who returns in the second part of the poem.

After a brief transition (2:9–10), the poem moves to a short section that articulates various reactions to the destruction (2:11–12), including, most important, the poet-narrator's own reaction (2:11). The poet then laments his inability to salve Zion's hurt (2:13) and asks rhetorically who can heal her wounds. The next three stanzas (2:14–16) survey possible candidates (prophets, passersby, enemy), all of whom are ultimately found wanting, and thus, in the end, Zion is urged to turn to the one who authored the destruction in the first place, God (2:17–19). Zion does address God, but not in the plaintive and petitionary tones suggested. Rather, her own speech (2:20–22) is more challenging, even accusatory, than anything else. She is buoyed, one senses, by her own anger, which, although not thematized overtly like God's anger, nevertheless has been seething throughout, as it were, under the surface of the poem and at last boils over briefly at the poem's end. The heroic defiance that feeds this anger actively resists the degrading effects of radical suffering; it enacts and recovers, however momentarily, human dignity, and in so doing it incarnates within the poem (and the poem's readers) a dangerous but potentially life-bequeathing memory of hope.

Lamentations 2:1–8
The LORD as Enemy

The central thrust of the poem's opening section may be simply stated: to show in no uncertain terms that God is the chief cause of Jerusalem's destruction. Its portrayal of God, as it accentuates God as Judah's champion-turned-enemy, God's unquenchable rage, and God's merciless destructiveness, is one of the darkest in all of biblical literature. It is unified by a parade of clauses exhibiting a remarkably uniform sentence structure (God as subject, a masculine singular verb, and the city or one of its parts as object) and a high density of common vocabulary and imagery (e.g., words for divine anger, God featured as warrior, prominent focus on the Temple Mount, and repetition of key words and phrases—"destroy," "strongholds," the "daughter Zion" type title). The enjambed second line of the poem (not evident in the NRSV's translation) effectively frames the main personae featured, God and Zion, and underscores the primary roles they play, actor and patient. Indeed, Zion's role as the object (even victim!) of God's attack stands out in the Hebrew as it is marked by a special (untranslatable) Hebrew particle that identifies definite direct objects (and otherwise is used only sparingly in poetry). Much of the imagery in the section is drawn from the ancient Israelite prophetic traditions about the "Day of the LORD." These traditions assert the belief that God will intervene in history and defeat God's and Israel's enemies in battle. They feature most prominently depictions of battle imagery, God envisioned as warrior, divine anger, fire, and darkness and gloom (cf. Isa. 13; Ezek. 7; Amos 5:18–20). The Lamentations poet, like Amos before him, takes the positive expectations popularly associated with the "Day of the LORD" and turns them on their head, using the concept to spectacularly figure God's battle against God's own people and beloved city.

79

The opening stanza (as in the first poem) is complex and finely crafted and impressively sets the stage for the loosely connected sequence of stanzas that follows, emphasizing God's role as warrior, God's anger, and the section's special concern with the demolition of the temple and its surrounding environs. A note of ominousness is sounded from the very outset, first in the poem's opening "How," which, beyond the sorrowful tonal shadings it imbues, suggests a note of horror, and then in the evocation of storm clouds, which as wielded by God "in his anger" can only portend ill (cf. Ezek. 1:4). The Hebrew verb that the NRSV translates as "humiliated" in 2:1a only occurs here in the Old Testament, and thus its meaning is disputed. The NRSV's "humiliated" assumes a derivation from a Hebrew root meaning "to show contempt" (see the common noun "abomination," e.g., Gen. 43:32, Jer. 44:4, Ezek. 8:6, and its related verb, Ps. 106:40). However, the larger poetic context of the present passage, in which the "day of the LORD's anger" and God's battle against Jerusalem factor so centrally, suggests the alternative understanding "to becloud, overcloud, engulf in clouds" (so Gk, Syr, RSV), a verb derived from the common noun "darkness, cloud." As a storm god, God's theophany is manifested amidst the dark clouds associated with thunderstorms (Exod. 13:21–22; 19:16–19; 1 Kgs. 8:10, 11; Ps. 78:14) and as warrior God either is enwrapped in clouds (2 Sam. 22:12, 13; Ps. 97:2; Lam. 3:44), rides upon clouds through the skies (2 Sam. 22:11–12; Pss. 68:4, 33; 104:3), or is otherwise associated with clouds (Judg. 5:4). And thus aptly, Joel (2:2) and Zephaniah (1:15) refer to the "Day of the LORD" as "a day of densest cloud," (NJPS; cf. Ezek. 30:3) and Ezekiel (30:18) envisions it as a time when "the city shall be covered by a cloud." Here, too, then, the image of the storm cloud evoked at the outset of the poem is most fitting, alluding to the advent of the "Day of the LORD" and the frightening onslaught it heralds.

Moreover, by specifically characterizing the "Day of the LORD" as a "day of anger" (2:1c; cf. 1:12c; 2:22b), the opening section's accent on God's awful fury is promptly signaled. References to God's anger frame the first stanza (like the poem as a whole, 2:1c, 22b) in a kind of enveloping structure, "in his anger" (2:1a) and "in the day of his anger" (2:1c), the stanza's linguistic artifice thus mirroring (mimetically) the larger thematic notion that God's anger is all-encompassing and provides the ultimate context within which the city's destruction is to be understood. And the repeated mention of divine anger throughout the section simply serves to underscore this notion: "*in his wrath* he has broken down/ the strongholds of daughter Judah" (2:2b), "He has cut down *in fierce anger*/ all the might of Israel"(2:3a), "he has poured out *his fury* like fire"(2:4c), and "and *in his fierce indignation* has spurned/ king and priest" (2:6c). Such strong emphasis on anger imputes to God felt pain and a belief that God has been wronged in a very serious way. And though such capacities elsewhere in the Bible are attributed to God, as biblical faith in general and Lamentations in particular steadfastly profess a God who is decisively impinged upon and affected by God's covenantal partners, they are not explicitly in evidence in this poem. That is, remarkably nowhere in Lamentations 2 are we shown any sign of God's felt pain or of God having been wronged. Thus, God's anger, as shaped by the poem's rhetoric, becomes noticeably one-dimensional, almost solely a source for hurtful action, and leaving the poem's readership, then, with the impression, as O'Connor observes, of an "out of control" and "mad deity" (1038).

Finally, the references to "daughter Zion," the "splendor of Israel," and God's "footstool" in 2:1 indicate the larger section's special interest in God's own dwelling place. "Daughter Zion," the most common type of epithet used of Zion in Lamentations, foregrounds the persona of the city-temple complex. The intended referent of the "splendor of Israel" is more ambiguous, constituting either another one of the personified city's titles (cf. Isa. 13:19; Lam. 2:15c) or a more straightforward (no personification implied) designation of Jerusalem, the temple, or even the ark of God (Ps. 78:61; Isa. 64:11; cf. Isa, 28:1, 4). And "his footstool," though most literally referring to the ark of the covenant (1 Chron. 28:2; Pss. 99:5; 132:7), also represents (through synecdoche) the Jerusalem temple as a whole (Isa. 60:13). In either case, the commonplace image of God invisibly seated on a cherubim throne with feet propped on a stool is consciously evoked (see Isa. 6). Two ideas about all three of these designations stand out. One, no matter the specific referent, whether Zion, Jerusalem, temple, or ark, focus is explicitly on the permanent residence of Judah's God, the special place of juncture between heaven and earth where Judeans gained access to God's divine presence. And two, whether "beclouded," "thrown down," or "not remembered," God clearly turns against and violently assails God's own dwelling place. Indeed, it is God's residence (in its various guises), the temple personnel, and even the temple services that come in for frequent comment in the poem's initial section (2:1b, c, 4a, c, 6a [2xs], b, c, 7a [2xs], c, 8a) and that ultimately bear the brunt of God's fierce fury, culminating in the graphic demolition of the temple itself (2:8).

The stanzas that follow 2:1 elaborate on this complex of images and ideas, providing detail and lending emphasis to the basic picture of God and God's harsh treatment of Zion already evoked. The initial couplet of 2:2 stresses that God destroys "without mercy" (literally counterpointing Zion's desire for "comfort" expressed throughout the first

81

poem), a sentiment that is not only mentioned two more times in the poem (2:17b, 21c), but is strongly realized in this initial section once again through the trope of repetition, as verbs of violence are piled literally one upon another (God is the overt subject of 29 out of the first 31 verbs!): God "destroyed," "broken down," "brought down," "cut down," "withdrawn (his protective hand)," "burned," "bent his bow," "killed," "poured out his fury," "become like an enemy," "destroyed," "multiplied . . . mourning," "broken down," "destroyed," "abolished," "spurned," "scorned," "disowned," "delivered into the hand of the enemy," "determined to lay in ruins," "stretched the line," "did not withhold his hand from destroying," and "caused . . . to lament." The intensity and mercilessness of God's assault is chillingly communicated through verbal repetition alone; in-depth commentary is not required, as even the most casual of readers cannot help but to sense and feel the savagery of God's attack.

The section's central concern with God's violent actions, as told through this long string of mostly active and transitive verbs, gains depth and substance through a rich play of metaphor and simile. Verse 3 features three such metaphors. The word translated "might" in 2:3a literally refers to a "horn" (of a bull or wild ox) and is always used as a metaphor for power and authority (with the Davidic monarch especially in mind, cf. Pss. 89:24; 132:17) and "is usually associated with divine deliverance from one's enemies" (Seow, 197). That God cuts down Judah's "might" and magnifies the "might" of the enemy (2:17c) encapsulates, emblematically, Zion's reversal of fortunes. Similarly, the hand of God, which in Hebrew literature is primarily a symbol of divine protection, power, and might (Exod. 15:6, 12; Ps. 89:13; Isa. 41:10), also has apparently undergone a "change" (cf. Ps. 77:10). In 2:3b, God's "right hand" is withdrawn from before the invading enemy, leaving the city defenseless and open to attack. Then in the second line of 2:4a we are told that God "sets (or readies) his right hand." The translation of NRSV disregards for no reason the lineation as preserved in the Hebrew—"like a foe" begins the third line of the stanza! A better rendering would be something like the following: "He bends his bow like an enemy./He readies his right hand.// Like a foe he has killed/ all in whom we took pride." The Hebrew verb translated "sets" and close synonyms have the sense of setting up or generally readying weapons or the like for operation (2 Chron. 26:14; Pss. 7:12, 13; 57:6; Lam. 3:1), which is appropriate here. The image is that of God readying his "right hand"—his weapon par excellence!—for battle. Thus, not only does God deny Judah divine protection, but the chief symbol of that protection, "his right hand," is now poised to do battle against Judah. And finally, in 2:8b, as if to bring the point home, God's protective "right hand," having been withdrawn from its defensive posture and then readied for battle, is finally engaged and not withheld "from destroy-ing," from displaying the full extent of God's brutal and disastrous power. The hand that saved Judah in the past is the same hand that now savages her.

Verse 3 closes by likening God to a consuming fire. Fire is a com-mon manifestation of divine theophanies (Exod. 19:18; 2 Sam. 22:9, 13), is used as a divine instrument of war (see the comment on 1:13a above), and frequently occurs as a symbol of divine anger (Ps. 89:46; Isa. 66:15; Ezek. 21:31). Though all three senses resonate here, it is the instrumental use that is most prominent. As O'Connor well notes, com-menting on the fire imagery that appears more generally in the poem, "God's presence is a consuming holocaust. The poem does not nuance references to fire, as for example, purgation, cleansing, or refining, as have some of the prophets . . . In Lamentations, fire is God's weapon to obliterate a world" (1038). All three images in 2:3—cut-down horn, withdrawn right hand, and consuming fire—symbolize negative impli-cations for Judah.

The poem's most radical metaphor, God as enemy, appears in verses 4–5. Here God is not only portrayed as the enemy (as in 1:13–15) but is also specifically named an "enemy"—not once, but three times (2:4a, b; 5a)! The most pointed of the three references is in verse 5a, as the "like" in NRSV is probably a later theological addition (as it is not pre-served in Syr) designed to stress that God is only acting "as if" he were an enemy, but has not in reality "become" an enemy (so Tgs). Only in Job (16:9; cf. Isa. 63:10) is God comparably designated. That a Judean poet could call God "enemy" is a telling sign of the deep distress and unparalleled suffering brought on by the catastrophe. As we have already had occasion to discuss the doublesided (anti/theodic) implica-tion of this kind of portrayal of God (see the Introduction above), it will suffice here to reflect on the surplus of meaning that specifically falls out from this poem's use of the enemy metaphor for God. Beyond por-traying God as poised to do battle (2:4a, b), the metaphor is never explicitly developed. Rather, it is left for the reader to fill in any signif-icance that might be attached to the poet's naming God thus. For ancient and modern readers alike there is little positive that is to be associated with referring to somebody as an enemy. An enemy is some-one who hates, despises, and curses and thus who is hated, despised, and cursed; someone who intends harm or injury, and therefore is to be harmed or injured; who is not to be trusted but feared. Paul Ricoeur defines metaphor as a "redescription of reality" (229–39; cf. Newsom

83

"Job," 416–17). The poet in Lamentations 2, by metaphorizing God as "enemy," momentarily shifts how the human-divine relationship is perceived. It now gains a pronounced adversarial coloring to it. God may remain potent, but it is a potency that, at times, is to be actively feared, guarded against, not trusted. Here we do not meet the kindly and compassionate God so often preached in church and synagogue. Nor do we even have to do with the fearsome but righteous God of justice whose punishments, though severe, are always just and appropriate. Rather, here the only presence of the deity available to the poet (and reader) is that which is manifested in the raw and malevolent power of an enemy. Here there is no consideration of just cause (recall the thematic prominence of God's anger and the corresponding absence of any mention of human sin in this part of the poem). Only Job's figuration of the Divine Enemy as a mad beast (16:9) is more terrifying. Through the enemy metaphor the poet finds a language that expresses a terror and hurt that is ultimately beyond expressing, that gives some bite to the heart and senses, that jolts and ultimately induces in the reader a "sense of complicity with the extremity" of the cruelty and suffering that the destruction of Jerusalem unleashed on the city's human population (cf. L. Langer, *Holocaust,* 175). The image of the familiar God of beneficence and compassion must be counterpointed (not overturned!) if the audience is to comprehend bodily and cognitively the extremity of the atrocity herein figured. This is definitely not a metaphor for God that either the church or the synagogue has shown any interest in developing or adapting. And it is certainly not my intention to advocate the normative use of such a metaphor for Christians and Jews. Yet I do value its presence in Scripture, as it reminds us both of the reality of suffering in extremity and its utter aversiveness and of the radical alterity of divinity, an alterity that is not always experienced as being hospitable to particular and individual human concerns.

Still, the metaphor of God as enemy is but a small part of the Bible's larger and more complex metaphoric figuration of the divine, and thus to call God enemy in this particular instance does not imply that such talk about God is always and forever appropriate. It is not. In fact, the poetry of Lamentations 2 itself actively resists attempts to overread the metaphor's final significance even in this instance. As noted, the metaphor is never really developed. God is named as enemy and then the poem moves on. This refusal to linger over the image blunts some of the metaphor's potential sharpness. A similar effect attends the impersonal (third-person narration) nature of the poem's presentation of the enemy metaphor. Here, again, one may usefully contrast Job's more personal and thus more intense depiction of God as enemy (Job

16:9–17). The poem's underlying lyric properties, especially its quintessential occasionalness and its nonlinear strategies of signification (i.e., the need of lyric poetry to be read prospectively and retrospectively, vertically and horizontally), further inhibit readers from overweighting the metaphor. For example, though human sin is nowhere in view locally, its reality is definitely acknowledged elsewhere in the sequence, and such knowledge undoubtedly will color how readers finally assimilate and interpret the poem's evocation of God as enemy. Therefore, part of what is right about the note that the poet achieves through his threefold naming of God as enemy has everything to do with the metaphor's local inflection and ultimately the reserve with which it is evoked. The metaphor evidently was not come to lightly and neither should it be reuttered lightly.

The last part of the section (2:6–8) focuses most specifically on God's destruction of the temple. In 2:6a the temple is likened to a "booth" (cf. Ps. 27:5) "as in a garden" (cf. Isa. 1:8; NRSV's "like a garden" is nonsensical), likely meaning the temporary booths or shelters that were erected in the fields for the duration of the harvest season and then afterwards demolished. Similar imagery comparing destroyed temples to dilapidated booths after their abandonment following the harvest is found in the Mesopotamian city laments. The Hebrew verb translated by the NRSV as "broken down" is always used to denote violent and hurtful actions (Job 15:33; Jer. 22:3; Ezek. 22:26), epitomized by the rape of a woman (Jer. 13:22). Only here in the Old Testament is this verb predicated of God, underscoring the severity of the catastrophe. Like the stanza's other references to the destruction of the "tabernacle," abolishment of (lit. "forgot," cf. 2:1c) "festival and sabbath," and spurning of "king and priest," the main point of the imagery is to underscore God's complete obliteration of all means of mediation between God and Judah.

In the reference to "clamor" being raised "in the house of the LORD" in 2:7, surely we are to see the realistic image of a boisterous enemy celebrating as they loot and profane the temple. However, it is not so obvious that this image is the one most prominently on display in the line itself. The enemy is nowhere specifically topicalized, God alone is the grammatical subject in 23 out of the first 24 couplets, and the idiom "to raise a voice or noise" commonly refers to the thunderous roar of God (2 Sam. 22:14; Pss. 68:33; 77:17–18; Amos 1:2), all of which strongly suggest that the "clamor" referred to here is that caused by God, and only secondarily by the enemy. Thus, ironically, another traditionally positive sign is turned on its head, and then in the next line ("as on a day of festival"), the irony turns tragic. The "house of the

85

LORD," which should be filled with shouts of jubilation (Ps. 26:7), instead is filled with the din of battle (Exod. 32:17; Jer. 50:22, 46; 51:55).

This section closes with a final, unmistakable reference to the temple's ruination:

> The LORD determined to lay in ruins
>   the wall of daughter Zion;
> he stretched the line;
>   he did not withhold his hand from destroying;
> he caused rampart and wall to lament;
>   they languish together.
>
> (2:8)

Here, the very architecture that served as the visible token of God's presence (Ps. 48:12–14) is razed. The language of intentionality (2:8a) and of stretching a measuring line (2:8b), though prototypically the vocabulary of building, on occasion (2 Kgs. 24:13; Isa. 34:11) is used, as here, to figure destruction and demolition, as "demolition itself requires careful planning" (Provan, 68). Thus, exactness and forethought went into God's actions; Jerusalem's destruction was no accident, nor some divine lapse of mind. And beyond the obvious literal resonances the image of razing and demolition conjures—a ruined Jerusalem completely devoid of any physical reminders of its glorious past, there is an allusion to, or even a parody of, the very kind of sanctuary-razing ceremonies for which the Mesopotamian city laments were originally composed. Before old temples could be renovated or completely rebuilt, any walls remaining visible would have to be demolished. During this demolition, offerings were made and lamentations (i.e., the city laments themselves) sung before a brick from the old temple until the foundations of the new temple were laid. The purpose of this ritual was to placate the anger of the particular god whose temple was being refurbished. Our poet, in the spirit of Second Isaiah's more famous parody of idol making (Isa. 44:9–20), though much more somberly, parodies this kind of sanctuary-razing ceremony. Here it is God, instead of the master builder, who does the necessary measuring in preparation for the demolition and, as noted, the first part of the poem is intent on showing that God's anger is anything but placated. The parody brings into relief the distinction between Lamentations and the classic city laments from Mesopotamia. The latter eventually look forward to renewal and rebirth. A similar trajectory is reflected in the latter part of Psalm 78 (esp. vv. 56–72), where, in good city-lament fashion, God abandons "his dwelling at Shiloh" and delivers "his glory" (same word that NRSV translates as "splendor" in 2:1b) into captivity.

Shiloh was destroyed (as the archaeological evidence well attests) and its inhabitants killed. And though Shiloh was not rebuilt, God chose a new dwelling place, Zion, and there he built a new sanctuary "like the high heavens,/ like the earth" (Ps. 78:69). In Lamentations, by contrast, the city and its temple once destroyed remain in ruins and there is no evidence of any kind of rebuilding. The razing of 2:8 is complete; God's onslaught has spent its fury.

Perhaps the single most striking feature of this opening section of the poem is its depiction of divine violence. This is the second of Lamentations' three extraordinary renditions of God's violence (1:13–15; 3:1–18). Unlike the other two, however, which foreground the personal experience of violence and gain much of their pathos from the fact that their accounts of victimization come from the victims themselves, 2:1–8 shows that God's violence in this instance affects more than particular individuals. It also overwhelms the material city itself—breaking down walls, tearing up roads, laying to ruins houses and palaces—and even swallows up the city's inhabitants (esp. 2:2b, 4b, 5c, 6c). Thus, 2:1–8 in a way is a perverse democratization of Lamentations' other more personally focused descriptions of God's victimizing presence. It also, by dint of the perceived objectivity inscribed in the section's predominant third-person styled narration, serves to corroborate and substantiate those more personal and biased accounts. And the poem's unique sense of pathos largely derives from its portrayal of the methodic and horrifyingly efficient march of the warrior God. By the end of the sequence God remains the central pillar of communal life but in so doing has become the God of both good and evil (3:36), and thus a force to be weary of and no longer beyond human reproach. Sadly, we who have just emerged from humankind's most violent century can empathize all too easily with this poet, feel and understand these sentiments.

The other notable aspect of this first section is the continued survival of the ruined city's persona even after the real city's ruin. If not as arresting as God's furious assault on Jerusalem, it is nevertheless every bit as theologically significant. As noted in the discussion of Lamentations 1, the metaphor of the personified city signifies at several different levels. In particular, there is the female persona who is brought to life in the opening stanza of Lamentations 1 and the physical, material city itself. In the first poem, both levels of meaning are consciously evoked, though it is the persona that is clearly foregrounded, especially as she is the speaker for the entire second half of the poem. But regardless of which is more prominent in particular contexts, both dimensions of the metaphor are always being juggled. The strategy in 2:1–8 is

87

noticeably different. The two levels of meaning are progressively and intentionally differentiated as we move through the section. Though the presence of the city's persona is kept alive throughout these first eight stanzas—principally through the sixfold use of her epithets (2:1a, b, 2b, 4c, 5c, 8a)—the focus is chiefly on the destruction of the physical city itself. Just note the high density of terms such as dwellings, strongholds, palaces, and walls. This shift in focus to the material city is already initiated in 2:1. Recall that Lamentations 1 ends with personified Zion groaning but still alive, exhausted by both what she has suffered and the articulation of that suffering. It is this sad figure, "daughter Zion," whom God so ruthlessly casts out of heaven at the outset of 2:1. The eviction dramatically symbolizes Zion's dethronement, if you will, the stripping away of her cosmic privileges and status. But it also symbolizes the poet's removal of the city's persona from the foreground of this part of the poem, a feat which is achieved linguistically in the first stanza by the progressive materialization of the names by which the city-temple complex is referred. "Daughter Zion" in 2:1a can only be predicated of a personified, animate figure. In 2:1b, the reference to the "splendor of Israel" is more (creatively) ambiguous. It is both another epithet of the personified city-temple complex and a more depersonalized reference to God's heavenly and earthly abode—thus both the persona and the material city are intentionally evoked. And in 2:1c, reference to God's "footstool" can only signify the actual temple, thus effectively pushing the city's persona out of view, at least for the time being. At this point the poem, moving in its highly uniform clause type, precedes in its description of a mostly bloodless (cf. 2:2c, 4b, 5c) demolition of the city's physical architecture, with special attention given to the temple itself (esp. vv. 6–8) and culminating in 2:8 with explicit reference to the ritualized razing of the temple.

The theological significance of first the separation of persona from material city and then the systematic wrecking of the latter is twofold. First, it displaces and decentralizes—literally demolishes!—the importance that was attached to the geographical location of God's holy dwelling. At issue is the potency of God and accessibility to God's presence in light of the fact that God's temple is in ruins. Other exilic writers respond to this same dilemma in a variety of ways. The Priestly writer, for example, refashions the temple as a "tabernacle," a specifically movable entity so as not to be tied down to one particular geographical location. Ezekiel, on the other hand, shows the "glory" of God abandoning the temple and Jerusalem (Ezek. 8–11) and has God declare that God has become either a "little sanctuary" or a "sanctuary for a little while" (as NRSV) for God's people in exile—in either case the availability of God's

presence is no longer dependent on the physical or geographical existence of the Jerusalem temple. Indeed, one of the principal ideological
premises motivating the composition of the classic Mesopotamian city
laments was to celebrate the restoration of the major cult centers that
had been destroyed at the end of the Ur III period, a kind of reactivation or revitalization of their sacral functions—a perspective these compositions share with the Priestly writer and Ezekiel, both of whom also
look forward to the Jerusalem temple's eventual restoration and reactivation. The tack taken in Lamentations contrasts significantly with these
biblical and extrabiblical compositions. The temple, like the city, is
totally demolished and God no longer is to be found there—as God was
the one who did the demolishing! In this respect, Lamentations very
closely resembles the "Curse of Agade," a city-lament kind of composition that memorializes the destruction of the ancient Mesopotamian city
of Agade instead of celebrating its eventual restoration.

One consequence of this accent on the temple's destruction in 2:1–8
is to greatly problematize the whole issue of accessibility to God's presence. While the poet represents God enthroned in heaven (cf. 3:44,
49–50; 5:19), there is no comparable representation of God's earthly
manifestation. The poet exploits the resulting tension in several ways.
On the one hand, it allows an implied rebuke to rise to the surface of the
poetry every time God is entreated and remains silent. The divine
silence results because God has provided no obvious means for access
to God's presence. On the other hand, the lack of an earthly abode—as
it was destroyed—also explains God's silence. But if the issue of accessibility is left unresolved at the representational level of the poetry, a
more concrete solution is hinted at rhetorically. Both Gottwald, in his
perception that Lamentations is struggling toward a "new ethical and
spiritual foundation for community" and Provan, in his feeling (never
elaborated upon) that the poet is somehow seeking "to lead Israel back
to faith in a person rather than a place" (21), appear, at least intuitively,
to sense the weight and direction of the poet's rhetoric without being
able to articulate it explicitly—which, in one sense, is rather appropriate
as the poet never explicitly articulates his rhetorical design, but only
enacts it. As suggested above (see the Introduction), one of the larger
accomplishments of the sequence as a whole is to give voice—rhetorically—to the community, to enable the poetry's readership to voice their
hurt and pain, and thereby to begin to move past their suffering into survival. This implies a conscious centering of the human element in the
poet's thought, and indeed, from this point on in the sequence the
poetry's focus narrows rather fixedly to the human consequences of
the destruction—first in the figure of the personified city (2:20–22), then

89

in the suffering "man" of Lamentations 3, and finally in the larger post-destruction community in Lamentations 4 and 5. The material city, with the exception of an occasional allusion here and there (e.g., 3:7, 9; 5:18), no longer represents a prominent concern of these poems. This clearly is a profound and empowering gesture for the poems' *human* audience.

But one may take this line of interpretation one step further and suggest that the poems' crystallizing focus on humanity from this point on implies a felt need that somehow the locus of divine accessibility and redemption, in light of the 586 catastrophe, had to move from geography to humanity. To be sure, such a move is only implied, gestured toward. It is more a consequence of reading between the lines of the poetry, a drawing out from the juxtaposition of the city and temple's explicit and fantastic destruction and the need to continue to address God, to cry till God looks down from heaven. Thus, Gottwald's stress on "struggling" is most appropriate. Whether the poet was fully conscious of the direction that he was guiding his poetry or that he only sensed the need intuitively but could not articulate it, cannot, of course, be determined, and ultimately is of little consequence. Some such move can be inferred from the poetry itself and has some striking parallels in exilic and later literature. For example, Jeremiah writes about a "new covenant" that God will write on the people's hearts (31:31–34) and Ezekiel speaks of God's giving the people a "new heart" and a "new spirit" (36:26–27). In Second Isaiah the figure of a "suffering servant" features prominently (esp. Isa. 52:13–53:12). But perhaps the most telling examples, especially for our appreciation of the personified figure of Zion in these poems, are the Hellenistic *tychē poleōs* and the Shekhinah of later Jewish mysticism. While both of these latter figures partake of the divine in ways not realized by personified Zion in Lamentations—the *tychē* becomes fully divinized, while the Shekhinah remains a hypostasization of God—their parallels to the figure of Zion in etymology and function are striking. Like Zion, both are abstractions of geographical phenomena (e.g., the name "Shekhinah" is derived from the Semitic root *škn* "to dwell," which suggests that she was originally that aspect of the deity that was apprehendable and accessible to humans, thus functioning very much in a way analogous to the older *miškān,* "sanctuary"), both are female personae, and both have compassionate natures and advocate on behalf of their human subjects vis-à-vis God (in the case of the Shekhinah) or other gods. All of these foreground to one degree or another humanity as the premier site for encountering divinity. The separation between the physical, material city and that city's persona in Lamentations 2 enacts a similar strategy for maintaining a connection with God (and God's connection with

90

humanity) in lieu of a temple or some other tangible means for mediating between the human and the divine. It is a strategy that promotes the needs and concerns of the human partner of the human-divine relationship, while dearly longing for the continued existence of the relationship itself. That the fictive figure of Zion ultimately is meant to be emulated by the poems' readers is implicated most strongly in the choice of diction and the pattern of allusion found in Lamentations 5— where the whole poem is expressed in the voice ("we") of the community (see below). But her example of heroic defiance in 2:20–22 and the memory of hope and liberation it constructs is sufficient warrant for our close appreciation of this bold and underappreciated figure.

Finally, for Christians, the human-centered notion of redemption embodied within the figure of personified Zion in this poem will recall the unique incarnation of the divine within humanity in the person of Jesus of Nazareth. The significance of the life, death, and resurrection of this one child of Israel, according to the Gospels, is precisely that God resolves to redeem humanity in an utterly and "thoroughly human way," and that God is at work in the arena of human history, embodied in what happens among and between people. And thus by preserving Zion's person, even as her material vestments of municipality are completely razed, the poem preserves for its readership a trace of the divine and a taste of redemption, which, if they cannot lessen the hurt of suffering or the sting of death, do nevertheless remind us where and for whom God is at work to overcome these evils (cf. Johnson, esp. 14).

Lamentations 2:9–12
Reactions to the Destruction

The next section of the poem (2:9–12) is loosely shaped by reactions to the destruction just reviewed. The transition to this new section is facilitated principally by a loosening of the highly uniform clause structure that typifies 2:1–8 and a noticeable shift away from city architecture to focus more intently on human casualties and their responses to the catastrophe. Verses 8c–9a form a hinge that joins the two sections and initiates the transition:

> He caused rampart and wall to lament;
> > they languish together.
> > Her gates have sunk into the ground;
> he has ruined and broken her bars.

The imagery throughout these couplets retains the architectural focus of 2:1–8, while the two outer lines (joined by matching nominal and verbal compounds) mime the opening section's tight clause structure. In the two inner lines that clause structure is exploded and the first three lines feature gestures of personification that anticipate the shift to a more human-centered focus in the rest of the poem. Good parallels to Jerusalem's groaning walls are found in the Mesopotamian laments. The city gate and surrounding walls were evidently characteristic sites for lamentation. The image evoked is like that of someone who, sitting far off in the dark of night, can only hear the lamentations emanating from the city's walls, but cannot see the lamenters, and thus it is as if the walls themselves were mourning. And of course the walls have reason to mourn, as they have been breached and destroyed. The closest parallel is Jeremiah 14:2 where Jerusalem's gates are said to be "languishing" and bowed down with the darkness of mourning (cf. Isa. 3:26). Otherwise "languish" is always predicated of organic—animal or vegetable—subjects. Here Jerusalem's multileveled identity comes to the fore again. The poet is thus able to play on both Jerusalem's physical and personal identities at the same time. The image of a languishing woman (1 Sam. 2:5; Jer. 15:9) stands behind this imagery, and the whole nicely anticipates the reactions of the elders, young girls, and the poet-narrator to come (2:10–11).

The image in 2:9a is of the destroyed gate structure, either of the battered gate doors themselves lying in the dirt, or perhaps of the ruined gate towers, whose decapitation would make them appear as if they had sunk down in the earth (Jer. 14:2). In either case, it does not appear, especially in light of the second line where the "bars" have been shattered or destroyed, that the poet has the image of a burned-out city gate in mind (cf. Nah. 3:13), a common military means in antiquity for gaining access through a bolted city gate. Rather, here the gates seem to be imagined as having been broken through by a battering ram.

Beginning with the next two couplets, the shift in focus to the city's population and their reaction to the catastrophe (just narrated in 2:1–8) is made complete. The depictions of the poet's internal, very visceral discomfiture (2:11a–b), the "elders" (i.e., the old men) and "young girls" (a merism meant to represent the entire surviving population) performing conventional mourning rites (2:10), and the paralyzation of the ruling elite ("king and princes" are in exile, the perishing of the Torah [NRSV "guidance"], and the failure of the prophets to obtain visions, 2:9b–c) represent a transformation of the Bible's otherwise highly stylized and conventional description of the reception of bad news (see Isa .13:7–8; 21:3–4; Jer. 6:24). Here the convention is made to depict the feeling of appallment at

Jerusalem's destruction and the horrendous suffering of its population. The inclusion of the poet-narrator's own reaction in 2:11 is specifically calculated to draw the reader in through a strategy of identification. Like 1:12a—where the apostrophe begging the passersby to witness Zion's pain functions as a covert address to readers in their capacities as witnesses of Zion's poetically mediated pains—the identification remains indirect. That is, readers are not yet inscribed explicitly or directly into the poetry's rhetoric (as they will be in Lamentations 3–5). Still, that the poet-narrator's response matches—almost verbatim (cf. 1:20)—that of personified Zion's validates and confirms Zion's own earlier response. Even though, as we have seen, the poet's rhetoric has been by no means neutral, the stretches of third-person discourse in these first two poems (1:1–11; 2:1–8), nevertheless, by dent of grammatical implicature, project a sense of objectivity that normally does not inhere neutrally in direct discourse. The modulation to direct discourse effected here explodes any such implications and aligns the poet-narrator solidly with Zion.

In fact, this is only the most conspicuous use of an identification strategy in this section of the poem. The king and princes find themselves "among the nations" just like personified Zion (1:3b). The elders' and young girls' performance of ritual acts of mourning reminds us of (and even mimics) Zion's own acts of mourning (1:2, 8c, 9b, 16a, 17a). And to make sure that we get the point, the Hebrew itself contains verbal cues designed to facilitate our making these connections. For example, the phrase "the young girls of Jerusalem" puns the kind of epithet used for naming the personified city elsewhere in the poem (e.g., "young girl of Judah" [2:2b, reading with Vg]; "virgin [lit. young girl] daughter Zion" [2:13b]). And the elders "sit on the *ground*" (2:10a) and the young girls bow "their heads to the *ground*" (2:10c); and even the "bile" of the poet-narrator "is poured out on the *ground*" (2:11b) in sympathetic identification with the fate of the personified city, who was "thrown down from heaven to earth (lit. *ground*)" (2:1b) and whose gates—symbolizing the city's architectural edifice as a whole—were "sunk into the *ground*" (2:9a). The poetry thus establishes a pattern of identification between the personified city and other figures in the poem which means to suggest the existence of a commonality of experience amidst diversity—a point that is ultimately aimed at the poem's divine and human audiences. That is, the intent is for the reader, and ultimately God, to extend the pattern exhibited in the poem to themselves.

Lamentations 2:12 is one of the more exquisite stanzas in the poem. It is also one of those lyric gems—characteristic of Lamentations more generally—that seems to explode onto the reader's consciousness as if out of nowhere. Aside from some similar phraseology ("in the streets of

93

the city," 2:11c, 12b), the stanza is tied to what precedes it mainly by the typically strong magnetic pull of stanzaic integrity in Lamentations and general subject matter—the "infants and babes" are only named explicitly in 2:11c. There the "infants and babes" function in apposition to the "destruction of my people," further specifying and intensifying the image (very much in the same vein as 1:18b–c where Zion's wound is described as her girls and boys being carted off into exile). The NRSV's "destruction of my people" sanitizes the image. The persona of the city is intentionally foregrounded through the use of another epithet, literally "the daughter of my people." And the Hebrew word translated as "destruction," while it does frequently connote the battering, crushing, and breaking involved in destroying and attacking a city, especially the breaking of the city gates and bars (Isa. 45:2; Lam. 2:9a; Amos 1:5) and walls (Isa. 30:13), also can signify the physical breaking, bruising, and maiming of the human body (Ps. 37:17; Jer. 14:17; Lam. 1:15b). Here, both meanings, of course, are intended to resonate. However, both the immediate and larger contexts suggest that it is the more personal imagery, the physical battering of the human body, that is stressed here—or at least, it is the latter that the reference to the "infants and babes" and the focus on their fate in 1:12 brings most jarringly to the surface of the poem at this point. Thus, the poet-narrator, more than simply reiterating the reason for his and his fellow survivors' distress (i.e., "because of the destruction of my people"), finely points the harsh and outrageous consequences of God's divine rampage, the starvation of the city's most innocent victims, the babies.

The stanza itself is unified through subject matter ("infants and babes"), a framing inclusio formed between the phrases "to their mothers" (2:12a) and "their mothers" (2:12c), euphony (though not visible in translation), and syntax (the stanza is formed as one long sentence). This poet's fondness for wordplay is exhibited in the phrase "as their life is poured out," which may be read in two ways, both activated by the larger context in the stanza. Elsewhere the phrase appears to have severe suffering in view (1 Sam. 1:15; Job 30:16; Ps. 42:5). Certainly the babies are presented here as declaiming their distress before their mothers (2:12a), much as Zion is beseeched by the poet in 2:19b to pour out her heart like water before God. And the "life" as the seat of emotions is frequently used for expressing sorrow and distress (Gen. 42:21; 1 Sam. 22:2; Job 3:20; Jer. 13:17). Yet the "life" is also the preeminent life force in human beings (Gen. 2:7), and this connotation is just as clearly in view. According to Deuteronomy (12:23, 34) and the Holiness Code (Lev. 17:10–14) "the blood is the life" and therefore must not be eaten, but poured out on the ground (esp. Deut. 12:24). Here, then, like the animals to be butchered for food in Deuteronomy, the pouring out of the "life" signals death. In Judges 9:17 NRSV's "risked his life" captures this nuance perfectly. In this more sinister light, note the play on the imagery in Lamentations 2: God *"poured out* his fury" (2:4c) against Jerusalem, the poet's guts are *"poured out* on the ground" in response to God's actions (2:11b), the personified city is requested to *"pour out"* her heart before God (2:19b), and here the infants' lives are *"poured out."* The lexical repetition joins all of these separate images, inextricably linking them. Here the action which caused the poet such distress is that that causes the babies to die. And not only to die, but to die in their mothers' "bosom," where they should find succor and security and life (Ruth 4:16; 1 Kgs. 3:20; cf. Job 3:12), and in the "streets," or better, "the city plazas"—the broad open places, typically located near the gate in Palestinian cities (Judg. 19:15, 17; 2 Chron. 32:6; Esth. 4:6), which were the very heart of city life and where, as noted in Zechariah 8:5, children should be running around and playing as their parents conduct business or catch up on the day's news. The horror of the imagery (i.e., dead babies expired on their mothers' breasts or their bodies littering the city's plazas) is simply evoked and left to linger without comment. The lexical play makes the point painfully obvious. One last twist is conjured as the suffering, distress, and death herein evoked are hauntingly counterpointed by the ghastly notion that the babies' poured out "life" could be an atoning sacrifice: "for it is the blood, as life, that makes atonement" (Lev. 17:11). Thus, the poet voices once again (cf. 1:11a–b), this time through allusion, the utterly abhorrent reality that preservation of life during the catastrophe was often purchased at the cost of another's death.

Lamentations 2:13–19
Asking Unanswerable Questions

As if unable to repel the assault on the senses that his own words have evoked, the poet-narrator addresses directly the personified city for the first time, rattling off a series of questions which are never to be answered directly:

> What can I say for you, to what compare you,
>   O daughter Jerusalem?
> To what can I liken you, that I may comfort you,
>   O virgin daughter Zion?
>
> (2:13a–b)

95

These questions constitute the most explicit expression of this poet's chosen task: to use language to witness (and thereby salve) the atrocities suffered by Zion. That is, it is the power of language that is the constitutive element in these poems. It is through language—these poems and their verbal artistry—that the burden of binding and salving the people's hurts and pains rest. As Francis Landy puts it, "The discourse attempts to explain, illustrate, and thus mitigate the catastrophe, to house it in a familiar literary framework" (329). But, as Landy also notes, any such linguistic gesture must necessarily fail, as this poet candidly recognizes, since no language has the capacity to encompass or contain fully and adequately (and thus assuage) such great hurt and pain. O'Connor well summarizes the thought that lies behind the poet's questions in 2:13:

> At last, the narrator confronts her [Zion's] sufferings in their totality, their incomparability, and in the inability of his words to bear witness. He needs a "language of the unsayable" but such a language of direct speech that can express and encompass her suffering does not exist for her suffering is "as vast as the sea." The narrator and the poet behind him confront the limits of language. Language "breaks" on account of her "breaking" [NRSV "ruin," 2:13c]. (1041)

Thus, if the poet's linguistic gesture that are these poems must finally fail, it is a spectacular failure nonetheless, one whose therapeutic reaches frequently hit their mark.

NRSV's translation of the stanza's initial clause, "What can I say for you," hides the fact that the Hebrew verb literally means "to bear witness." Witnesses were required for any number of legal transactions in antiquity and their names were often recorded at the ends of contracts (cf. Isa. 8:2; Jer. 32:10, 25, 44). The idea of "witnessing" usually bears a negative nuance, either "to bear witness against" (Deut. 32:46; Pss. 50:7; 91:9) or, when predicated of future actions or events, "to warn" or "to admonish" (e.g., Deut. 8:19; 2 Kgs. 17:13; Jer. 6:10). Only in Job (29:11) is a comparably more sympathetic kind of witnessing implicated. The poet-narrator is represented within Lamentations 2 as wondering how he can appropriately witness (memorialize) Zion's suffering, but it is in fact the poem itself—the literary artifact—that does the actual witnessing. Here the poet trades on the illocutionary force granted to legal documents in the ancient Near East. But such force is not confined to legal documents alone. Proverbs 4:20–22 beckons the student to be attentive to "words": "For they are life to those who find them,/ and healing to all their flesh." An inscribed letter from the excavations at Arad in southern Judah also well illustrates the performative power of the written word: "I hereby send to witness to you (i.e., to warn

96

you)" (Arad 24, lines 18–19). And like Arad 24, which concerned "a life and death matter" (lines 17–18) at some point during Nebuchadnezzar's invasion of Judah, Lamentations' act of "witnessing" is no less urgent or life threatening.

The first line of the third couplet, "For as vast as the sea is your ruin," serves to explain why the poet's words can never adequately contain Zion's hurt. The "sea" is a traditional metaphor for immeasurable size or breadth (Job 11:9). "Ruin" translates the same Hebrew word as "destruction" in 2:11b, which, as noted above, can signify both the breaking of the city (i.e., its walls, gates) and the breaking of the body. But it is the latter that the final line brings into sharp focus: "who can heal you?"

The final question of 2:13 is shifted to the last line of the stanza both to underscore a strong sense of stanzaic closure and to structure through juxtaposition the immediately succeeding stanzas, which present, as it were, a quick succession of potential "healers." Each stanza focuses on a single group. The first three—prophets, passersby, and enemies—we are to infer are not especially likely to minister to Zion's wounds. The prophets, according to 2:14, have proved, at best, unreliable and at worst impotent. Given the hazy temporality of these poems, this stanza may either hearken back to before the catastrophe, in which case the prophets are being indicted for their failure to foretell the disaster (so Hillers, 107), or speak to the prophets' present inability to see visions that would console Zion, or both. Of the two, the latter is surely the most prominent (cf. Hos. 6:11–7:1), especially in light of "to restore your fortunes" in 2:14b, which basically means "to change things back to the way they were" (cf. Job 42:10) and is frequently applied to peoples who have suffered displacement (Deut. 30:3; Jer. 46:26). The passersby, whom Zion looks to for sympathy and support earlier in Lamentations 1 (1:12a), are shown in 2:15 (especially retrospectively in light of 2:16), to act no better than the enemies. "Clap their hands," "hiss," and "wag their heads" are gestures of derision and contempt. The enemies, who are the subject of 2:16, as expected, are also not painted as sympathetic figures to whom Zion might be able to turn for help and consolation. "Open their mouths," "hiss," and "gnash their teeth" match the derisive gestures of the passersby. "We have devoured" mimics the language predicated of God earlier (2:2a, 5b) and "the day" alludes to the "Day of the LORD" motif (1:12c; 2:1c).

Lamentations 2:17, by extension of the paratactic pattern of successive stanzas focusing on groups of potential healers, presents yet a fourth candidate, God, who—ironically—appears to have much in common with the three earlier candidates. That is, God, too, is not portrayed as a figure likely to be sympathetic to Zion's cause. After all, God is the

97

one who caused Zion's suffering in the first place. Indeed, the language throughout this stanza intentionally alludes to imagery found in 2:1–8: "demolished without pity" (cf. 2:2a, 21c), "made the enemy rejoice" (cf. 1:7d; 2:16), and "exalted the might of your foes" (cf. 2:3a). "As he ordained long ago" (lit. "from olden times") is a bit of hyperbole that shifts God's planned devastation back into the myth-shrouded *illo tempore* and recalls the image of the pyrotechnic God of old whose stories Judeans had passed down from generation to generation (Pss. 44:1; 74:12; 77:5, 11; 78:3). The message of the poetry's fabric of allusion here: Zion is not likely to fare any better in God's hands than she would in the hands of the previously mentioned prophets, passersby, and enemies.

But this irony is twisted and deepened further in 2:18–19, for it is precisely to God whom Zion is instructed to turn for help and healing! Considering the representation of God as enemy earlier in the poem, the choice is not only ironic, but also extremely profound. The poet's presentation of God as enemy in 2:1–8, and as reprised in 2:17, is explicit and calculated. God is a god to be feared. The poet's advice, appeal for mercy from the conquering general. Do anything to get God's attention, to staunch the wounds of suffering. Scream, fuss, carry on, act out. The more hysterical the better. He advises Zion literally to "arise" (2:19a) from the ground/earth from which she was cast (2:1b) and to cry and weep unceasingly (2:18b–c, 19a). The "heart" that was "wrung within" Zion because of her suffering and the hurt of her people (1:20b), the poet now implores should measure the depths of her crying (2:18a; NRSV "aloud") and should be poured out "like water" (2:19b). The "wall" in 2:18a is a synecdoche for Zion as a whole and was a prominent site for the uttering of lamentations in antiquity—not to mention that it was "the wall of daughter Zion" that God laid in ruins (2:8a) and that it is only Zion's broken and collapsed walls that remain standing. And just as a bit of extra incentive, the poet tells her to do this "for the lives of your children/ who faint for hunger" (2:19c–d), reprising the language from 2:11c–12c and thus replaying the very images that ignited his own reaction. Thus, the section ends as it started, with images of dead babies haunting the poet's (and our) memories.

Lamentations 2:20–22
Zion's Words of Resistance

The poem's concluding section (2:20–22) deftly draws on all that has preceded, including Lamentations 1, providing the poem with a satisfying and climactic finish. After Zion's extended and poignant speech in the latter half of Lamentations 1 (vv. 12–22) and given the persistent allusion to her in 2:1–8 (via her epithets) and the poet-narrator's direct address to her in 2:13–19, the pressure of expectation to hear again from Zion directly has been building steadily throughout the poem, until, as if at the last possible moment, the poet finally gives the reader what she or he wants. The reader's pent-up expectations and the highly charged rhetoric of the speech itself combine to give Zion's only speaking appearance in this poem an explosive feel that goes well beyond the content of her words.

Zion finally responds—how could she not—but not as a contrite and defeated prisoner of war, or even as a convicted felon pleading on the mercy of the court. There is none of the hair tearing, skin gouging, or loud hysterics that comprise the conventional literary portrayal of mourning women (and goddesses) in antiquity. Nor do we even meet the broken and spent persona who concluded the previous poem. Instead, the words that we hear are cold and pointed, steeled, it would seem, by the flames of Zion's own anger that, while not prominently displayed on the surface of the poem, like God's, has evidently been simmering underneath and at last boils over. She opens with the same insistent address that was heard throughout Lamentations 1, "Look, O LORD, and consider!" (cf. 1:9c, 11c, 20a), confident that to see suffering embodied in real people is, de facto, to respond compassionately to end that suffering. "To whom have you done this?" (though not necessarily a question as in NRSV, but more the object of the initial address), echoes again language from Lamentations 1. Here the poet chooses the same verb of violence, *ʿll* (and again NRSV anesthetizes the violence in their translation as "done"), that he used so strategically in the first poem (1:12b, 22a–b). Indeed, it matches the very charges leveled in 1:12b: "which you have done to me"(1:12b) // "to whom you have done this" (2:20a). The only difference is that in the former the reference was to Zion's own pains, while here it is in reference to the pains of her inhabitants. The similarity of language equates the two in a way implied by Zion's identity as the personification of her people: Zion's pains *are* her people's pains, and vice versa. And once again the poet matches the violence (*ʿôlaltā* "you have acted violently," 2:20a) and the victims of the violence, the children (*ʿōlălayik*, 2:19c; *ʿōlălê*, 2:20b) by a horrific pun. In the rest of this stanza Zion asks her own rhetorical questions, which match those of the poet-narrator, though they are noticeably less frenzied, more measured, sure, and insistent. The answers to these, though literally withheld like the poet-narrator's, are only too obvious. Lamentations 2:20b raises once again the specter of cannibalism and with it the heinous thought that one person's life can be purchased at the

99

expense of another's. The added horror here is that those who die are babes—the community's literal and physical future—and they are killed by their own mothers! We have already called attention to the poet's evocative choice of diction, which presents the mother's act of cannibalism as if it were an everyday event, like eating fruit (see the Introduction above). The answer to the question is of course, no, women should not have to eat their own (or anybody else's!) children in order to survive, and at such a price—with the knowledge of so heinous an act—what would the quality of survival be? The whole image is grotesque and revolting. That it could be thought, let alone voiced, again speaks volumes about the depth of Zion's misery—and, now, the depth of her anger.

In the next question, Zion asks should "priest and prophet" be murdered (NRSV "be killed") in the very place where presumably they were to serve God and expected God's divine protection, "in the sanctuary of the LORD." Again the negative answer is only too obvious, and the chief culprit is implicit (in both questions) in the address to God. In the first two couplets of 2:21 Zion continues to identify human casualties, though she has now dropped the false face of the earlier rhetorical questions. Young and old lie dead "on the ground"—again alluding to Zion's own treatment at the beginning of the poem. Young men and women—those in the prime of their lives—fall by the sword. This abbreviated catalog, which moves from rhetorical questions (2:20b–c) to plain declarative statements (2:21a–b), ends in direct accusation: "You killed on the day of your anger!/ You slaughtered without mercy!" (2:21c; NRSV's "in the day of your anger you have killed them,/ slaughtering without mercy" misses the passion and directness of the original Hebrew). Elsewhere in the Bible, God's sacrificial victims are usually envisioned as Israel and Judah's enemies (Isa. 34:6; Jer. 46:10; Ezek. 39:17), though in Zephaniah 1:7–8, as here, Judah and Jerusalem, too, become sacrificed. Though, here, too, God's anger continues to be figured explicitly at the poem's surface, it is Zion's anger, implicated in the fact and tone of and the reasons given for her accusation, that resonates most clearly and most loudly. And thus, God's day of anger is transformed rhetorically into Zion's speech of wrath.

The final stanza is one long complex sentence, which sets it apart from the poem's tendency to keep sentences confined mostly to lines and couplets. This change of pattern helps signal the poem's impending conclusion, but it also underscores the feel of climax. Parataxis joins the separate clauses, piling one thought onto another, until they overwhelm Zion and simply need to be gotten out. It begins ("You invited . . . as if for a day of festival") by continuing to play on the image of

100

sacrifice. The announcement of a festival (cf. 2:7c) is normally a joyous event, involving festivities of all sorts, including a festal meal. This day of festivities, however, takes a phantasmagoric turn in the second line. Instead of calling all (surviving) Judeans to a celebratory feast, God calls Zion's "enemies from all around" (cf. 1:17b) to make a feast of the city's inhabitants. That this "day of festival" is in reality the "Day of the LORD" is made clear by the explicit references to the latter in 2:22b and the lexical play on the earlier phrase "the day you have announced" (1:21c; cf. Gk). "Enemies" of NRSV is a gloss for an obscure Hebrew word. Suggestions for its meaning include "those who lie in wait" (cf. Ps. 59:3), "attackers" (cf. Job 18:19), or "dread, terrors," with particular reference to the "terror on every side" found frequently in Jeremiah (6:25; 20:3, 10; 46:5; 49:29). Whichever of these is correct, the Hebrew bears connotations of a surrounding enemy and the feelings of terror that this would arouse.

In 2:22b, by delaying the substantivized adjectives till the second line of the couplet, the poet enhances the syntactic pull felt in the couplet and effectively renders, through juxtaposition, the final couplet ("those whom . . .") as an appositive (this sense is further enforced through implication associated with the use of the standard Hebrew relative particle [ʾăšer], which here functions almost like a substantive). The first line of the last couplet contains the same rare verb for "child rearing" *(tph)* found in 2:20b, thus effectively alluding back to the portrayal of cannibalism there. The verb also plays on (through a change in the middle letter) the verb for "slaughter" *(tbḥ)* in 2:21c. Thus, as with the wordplay in 2:20, victimizing activity and victim are equated here, further heightening the incongruity and horror of the situation. The word order of the final couplet is also important. First, by demoting the verb to final position, the poet effects the most violent form of enjambment found in Lamentations, and thus increases yet again the palpability of the syntax's tug as it drags the reader ever more insistently through to the stanza's end. It is as if it were to the end that the poem had been heading all along—that is, a certain naturalness attends the poem's denouement, even though, as we will see, in one sense the end is anything but natural. Second, this use of verbal enjambment further enhances the sense of closure in the poem by effecting a chiasm in word order with the poem's opening couplet.

This long-range chiasm also establishes a set of correspondences that further complicates the poem's meaning. Both verbs ("beclouded"//"destroyed") are destructive in nature and the poet's pattern of identifying Zion's experience as victim with that of her inhabitants is exemplified once again (Zion is victimized by God's beclouding in the

101

same way that those whom Zion bore and reared are destroyed). This leaves the final correspondence to relate "my Lord" in 2:1a with "my enemy" in 2:22c. The equation is quite striking at first glance, but after some consideration, quite brilliant as well. Throughout Lamentations the identity of the enemy is constantly and intentionally blurred (e.g., 1:2). In this poem alone, in addition to references to Zion's historical enemies (2:3b, 7b, 16a, 17c), God is called an enemy (2:4a, b, 5a) and shown both acting like an enemy (esp. 2:1–8) and collaborating with the actual (human) enemy (2:3b, 7b, 17c). Through such strategic lexical manipulation, the poet gives this final reference to the "enemy" the capacity to refer to both Zion's actual human enemies and God. And of the two it is the latter, God, who is most prominently in view here, as suggested by the chiasm with 2:1a, the more immediate context of 2:20–22 in which only God is addressed, and the specific reference to "enemy" in the singular (contrast the plural of Syr and Tgs, and, for example, 1:21b). Here Zion dramatically affirms the designation given to God in 2:1–8.

The poem's final word, the verb that NRSV translates as "destroyed," provides one last twist. The verb itself literally means "to bring to an end, complete, finish"—and thus is mimetically fitting as the poem's concluding word!—and the NRSV is quite right that the kind of completion in mind here involves the destruction of human life. But this misses the sad irony of the poem's diction. The feat of child rearing that Zion had begun—giving life and then giving the cultural and physical means to live that life—God literally and ghastly completes, not by producing healthy and productive adults, but by murdering and killing.

Zion's rage seems to have reached its peak with the direct address to God in 2:21c and 2:22a. The shift to third-person reference afterwards robs the poetry of some of its poignancy and bite. The effect is to cast the remainder of the stanza almost as an afterthought, which in the case of the final couplet (2:22c) has the confounding effect of making Zion's observation all the more stinging. Imagine Zion throughout her speech as confronting God in person, first with the rhetorical questions of 2:20b–c, then with the observations of the dead and murdered in 2:21a–b, and culminating in the very forceful accusation of 2:21c: "You murdered on the day of your anger! You sacrificed without mercy!" In the heat of the moment she continues to address God directly in 2:20a. But then with the shift away from direct address, it is as if Zion begins to slowly turn and walk away, perhaps shaking her head and mouthing the last couplets with a falling voice and in utter disgust. The effect is strengthened, contradictorily, by the subsidence of rage, the lack of the felt need to address God directly, face to face. It reminds me of how I felt and how I knew when my Dad was the angriest with me. He would not yell at or threaten or discipline me. He would simply be quiet and look away. The poet's manipulation of rhetoric here at the poem's end has something of this same effect, though it is achieved lyrically and not dramatically like my exposition.

These final three stanzas constitute one of the sequence's undisputed high points, one of those centers of "emotionally and sensuously charged awareness" that so quintessentially epitomizes the lyric moment. Their importance to our appreciation of Lamentations as a whole cannot be understated. In many respects, Lamentations seeks to preserve for future generations (for us!) the memory of the suffering unleashed by the Babylonian destruction of Jerusalem. The success of the poet's exquisite and painful accomplishment can already be appreciated on the basis of these first two poems alone. But Sharon Welch reminds us that "in order for there to be resistance and the affirmation that is implied in the preservation of the memory of suffering, there must be an experience that includes some degree of liberation from the devaluation of human life" caused by suffering (39). In the figure of personified Zion as she speaks in these final stanzas, the poet incarnates that experience of liberation, and constructs a counter memory of resistance and transcendence. Zion's words are laced throughout with convicted if understated defiance. That hint of defiance—which hides behind the thin veneer of the rhetorical questions of 2:20b–c and explodes ever so briefly in the acrid accusation of 2:21c—creates the necessary space for an emergent sense of resistance that gestures ever so faintly toward the non-finality of suffering and the evil that caused it. Suffering and destruction constitute the tragic dimension of human existence that can never be completely overcome or abolished. But they can be resisted and therefore transcended. The maintenance of human dignity embodied in Zion's final words not only creates a basis for resistance, but is already a part of such resistance (cf. Farley, 57). W. Lee Humphreys likens the persistence of tragic suffering in created existence to a stone in a path and he suggests that those who would survive and even flourish are those who are able "to take up the stone" and "set it as the cornerstone of their structure" (140). The metaphor is an apt one for what our poet accomplishes in this poem. In eschewing—intentionally—the material act of rebuilding temple and city, physically gathering up the scattered and battered rubble and reforming them into a new structure, our poet opts for the more durable feat of linguistic construction that is this poem. And in particular, it is through the defiant voice of personified Zion that the poet seeks to enliven her now metaphorical stones and to incarnate within the poem's readership the

103

actuality of resistance and the dangerous memory of hope that resistance houses. Thus, if we tune ourselves into the poem's language, we glimpse, albeit briefly, something of Zion's noble and heroic stature. It is in the likes of such a woman, hurt and hurting as she is but able to rise in the midst of suffering to confront her God with the felt wrongness of that suffering, that the poem finally stakes its chance for survival and new life. The image that lingers after this poem's final word is that of a defiantly alive woman, hurt and broken though she may be, and it is the hope that inheres in such defiance that haunts this poem's silent aftermath and revivifies our retrospective experience of the suffering otherwise figured in the poem.

POEM 3

An Everyman

LAMENTATIONS 3

The formal patterns of repetition are noticeably intensified in the third poem (e.g., the acrostic now effects the first line of every couplet and the unbalanced rhythm and prominent enjambment of the qinah meter are pervasive), bringing the sequence to an emotional climax. This poem, like each of the others, tries to confront and come to terms with the painful reality of suffering. Unlike the other poems, however, there is little explicit mention of the actual fall of Jerusalem, the poem's language being shaped chiefly by the highly conventional, even stereotypical, and thus more generic cadences of the psalmic laments. The poem's only speaker is an unnamed man who introduces himself at the beginning of the poem (3:1). This distinctly male voice complements and contrasts with Zion's equally distinct female voice, providing the sequence with a feeling of gender balance—the suffering and misery engulfed men as well as women. The poem itself is a rather baroque composition that combines a variety of genres (featuring most prominently the individual lament) and breaks down into five major sections. In the opening section (3:1–18), the man, speaking in the first-person singular ("I"), rehearses the horrors of his treatment at the hands of God, who is referred to only obliquely until the last word of the section. The section stands as a counterpart to Zion's speech in 1:12–22, only it uses the language and motifs common to the individual lament well-known from the Psalms. In 3:19–24 the man asserts his resolve to hope. These stanzas form a bridge to the second major section (3:25–39), in which the man contemplates reasons to hope in God in the face of adversity and suffering. This section draws most noticeably on wisdom-inspired traditions. The man's voice in this section becomes more expansive, more inclusive. Many of the individual sentiments expressed throughout this section contradict or conflict with sentiments and ideas expressed elsewhere in Lamentations. These correspondences are intentional. They force the reader to measure and compare traditional attitudes and dispositions with the suffered reality that comprises the fabric of these poems. Lamentations 3:40–47 is set apart by its use of the first-person common plural voice ("we"). The transition, though, is unobtrusive because it has been prepared for by the gradual expansion of voice accomplished in the preceding section. Here the speaker is using a hortatory plural and speaks as one among a larger group. The section draws specifically on traditions associated with the communal lament. The "I" of the first-person singular returns for the duration of the poem in 3:48, though it is clearly a more expansive, more inclusive "I" than that of 3:1–18. The shift in voice reasserts the utterly personal dimension of suffering. This final section moves from complaint and lament to supplication and imprecation. The transparent nature of the seams joining the poem's various constituent sections has prompted some to question the compositional integrity of the whole. However, the triply reinforced acrostic and the high frequency with which thoughts and ideas carry over couplet and stanza boundaries (3:3–4, 6–7, 12–13, 28–36, 42–43, 48–51, 53–55, 60–63) strongly assert the poem's unity and integrity.

Excursus: The Everyman

The identity, number, and general nature of the speaker(s) in this poem has generated some debate among scholars. The obvious mixture of genres evidenced in the poem and especially the shifts in voice from first-person singular ("I") to first-person plural ("we") at 3:40 and back to first-person singular at 3:48 have provided the basic stimulus for the discussion. Some scholars, feeling that the degree of fragmentation present in the poem is simply too great to sustain the hypothesis of a single speaker, posit more than one speaker, while others, striving for a more holistic reading of the poem, offer a range of scenarios in which there is only one speaker, either a collective figure, perhaps even another personification of the community, or an individual who is specifically a representative of the larger community or whose experience is paradigmatic of and for the larger community. In the end, however, one may concur with Hillers' observation "that for all the variety of opinion represented there are often considerable areas of agreement between one scholar and another—the various approaches are not always mutually exclusive alternatives" (120). What may be most plausibly said about the the speaking voice in Lamentations 3 is as follows. First, the voice is distinctly male. Here NRSV's translation of the poem's opening line, "I am one who has seen affliction," though well intentioned in its attempt to utilize inclusive language, obscures the important fact that the speaker is specifically a "man" (*geber* in Hebrew). That

106

is, the speaker is explicitly gendered, lit. "I am the man," and thus effectively counterbalances Zion's equally gendered and specifically female voice. By the end of the poem the man's voice will become more inclusive, but not initially. One of Lamentations' key accomplishments is to fashion an inclusive and communal voice and response that can only be accessed through human individuality and which is, therefore, necessarily gendered.

Second, there is no good warrant for seeing more than one speaker in this poem. As noted earlier, generic mixture of the type evidenced in this poem and in Lamentations more generally cannot *by itself* implicate differences in authorship or even speaking roles. Neither does the modulation in voice between singular and plural provide sufficient ground for positing more than one speaker. In fact, the move is integral to the poem's larger rhetorical project. As with the frequent interchanges between "I" and "we" in the Psalms (e.g., Pss. 44, 74, 83, 89, 123), we need not take this "I" and "we" at face value, as literally indicating different speakers. Recall the experience of listening to a public speaker. The speaker will quite naturally refer to himself or herself in the first-person singular. However, if the speaker should at times shift to the first-person plural in order to better identify with his or her audience, say as in a political speech, this would give no reason for pause on the audience's part. That is, one would not have to posit that the speaker is fictively taking on another persona in order for the shift from first-person singular to first-person plural to be comprehensible. This shift simply reflects a rhetorical device designed to press the speaker's point a bit further. The various modulations in voice in Lamentations 3 achieve similar rhetorical aims. The man's suffered reality is related at first in utterly personal terms (3:1–18) and then over the middle course of the poem (3:25–39) his voice gradually broadens (through use of third-person verb forms and a succession of more general terms for man or human being) to include human experience more generally, and thus we ultimately come to read the opening litany of suffering, retrospectively, not only as the experience of a particular individual, but also as the experience of a man who is more broadly representative of "everyman," to use Hillers's term (122). The high point of the poem's rhetoric comes in 3:40–47, where the poet shifts into the first-person plural voice. The man's experience, his sufferings as well as his hopes and longings, are now our experiences; his voice is our voice. The merger between individual and community is complete. When the singular "I" resumes (3:48) it has become more inclusive, resembling in many respects the all-embracing voice that Whitman achieves in much of his *Leaves of Grass*.

Finally, while the use of traditional, figurative, and metaphorical language throughout this poem makes any attempt to identify the man with a known historical person problematic, nonetheless some aspects of the poem's language do allow us to speculate more specifically about the man's nature, and thus deepen our understanding and appreciation of this important figure. For a poem that draws so self-consciously on the individual and communal lament genres from the Psalms, it is remarkable that no other psalm opens in a way analogous to Lamentations 3. In fact, the best-known parallels to the poem's opening "I am the man who has seen affliction" come from the self-presentation formula of kings in royal inscriptions from the ancient Near East (e.g., "I am Azitiwada, the blessed one of Baal, a servant of Baal, whom Awarku, king of the Danunians, made powerful" or "I am Zakkur, king of Hamath and Lucath. A humble man am I!"). Other aspects of the poem can be construed as pointing toward a royal genealogy as well. The reference to the "steadfast love of the LORD" (3:22; cf. 3:32) suggests the language of the Davidic covenant (cf. Ps. 89:2, 3, 24, 28, 34, 49), and the use of "rod" (3:1) and "transgressed" (3:42) recalls God's promise to David to punish any breach of covenant with a rod (2 Sam. 7:14; Ps. 89:34). Also the combination of "I" and "we" language in the royal psalms (e.g., Pss. 44, 89, 144), where the king presumably stands in as the community's representative, is reminiscent of this poem. And the notice that the man is mocked by his own people (3:14) is perhaps less objectional as a remark from a king (cf. Ps. 89:41, "he has become the scorn of his neighbors"). Lastly, there are notable resemblances between the man of Lamentations 3 and the Mesopotamian laments' depiction of the king, variously referred to as "a humble man," "the man of the offering," and "the man who speaks the prayer," or more simply as just "a man" or "that man" and described as a lowly and sinful person, who frequently presents the lament itself as an offering intended to soothe the anger of the aggrieved god (for details, see Dobbs-Allsopp, "*haggeber*"). One need not identify the man so specifically, of course, as it is likely that as with the other voices in Lamentations the poet is effecting in him a persona. Nonetheless, one might not unreasonably suppose that some archetypal communal figure like the king does in fact stand in the distant background of the man of Lamentations 3.

In Lamentations, of course, the king is no longer the kind of heroic figure imagined in other city laments. Indeed, in the postcatastrophe Judah envisioned by our poet none of the classically heroic figures remain: the princes have fled (1:6), the warriors are defeated (1:15), the priests and prophets have been killed (2:20), the well-to-do sit in shame on ash heaps (4:5), and the king himself has been taken into exile (4:20).

Thus, even if the figure of the man is predicated on the archetypal example of the king, a more particular embodiment of the king has (by necessity) been intentionally suppressed, as perhaps indicated most clearly by the speaker's presentation of himself with the Hebrew term *geber* and not as a king (cf. Qoh. 1:12). The Hebrew noun is usually translated simply as "man," but as O'Connor suggests, the term is not simply generic for a male person. Taking her cue from the word's etymology, O'Connor suggests that the noun here should be understood with the nuance of a defeated "strongman" (1046). What is especially attractive about this suggestion is that it calls attention to the etymology of the Hebrew term and emphasizes the sense of defeat and humiliation that are clearly portrayed within the poem itself. However, instead of reading a strong sense of the root's etymology into this specific word, for which there is no real positive evidence, I would suggest that we see in the poet's choice of diction an intentional play on the earlier use of the related verb "prevailed" (1:16c) and a kind of refraction-through-absence of the etymologically related terms "strength," "strong man or warrior," and "lady or queen." That is, the poet's choice of the Hebrew word *geber*, in addition to reflecting the positive sense of "man," also reflects the absence of the more specifically royal connotations associated with the related words "strong man or warrior" and "lady or queen" (cf. 2 Sam. 2:31 where the same Hebrew term specifically means to highlight David's nonroyal and hence usurper status). And thus, the man of Lamentations 3 is every bit of Hillers's "everyman," just a regular guy whose chief distinction—his suffering and the accident of his survival—he shares in common with the other members of the post-destruction community.

Lamentations 3:1–18
A Man's Complaint

The poem's initial section constitutes Lamentations' third and final depiction of God as adversary. In its vivid portrayal of God's personal attack on the "everyman," voiced by the man himself, 3:1–18 forms a fitting counterpart to Zion's own testimony to divine violence (1:13-15). As O'Connor observes, the man's "voice is as intimate, personal, and anguished as that of Daughter Zion" (1046). And the two together, the "everyman" and "Daughter Zion," sandwich (envelope) the more objective account of God's brutal overthrow of Jerusalem in 2:1–8. The basic tenor of the section has much in common, as well, with Job's great complaint about God's violent behavior (esp. Job 16:7–17). Indeed, like Job, who himself sits "among the ashes" (Job 2:8), the "everyman" of Lamentations 3 is physically bent (NRSV "made me cower") by God and ground into the "ashes" (3:16). The section is shaped as one long complaint, a staple feature of individual laments, and is unified through a twofold pattern of pronominal repetition, first-person forms of the "everyman" counterpointing third-person forms of God. References to the "everyman" as subject enfold the section as a whole ("*I am* the man," 3:1; "so *I say*," 3:18), otherwise God is mostly the author of the harmful actions depicted throughout and the man God's unwitting victim, marked in 3:2 by the same prosaic particle that identified Zion as the object at the beginning of the second poem (2:1a).

The third poem opens most dramatically, "I am the man who has seen affliction." The use of an initial identifying verbless clause, "I am the man," fixes immediately on the question of the speaker's identity and concomitantly asserts the utterly personal nature of the poem, a sense reinforced by the placement of the first-person personal pronoun ("I") in initial position, the position effected by the acrostic. Such prominence given to the speaker is unique for the opening of a psalm or a psalm-like composition. Even the dark Psalm 22 opens by addressing God, "My God, my God, why have you forsaken me?" Indeed, it is customary (and almost obligatory!) to name God explicitly in some fashion in the opening line or couplet of a psalm. Here, by contrast (and again similar to Job 16:7–17), explicit reference to God is suppressed until 3:18, effectively decentering God from this portion of the poem and focusing instead on the "I" of the speaker and his hurt. NRSV's insertion of "God's" into the text at this point, making the implicit referent of the poem's third-person forms explicit, destroys this decentering effect. It is not so much that the source of the speaker's distress is in doubt. Anyone coming to the poem from Lamentations 2 will naturally associate "the rod of his wrath" with the "day of the anger of the LORD" from 2:22b. But even when encountering 3:1–18 on its own the metaphors are such that their divine antecedent is never really obscured. Rather, it is precisely in the refusal to name God even though God's identity as the man's chief tormentor is so readily apparent that the poem foregrounds the experience of physical pain. Concomitantly, the suppression of God's name until the section's very last word ensures that the naming of the "LORD," when finally delivered, receives added emphasis.

110

These lines also assert the man's status as both witness to and survivor of horrendous suffering. Here the poet's attention to language is characteristically meticulous. In having "seen affliction" the man does what God fails to do. The language used here is otherwise predicated only of God in the Old Testament (Exod. 3:7; 4:31; Job 10:15; Pss. 9:13; 31:7) and thus specifically calls attention to the repeated unanswered requests for God to "see" in Lamentations (esp. 1:9a) and indeed pointedly if subtly indicts God for this divine lapse. Thus, the man serves literally and figuratively as the poetry's much-sought-after witness to Jerusalem's horrors, and his words, like the larger poetry of which they are a part, serve to comfort and assuage the pain, as O'Connor says, by creating "a world of language that mirrors suffering back to the brokenhearted and hopeless" population (1044). But the man is more than a mere witness—he himself has also experienced suffering's heinous grip. In addition to its obvious reference to visual acuity, the Hebrew verb "to see" also carries the nuance "to experience, know" (Esth. 9:26; Ps. 89:48; Jer. 20:18; cf. Lam. 2:16c), and thus the man's assertion to have "seen affliction/ under the rod of his wrath" is also an assertion to have experienced the same himself. The sentiment is underscored for good measure by the intentional chiming in the Hebrew of the beginning and ending of this first line (ʾănî "I" and ʿŏnî "affliction"), exhibiting once more this poet's habit of matching linguistically the hurt with the one who is hurt. And thus the man's authority "to speak, to give voice, to testify from inside the pain of his affliction" (O'Connor, 1048) is firmly established here at the poem's outset. The sentiment and feel is not unlike that of Jew Klein's self-presentation in Celan's "Conversation in the Mountains": "I'm here, I've come. . . . I and no other, I and not him, I with my hour, undeserved, I who was touched, I who was not touched, I with my memory, I feeble-memoried, I, I, I . . ." (as cited in Felstiner, 143).

The sequence of images that follow, though tied together formally through the acrostic, the play of pronouns, and the overlapping and interweaving of couplets and stanzas, is not developed in any overtly logical or systematic way. Instead, the poet heaps metaphor upon metaphor, drawing images, as it were, from whatever realm imaginable, in an effort to articulate and thus circumscribe and encompass the man's pain. The first four couplets focus especially on the man's physical distress, isolating the utter passivity that characterizes suffering, its felt sense of being violated from without. The "rod of God's wrath" is figurative language for divine punishment (Job 9:34; 21:9; Ps. 89:32; Isa. 10:5), but as 3:2 makes clear, the "rod" is also a shepherd's tool (Ps. 23:4; Ezek. 20:37; Mic. 7:14), normally used to guide and lead the flock. Here, however, the shepherd's "rod" is wielded in anger and God leads the man not into safety (Exod. 15:13; Ps. 77:22; Isa. 63:13–14), but, contrary to expectation (Isa. 9:2), into "darkness," figurative language for imprisonment (Pss. 43:3; 107:10–16; Isa. 42:6–7, 16; 58:9–12), which also echoes the foreboding darkness associated with the storm cloud of 2:1. The unique "against me alone he turns his hand" (cf. Job 19:19) explicitly picks up on the hand imagery from Lamentations 2. The hand that God withheld from before the enemy (2:3b) here pummels the man (cf. Ps. 39:11) "again and again." The Hebrew root of the verb "turns" also bears nuances of a city's overthrow (Gen. 19:21, 25, 29; Jer. 20:16; Lam. 4:6; Jonah 3:4) and of perversity more generally (Isa. 29:16; Ezek. 16:34)— God is not acting in his normative capacity and the suffering he causes is antithetical to the goodness of God's creation. The Hebrew of the phrase "all day long" also alludes to the "day of anger" passages in the two earlier poems (1:12c; 2:1c, 22b), thus explicitly linking Lamentations' three prominent depictions of divine violence. The imagery of physical violation comes to a momentary head in 3:4 with references to the man's wasted away flesh and broken bones (Job 13:28; Pss. 32:3; 38:3–4)—the latter recalling Zion's own burning bones in 1:13a.

The images of 3:5–9 cluster around ideas of isolation, abandonment, and encirclement. The series of verbs used in these lines (being besieged, enveloped, imprisoned, walled about, shut out, and blocked) poignantly articulates the extreme helplessness, abandonment, and solitude that are among the chief burdens of suffering and for which there is no way out except from a beyond that stands outside the suffered experience. Indeed, as Levinas stresses, the evilness of such suffering itself constitutes the original call for help and salvation, and thus these verses not only give voice to and protest the direness of the man's situation, they also mean to cry out (3:8) thereby to the beyond "whose exteriority promises salvation" and consolation (93). The Hebrew that the NRSV renders as "besieged" in 3:5 literally means to "build against me." It is the evocation of building imagery here and in 3:7 which, in light of Lamentations' overarching affiliation with the city-lament genre and the earlier allusion to foundation-razing (2:8), resonates ironically. Normally, rebuilding would follow razing, but here building activity becomes just another metaphor for destructiveness. In 3:6 "darkness" refers to the netherworld (Ps. 88:18), where "those long dead" (NRSV's "dead of long ago" misconstrues the Hebrew, cf. Pss. 31:12; 88:5–7; 143:3; Isa. 59:10) are forgotten and cut off from God. The imagery in 3:7 and 9 plays on Jerusalem's ruined topography. "He has walled me about" (3:7) suggests the image of the destroyed city and temple walls (Ezek. 42:7, 12; Mic. 7:11) being rebuilt (Amos 9:11) as a prison. The "hewn stones" of 3:9, which should be used in relaying the foundation for the temple (1 Kgs. 5:31; 1 Chron. 22:2), are instead scattered in the road to block the man's path—realistically evoking the rubble strewn roads of destroyed Jerusalem and the surrounding countryside, but fig-

112

uratively symbolizing the perversion (through suffering) of the goodness of creation (Job 19:8; Hos. 2:8). The latter is underscored by the
image, which is also evoked by the language of the couplet, of the field-
stone fences used to block roads instead of bordering them (as they pro-
tected the vineyards, orchards, and gardens along the roadside, cf.
Num. 22:24; Qoh. 10:8). The references to crying out and "prayer" in
3:8, finally, underscore the radical importance this poem (and Lamentations as a whole!) invests in language, the intuitively felt conviction
that it is only through the language of prayer, lament, and complaint
that suffering can be overcome and the "mute God" transcended
(Soelle, 78).

In 3:10–11 the imagery changes once again, this time reenvision-
ing the divine assault as an attack of wild animals. In the Old Testament,
bears and lions commonly occur as the animal (non-human) embodiment of that which is most feared by human beings (Prov. 17:12; Hos.
13:8; Amos 3:8), and as such are commonly used as figurative representations of the enemy (e.g., Pss. 10:9; 22:13). "Led me off my way"
apparently continues the predatory imagery from the previous couplet (the Hebrew is not completely certain) and plays on the path-
perverting imagery of 3:9. "Has made me desolate" recalls (especially
in the Hebrew) Zion's self description in 1:13c. The poem's kaleido-
scopic poetics take another turn in 3:12–13, foregrounding the image
of God as divine archer who uses the man for target practice (Job 6:4;
16:12–13; Ps. 38:2). The word "bent" comes from the same Hebrew
root as "ways"/"way" in 3:9 and 11 and is the same verb used to portray
God's assault on Zion in 2:4a (cf. "trodden" in 1:15c). The "vitals" or,
more literally, the "kidneys," were considered in antiquity as a sensitive
and vital organ (Job 16:13; Ps. 139:13), the seat of the emotions (Job
19:27; Pss. 16:7; 73:21; Prov. 23:16; cf. Lam. 1:20; 2:11), and thus a chief
symbol of human intimacy. Here, then, the divine assault penetrates (as
an arrow) to the very core of human intimacy. The "laughingstock"
imagery of 3:14 is a commonplace in laments (e.g., Ps. 22:13–14),
though here the mention of "all my people" (if correct) turns the image
sardonic, as the man is imagined as the butt of his fellow sufferers' jokes.
It underscores the man's social isolation, shame, and utter lack of
human compassion, while recalling the same cruel treatment suffered
by personified Zion (1:7d; cf. 2:15–16). The references to "bitterness,"
"wormwood," "teeth" grinding "on gravel" (the Hebrew here again is
not entirely clear), and "ashes" are similarly proverbial, symbolizing
deep sorrow and/or calamity.

113

In 3:17–18 the man, as initially in 3:1, is once again cast as agent
and subject, providing this section with a certain symmetry and a

noticeable sense of closure. "My soul," though frequently used in poetry as a circumlocution for a personal pronoun (3:20, 24), also carries here the sense of a person's essential life force (1:11b, 16b, 19c; 2:12c, 19c). The NRSV's "is bereft of peace" misses the force of the original Hebrew, which is more vigorous and places the accent on the man's movement: "I reject peace," i.e., despair of ever having peace or well-being. Indeed, the statement counterpoints God's rejection (2:7a; 3:31; cf. Ps. 88:14) which has caused the man's distress in the first place. Here we meet a suffering so extreme that it leads to the abandonment of all hope and an inability to entertain the very idea of (bodily) goodness and health (NRSV "happiness"). The final couplet names God for the first time and stresses that God is the chief cause of the man's torment. Unfortunately, the NRSV's rendering of the couplet obscures important nuances in the Hebrew and totally muffs the crescendo that is reached here. First, the Hebrew verb translated as "gone" means "to perish, destroy," which carries a special nuance of death and human mortality that is surely in view here but completely missed by the NRSV. Second, the verb phrase itself is multivocal and can mean either "perish from or in," where the Hebrew preposition designates the source (Jer. 49:7; Amos 2:14; Mic. 7:2; Zech. 9:5), or "to perish because of," where the preposition designates the agent (Job 4:9; Ps. 80:16). The context opens onto both meanings, only the former of which is realized in the NRSV. Together the two express the compound sentiment that the speaker's "glory and all that" he "hoped for" ("my lasting hope" is a simpler and more faithful rendering of the Hebrew) *from* God has perished specifically *because* of what God has done to him. But it is, of course, the phrase's causal sense that this opening section has gone to such lengths in its polychromatic play of imagery to stress and that when properly understood culminates fittingly in a climatic and emphatic declaration: "So I say, my lasting hope/ has perished because of the LORD!"

Excursus: Conventional Language

The stereotyped nature of the language used in Lamentations 3 and the poet's obvious dependence on other well-known genres, such as the individual and communal laments, often have led scholars to question the poem's historical connection to the events of 586 and to downplay its emotional and aesthetic achievement. Such tendencies belie a fundamental misunderstanding of this poetry. In the first place, the language used is above all a function of genre. In the case of the psalms of lament, as Miller rightly stresses, the language is characteristically stereotypical, generalizing, and figurative. Miller writes:

> The individual laments are in many ways strongly stereotypical. That is, in moving from one lament to the other, one can encounter much of the same structure and content repeated, with some variation in the images and primary metaphors used. The enemies themselves are talked about in very typical stereotyped language. Cliches of all sorts are used throughout the psalms.
>
> (50)

This strongly stereotyped and figurative language has confounded scholars' attempts to identify more specifically groups of peoples who, such as the enemies, repeatedly appear in lament after lament, or even to identify the probable setting in life in which these laments were used. However, if the language obscures the identity of the enemies or a particular psalm's original setting, it also opens up the possibility for a multiplicity of identities and settings. That is, because of the metaphorical and figurative nature of the language—it is poetry after all!—the language remains open for different people to use and appropriate in accordance within whatever situations they find themselves. As Miller observes, "the enemies are in fact whoever the enemies are for the singer of the psalms. . . . The laments become appropriate for persons who cry out to God in all kinds of situations" (50–51). That this was the understanding of the biblical writers would seem to be confirmed by the many times psalms are historicized and embedded in narratives (e.g., 1 Sam. 2:1–10; Isa. 38:10–20; Jer. 11:18–12:6). In such cases, the stereotypical language takes on a particularity that is imparted to it by the surrounding narrative context. Thus, the frequent observation that there is "very little specific reference to the fall of Jerusalem" in Lamentations 3 (Hillers, 120), for example, should not be interpreted as necessarily casting doubt on the poem's historicity with reference to the destruction of Jerusalem in 586. On the contrary, the language is a function of the particular genres utilized, and because of the language's stereotypicality it is open to appropriation in just such a context. Thus, the best clue to the date of Lamentations 3 is the context in which the poem is embedded, namely within the sequence as a whole.

Moreover, it may be that traumatic times in particular require the use of traditional expressions and rhythms. Citing an analysis of texts written by Polish victims of the German occupation during World War II, Czeslaw Milosz observes that these peoples couched their grief, anger, shame, etc. in utterly conventional expressions:

> As to the manner of style, we observe in general a tendency to simplify the style. The "novelty" of the matter finds reflection both in

115

> "small devices" of expression (metaphors, comparisons, etc.) and in formulas of certain works, as well as in their fabric and their internal components. Those results enrich a familiar repertory, without, however, going beyond the framework of perfectly explicable changes. On the contrary, there is not even one work deserving attention, where the author tries to express horror by going beyond the traditional communicative language or by disintegrating it.
>
> (68)

In response to horrific situations, people draw on the traditional motifs they know well and that are ready to hand. One gains a certain poignancy from such "topoi polished by long use like pebbles in a stream" (Milosz, 65). Put differently, the representation of extreme events typically (and perhaps necessarily) is lacking in innocence. In many respects the above description accurately represents what is going on in Lamentations 3. The poet labors and schemes "to exploit in new ways the devices of language available to [him] in order to mount a successful literary representation of primal outrage" (Mintz, 1). Thus, one should not allow the stereotypicality of the poem's words to dull the point or power of their message. To say that the language of Lamentations 3 is "traditional is not to say that it is flat or insincere" (Hillers, 122). One cannot deny, for example, the bitterness and accusatory tone of the initial complaint section in particular (3:1–18). Thus, we would do well to follow the counsel of the likes of Milosz and Miller and not let the poet's dependency on tradition blind us to his heartfelt expression of pain and agony. Indeed, it is the poetry's stereotypicality that has preserved these words' life-enhancing capacities, making them reutterable, reusable, able to be fitted even today for the saying of the unsayable.

Lamentations 3:19–24

To Hope

This short section composed of only two stanzas and unified by the refrain "therefore I have/will hope" (3:21, 24) forms a bifold hinge (cf. Ps. 77:11–12) that joins the poem's first two movements (3:1–18, 25–39). But neither the brevity of this section nor its highly transitional nature should be allowed to detract attention from the section's pivotal theological significance. If Lamentations' lyrics are dark and take as their most prominent subject matter an aspect of human existence that we find offensive and terrifying, they are for doing so by no means

116

morose or mired in melancholia. To the contrary, as I have tried to make clear throughout, Lamentations "is a most profoundly life-embracing work," one whose confrontations with death and suffering, for the most part, stand as "memory's beginning" to new life. As we have seen, Lamentations' hope is mostly fragmented and mostly communicated through innuendo and implication in the poems' lyric play and the like. But here, in these brief stanzas, Lamentations articulates most explicitly its resolve "to hope," a resolve that, if not yet a full-throated expression of hope, is nevertheless substantial enough to matter. It is a hope, as we will see, that is not facile, easily come to, but one born out of pain.

The section opens with the same strong assertion of the speaker's presence as in the opening and closing of the preceding section, "I remember" (following the Gk instead of NRSV's "the thought," cf. Ps. 77:12). The first two couplets (3:19–20) allude specifically ("affliction" [cf. 3:1] and "wormwood" [cf. 3:15]) and more generally to the distress recounted in 3:1–18. The image of the man's "soul . . . bowed down within" himself in particular is an image of inner despondency, intimately felt oppression, even sorrow (cf. Pss. 42:6, 7, 11; 43:5). Next comes a remarkable couplet. There is nothing in the Hebrew of 3:21 corresponding to NRSV's "But." The line simply begins with "this," which refers both retrospectively—back to the suffering (3:1–18)—and prospectively—forward to God's "steadfast love" (3:22). Before encountering 3:22, however, the reader can only understand "this" as pointing backwards to everything the speaker has just recounted, namely, the hurt of the preceding section. This, in turn, gives the couplet a highly radical inflection. It is in turning his "mind" (lit. "heart") to "this," his suffering, that the man fixes on "hope." Here we come face to face with the peculiar biblical idea that hope is born out of pain. As Brueggemann writes, such a hope is "a profound, elemental, material yearning rooted in the very bodies of the hurting ones, a yearning that moves with authority from hurting bodies to hoping lips" (*Old Testament Theology*, 50). The aversiveness of pain is such that it "cannot be felt without being wished unfelt," and thus once noticed, pain can only be realized as the voiced hope of pain's alleviation and medication (Scarry, 290). Here, the man "calls to mind" (lit. "this I cause to return to my heart")—notices!—his felt pain and "therefore" he has hope! This is not a smug or naively optimistic hope, but a serious and profound act of expectation that is only too aware of the hurtful reality from which it demands deliverance. This first part of the hinge, then, looks backward to all that has come before in the poem, grounding its inflection of hope in the man's expressions of hurt and complaint.

117

The next stanza, the second fold of the hinge, in its obvious propositional and tonal affinities with 3:25–39, looks forward to what is to come. This is usually understood as one of the poem's principal turning points, where the speaker makes a stunning about-face, what O'Connor describes as a "sudden emotional reversal" (1051). Having reached the nadir of despair, the man turns his thoughts to God's "steadfast love" and thus emboldened eventually, as Hillers puts it, "wins through to confidence" in God's mercies (6). Indeed, beginning here and carrying forward through the immediately following section there is a noticeable change in mood and feel, a change represented emblematically in the image of the man's "soul" in 3:24, which earlier was "bereft of peace" (3:17) and "bowed down within" the man (3:20), but now is plainly invigorated and even speaks. The gesture of hope implicit in the image, and indeed in the stanza as a whole, is unmistakable. This hope has two outstanding features. On the one hand, it is clearly rooted in God. This is well evidenced in 3:24 both in the man's explicit affirmation "I will hope in him" and in the phrase "the LORD is my portion," which arises from the traditions about the allotment of the land in which all Israel received portions of land from which to gain their livelihood, save the Aaronite priesthood whose portion and livelihood was to be solely dependent on God (Num. 18:20). The latter phrase ultimately becomes a statement of faith in the face of the most dire of circumstances (Ps. 73:26). But if firmly rooted in God, the man's hope is neither wholly pacific nor inherently optimistic. This man is definitely not the Pollyanna he is sometimes made out to be. Though firmly convinced that God's "final, inmost will for man is not suffering" (Hillers, 6), the hope voiced here is neither innocent nor lacking in its own claims on God. The references to "steadfast love," "mercies," and "faithfulness" in 3:22–23 allude to God's covenant loyalties as stipulated according to the Davidic grant (e.g., 2 Sam. 7:15; 1 Kgs. 8:23; Ps. 89:2, 14, 24–37; Isa. 55:3). Among the differences between the Davidic and Mosaic covenants, one stands out: the Davidic covenant is promissory in nature, an oath undertaken by God obligating God to Judah irrespective of the latter's behavior. Psalm 89:28–37 well expresses the central thrust of God's promise to David:

> Forever I [= God] will keep my steadfast love for him [= David],
>   and my covenant with him will stand firm.
> I will establish his line forever,
>   and his throne as long as the heavens endure.
> If his children forsake my law
>   and do not walk according to my ordinances,
> if they violate my statutes
>   and do not keep my commandments,
> then I will punish their transgression with the rod
>   and their iniquity with scourges;

> but I will not remove from him my steadfast love,
>   or be false to my faithfulness.
> I will not violate my covenant,
>   or alter the word that went forth from my lips.
> Once and for all I have sworn by my holiness;
>   I will not lie to David.
> His line shall continue forever,
>   and his throne endure before me like the sun.
> It shall be established forever like the moon,
>   an enduring witness in the skies.

It is this overt promissory aspect of the Davidic covenant that renders the man's hope more than a simple affirmation of confidence in God. By specifically grounding hope in the promises made to David, the man lays claim to those promises and places the onus on God to live up to God's covenantal obligations and to remedy the present situation of hurt. That is, such hope both indicts God for the current miseries that imply God has in fact "renounced his covenant" (Ps. 89:40) and calls God back to covenantal faithfulness. And thus, if willing to stake all on God, the man boldly insists as well that God does God's part. Here, then, as elsewhere in the Old Testament, hope voiced by "those who genuinely hurt" dares "to speak a command, even to the throne of God" (Brueggemann, *Old Testament Theology,* 51).

Lamentations 3:25–39
Sapiential Consolation

The next section is unified by viewpoint, mood, and subject matter, all of which differ from 3:1–18. After his long complaint, the man's focus shifts from depictions of the suffering itself to contemplation of traditional attitudes about how to cope with suffering. The series of reflections collected here is diverse and eclectic, but most draw loosely on aspects of Judah's wisdom tradition. Building on the immediately preceding assertion of the perpetuity of God's compassion and steadfast love (3:22–24), they generally counsel patience and long suffering, confident that God will eventually help those who wait for God's salvation. More specifically, they assert that God does not capriciously inflict suffering without also effecting mercy (3:31–33); neither does God oppress the captives (3:3; cf. Pss. 68:6; 69:33; 107:10–16), nor pervert justice (3:35). The use of God's epithet the "Most High" specifically foregrounds the image of God as one who establishes and sustains justice (Ps. 82:1–8).

119

God is in complete control and all powerful. What God says, God does (3:37)—an allusion to God's "good" creation (Gen. 1)—and both good and evil are attributable to God (3:38). Therefore why should one complain about just punishment for sin (3:39)? Rather, one should bear one's suffering quietly (3:28–30; cf. Pss. 4:4; 35:13, 14; 37:7; 62:5) and wait for God's deliverance (3:25–27; cf. Pss. 25:3; 39:7; 52:11; Prov. 20:22). "To put one's mouth to the dust" is an act of obeisance and of humiliation before God (cf. Ps. 72:9; Mic. 7:17), stressing the idea that such suffering should be passively accepted.

We may notice several aspects of this section. First, it propounds a general view about the proper conduct for a person in suffering, which teaches that suffering, like good fortune, comes from God and therefore is to be borne in confidence that God will eventually restore well-being. Implicit in such a view is the rightness of God's actions; God's goodness and justice are axiomatic. As such, the section shares the basic outlook of the friends in Job. Indeed, the section's choric function is essentially that of Job's friends, only enacted on a much smaller scale. It should be remembered, however, that, while Job is the hero of the book that bears his name and his perspective on suffering is radically different from that of his friends in important ways, nevertheless in the end Job, like his friends, is unwilling to give up the notion of a good and just God. Similarly, the view of God and the stance toward suffering adumbrated in 3:25–39 and the hope they inspire are aspects of Judah's religious heritage that this poem affirms. In the paratactic and concatenating logic of the poem, 3:25–39 serve as an extended elaboration of what the man calls to mind (3:21) and of why he settles on hope. One senses in these lines a genuine belief on the part of the man that if he can only endure his suffering long enough, God will eventually come to his rescue.

But the view of suffering and God realized in Lamentations 3 as a whole finally proves broader, more complicated than that reflected by the poem's middle section alone. As we have seen, even the man's expressed resolve to hope is not unmindful (not even for a moment) of the suffering out of which that resolve emerges, and the last half of the poem will eventually return to the subject of the man's affliction. Indeed, the power and success of this poem, again evincing a certain affinity with Job, derives in no small part from its ability to hold and affirm conflicting and contradictory truths without eventually surrendering either—the bifold hinge formed by 3:19–24 securely linking complaint (3:1–18) and hope (3:25–39). The first intimation within the section itself that the perspective championed at the level of propositional content is not wholly compelling arises syntactically. There are a number of places in 3:25–39 where the syntax is convoluted and even problematic. The most glaring example is in 3:28–36. The syntactic relationship of these three stanzas is complex and not completely certain. Each stanza appears to contain similar kinds of clauses that, while not dependent syntactically on each other, are dependent on the clauses in the other stanzas. This kind of clause mixing appears elsewhere in Hebrew poetry (Deut. 32:30; 33:4–5; 2 Sam. 1:20; Ps. 106:47). One effect of the density and complexity of this syntactic structure is to disrupt subtly but distinctly the ease and forthrightness of the poetry's meaning at this point, to slow the reading process down and to require our closer attention, if for no other reason than to decipher the syntax. Dissonance thus enters into the poetry's message at this point, like the sudden and unsettling rustle of the wind on an otherwise calm day that bears only the faintest echo of oncoming bad weather.

Another especially obvious example of syntax disturbing meaning occurs in 3:36. Lineation and syntactic difficulty combine to ensure that the line, regardless of how the syntactic issue is resolved, reads (in the Hebrew) as a straightforward declarative clause: "the LORD does not see"—NRSV's interpretation as a rhetorical question is but one (awkward) attempt to resolve the larger syntactic issue. Such a sentiment is not reassuring in the least (Ps. 94:7; Ezek. 8:12; 9:9). There are also other minor touches by which the poetry's surface meaning is decentered, even if only slightly. The parenthetical (according to NRSV) "there may yet be hope" in 3:29 hedges in a way that is remarkable in a psalmic avowal of confidence. Even more straightforward challenges to the section's ideology of suffering come in the poem's diction, which frequently and directly contradicts sentiments expressed elsewhere in Lamentations (reminiscent of how the friends' speeches are often diametrically opposed to those of Job). For example, the image of the passive sufferer patiently waiting for God's deliverance stands in stark contrast to the active laments and protests of the personified city in the first two poems, the community in Lamentations 5, and even the man himself in this poem's opening section. Note especially how the language of 3:28 ("to sit alone in silence") recalls and contrasts with that of 1:1a ("How lonely sits the city"). In the latter, Zion's "aloneness" is due to abandonment and she is anything but silent. In 3:31 the poet denies that God "will reject forever." Yet this is contradicted directly in 2:7a ("the Lord has rejected his altar," NJPS) and more generally in 5:20 and 22. The claim that if God causes suffering he will eventually have compassion (3:32) is refuted in four separate places: "killing without pity" (3:43), "the LORD has destroyed without mercy" (2:2a), "he has demolished without pity" (2:17b), and "slaughtering without mercy" (2:21c). The hyperbolic claim that God does not see (3:36) serves to point up all the places in Lamentations where God is requested to see and look upon the destruction (1:9c, 20a; 2:20a; 3:59–60, 63; 5:1). The phrase "to bear the

121

yoke" implies that suffering has some beneficial value (cf. Prov. 13:24; 23:13–14), which contrasts with the use of yoke imagery as a paradigmatic symbol of suffering in 1:14b and 5:5. The language throughout this section, then, forces the reader to evaluate the claims made by comparing them with counterclaims voiced elsewhere in Lamentations. There is no explicit attempt within the poetry itself to resolve the contradictory nature of this use of language; claims and counterclaims are given equal linguistic weight.

A final characteristic of note regarding the poem's middle section is its more expansive voice. These wisdom-inspired reflections are cast more broadly, as is typical of their genre, to reflect human experience in general, and thus, the speaking voice in this section becomes more expansive, more inclusive, though less personal—there are no first-person references to the speaker. The latter has a pronounced distancing effect. The poet effects this more inclusive and expansive voice by presenting the reflections using third-person forms (instead of the first-person forms of 3:1–18), by casting some thoughts as rhetorical questions (3:37, 39), which by virtue of the nonspecificity of their address lure readers into the poem's discourse, and by employing a succession of terms for human being or person more generally: "soul" (3:25) in its generic sense of "any soul" (contrasting with the earlier threefold [3:17, 20, 24] personal, self-referential use of the term); "one" and "human" (3:27, 35)—both translations of the same Hebrew word (*geber*) as in 3:1, though here with the more generic connotation implied by NRSV's translation (the same term occurs again in 3:39, but is left untranslated in NRSV); "anyone" (3:33); "one's" (3:36); and "any" (3:39). The net effect of these strategies is to broaden the poem's perspective to include humanity in general, of which, of course, the audience is a part. The explicit use of the Hebrew term *geber,* both at the beginning (3:27) and the end of this section (3:39), intentionally links the section with the poem's opening line. We read, then, the litany of suffering in 3:1–18 retrospectively, not only as the experience of a particular individual, but also as the experience of a "man" who is more broadly representative of "everyman." The poem, ever so subtly, becomes *our* own discourse of pain and hope.

Lamentations 3:40–47

"But You Have Not Forgiven"

Formally, this section is set apart by its use of the first-person common plural voice ("we") and its obvious dependence on elements of the communal lament. In other respects, however, it is integral to both what precedes and what follows. On the one hand, 3:40–41 constitute the conclusion to the previous section. In fact, it is only with these couplets that that section reaches its climax. The transition in voice is unobtrusive as it is experienced principally as a heightening of the poem's rhetoric. The man, caught up in the passion inspired by his own reflections on God's goodness and care of the faithful, persuaded by the sapiential admonitions recited in 3:25–39, calls for self-examination, repentance, and contriteness (3:40–41). One can almost hear the pitch of the man's voice rise. The poem's readership now is written directly into the poem. The verbs "test" and "examine" in 3:40 occur frequently in wisdom material (e.g., Job 5:27; 28:3, 27; Prov. 2:4; 20:27; Sir. 13:11; 42:18), carrying the wisdom focus forward into this next section. The exhortation to "lift our hearts as well as our hands" (3:41) calls for a full commitment of body, heart, and mind in prayer to God. On the other hand, through the force of juxtaposition, the remainder of the poem takes on the character of the prayer requested: complaint (3:42–47), expression of grief (3:48–51), and extended appeal to God for help (3:52–66). The confession of sin in 3:42 ("we have transgressed and rebelled") flows seamlessly from the preceding couplets. Indeed, it is just what might be expected in a penitential prayer of the kind that is called for as the logical conclusion of 3:25–39 (cf. Ezra 9; Neh. 9).

But the penitence is short-lived, and here the poem enjoys another of its momentary peaks. NRSV's translation completely misses the accusatory force of the following line. There is no conjunctive "and" in the Hebrew. To the contrary, the line has a pronounced adversative sense, communicated through the antithetical use of the pronouns "we" and "you" (the only place in the poem, except for "I" in 3:1 and 63, where independent pronouns are used) and the contrast set up between the positive confession and the negative framing of God's actions, which is better captured by the translation "but you have not forgiven!" The latter is more accusation than complaint. The cultural assumption that sin triggers divine anger and punishment was matched in antiquity by an equally strong assumption that repentance should bring about divine compassion and forgiveness (cf. Ps. 32:5). The God to whom loyalty and obedience are owed on pain of punishment is also the God who undertakes to care responsibly for his (or her) human subjects. Thus, the man comes to the brink of being consoled by the sentiments of 3:25–39 only to have them dashed by the continuing reality of God's silence and absence and the awful persistence of suffering, which forms the chief focus of the man's words for the remainder of the poem.

Fragments of complaint follow quickly. The next stanza (3:43–45) refocuses on God as the community's main adversary. The language echoes the language of divine violence found in both 3:1–18 ("anger," cf. 3:1; "pursued us," cf. 1:3c; "no prayer can pass," cf. 3:8; "made us filth and rubbish," cf. 3:14) and 2:1–8 (especially the cloud imagery, 2:1; "anger," cf. 2:1a, c, 2b, 3a, 6c; "killing without pity," cf. 2:2a, 17b, 21c). In this way the poem's larger community of readers is included in miniature within the circle of God's violence. Lamentations 3:46–47 shifts perspectives again, this time fixing on the hurtful actions of the enemies—the main topic of this latter half of the poem. But however fragmentary and whether at the hands of God or the enemy, the communal voice pointedly reminds us (and God!) of the hurt of the poem's present reality.

The kind of jarring juxtaposition of hymnic affirmation of God's goodness and the bleak and hurtful reality of historical experience found here in Lamentations 3 is not unique. It appears in other poetic compositions of the Bible as well, especially in the Psalms. Psalm 89, from which we quoted above, is a particularly instructive example. Immediately following the psalmist's recitation of God's pledge to guarantee the eternity of David's posterity and throne (Ps. 89:19–37), the psalmist shockingly reproaches God for repudiating the covenant, for not living up to God's oath:

> But now you have spurned and rejected him;
>   you are full of wrath against your anointed.
> You have renounced the covenant with your servant;
>   you have defiled his crown in the dust.
> You have broken through all his walls;
>   you have laid his strongholds in ruins.
> All who pass by plunder him;
>   he has become the scorn of his neighbors.
> You have exalted the right hand of his foes;
>   you have made all his enemies rejoice. . . .
>
> Lord, where is your steadfast love of old,
>   which by your faithfulness you swore to David?
>
>   (Ps. 89:38–42, 49)

The section's opening "But now you" (Ps. 89:38) is analogous to the "but you" in 3:42. The "remarkable point" of the juxtaposition in Psalm 89, as explained by Levenson, "is that the author or redactor refuses to choose between faith and realism or to beat one into the mold of the other. Indeed, as v. 50 [Eng. v. 49] shows, the speaking voice of the psalm dares to reproach God for the incongruity of the two" (23). Similarly, our poet, through the voice of the man and through the force of his counterposing poetics, insists that the affirmation of God's ultimate goodness and compassion toward humanity must be interpreted in light of the historical reality of the pain and suffering brought on by Jerusalem's destruction. The gap between the two realities is too great to be ignored. The poet of Lamentations, like the psalmist in Psalm 89, "refuses to deny the evidence of his senses in the name of faith, to pretend that there is some higher or inner world in which these horrific events are unknown" (Levenson, 19). But neither will he surrender the conviction that God's innermost will for humanity is not suffering but love and well-being. If the reality of pain and suffering must be squarely faced, it need not be accepted as final and absolute. To the contrary, it is to be resisted actively. The words of this poem constitute the stuff of that resistance, both in their protests and in their calls of faith for God's attention.

Lamentations 3:48–66
Grief, Supplication, and Vengeance

Another modulation in voice occurs in 3:48, the singular "I" of the man reemerging for the remainder of the poem. The shift is eased considerably by effecting the transition in mid-stanza and then by foregrounding images of crying "eyes" in the next several lines (3:48–51). Here there is no question of a second experience of suffering or the appearance of another speaker, though the "I" that we now hear is clearly more expansive, more inclusive than that of 3:1–18. The expansion of voice effected over the course of 3:25–47 distinctly colors how the singular "I" is now heard, as one among a larger community. The shift in voice also reasserts the utterly personal dimension of the suffering. As with Zion (1:16) and the poet-narrator (2:11) previously, the depiction of hurt in complaint ignites the man's grief and sorrow at the fate of his people (3:48–51). He not only laments the "destruction" of his people, but more particularly, the physical hurt of personified Zion. The phrase that NRSV renders only as "my people" is the same epithet for Zion that appeared in 2:11b (lit. "Daughter of My People"; cf. 4:3, 6, 10). The object of the poet's art is explicitly related in 3:49–50: "My eyes will flow . . . until the LORD from heaven looks down and sees." The poem's flood of words match the man's flood of tears in an effort to goad, flatter, shame, or otherwise compel God into acting in deliverance (cf. Pss. 14:2; 33:3). The Hebrew of 3:51 is more violent than suggested by NRSV's "my eyes cause me grief." The intended sense is more like "my eyes assault my very being (lit. soul)." The verb is the same verb of

125

violence as found in 1:12b, 22a, b, and 2:20a. The sense is either that the man's eyes are worn out from crying, or that the eyes are assaulted by the knowledge they give of the terrible events that have happened (specifically to the "women in my city," cf. 1:4, 18; 2:10, 21; the Hebrew alludes obliquely to the personified city). Thus, the depth and profundity of the man's grief matches that of Zion and the poet expressed earlier in the sequence.

The next stanza (3:52–54) briefly continues the complaint against the enemy. The notion of being hunted like a bird (1:6; cf. Pss. 11:1; 124:7; 140:5) and the protestation of innocence (3:35; cf. Ps. 69:4) are traditional. The hunting metaphor itself focuses the purely (i.e., lacking the civilizing characteristics that define humanity) animalistic status to which the victim has been reduced. The images of death in 3:53–54 stress the severity of the man's situation. The enemy tries to extinguish the man's life by flinging (cf. Pss. 18:41; 69:5; 73:27; 94:23) him into a "pit." "Pit" is also another term for the netherworld, Sheol (Pss. 30:3; 88:3, 4; Prov. 1:12; Isa. 14:15), and the "water" of 3:54 likewise is commonly associated with the netherworld (Pss. 42:7; 69:2–3, 14–15; 88:6–7; Jonah 2:3–6). The "stones" may well have a similar association (as in Isa. 14:19). If so they likely imply either stoning (as in NRSV) or some kind of sealing in by way of stones, similar to how "bars" (Job 38:10; Jonah 2:6) and "gates" (Job 38:17; Pss. 9:14; 107:18; Isa. 38:10) are more commonly pictured as blocking escape from the netherworld. In either case extreme, life-threatening distress is in view, as confirmed by the man's self-quotation, "I said, 'I am lost'" (lit. "I am cut off," i.e., dead, cf. Ps. 88:6; Isa. 53:8). As earlier (3:18), self-quotation marks a turning point in the poem, but this time complaint is followed by supplication.

The character of 3:55–63 as a petition to God is usually missed (as in NRSV) because the passage prominently features one of the Hebrew verb forms (the so-called "perfect") used in prose narrative to render events in the past tense. But the verb form itself is very flexible and can take on different nuances depending on context. Sometimes it can even express a wish or request (cf. 1:21c; 4:22b). The interspersed presence throughout this section of actual imperatives ("do not close," 3:56; "do not fear," 3:57; "judge," 3:59; "see," 3:63) and of other volitive forms (3:64–66) and the framing of the entire passage as a speech-act ("I hereby call," 3:55; NRSV "I called") occurring at the present moment (cf. Pss. 17:6; 88:9; 119:145–46; 130:1; 141:1) are broadly indicative of this latter (precative) use of the perfect. Therefore, in the following places where the NRSV gives a past translation, the Hebrew "perfect" should more accurately be rendered as an imperative:

3:56 "you heard my plea" = "hear my plea"
3:57 "You came near" = "Come near"
     "you said" = "say"
3:58 "You have taken up" = "Take up"
     "you have redeemed" = "redeem"
3:59 "You have seen" = "See"
3:60 "You have seen" = "See"
3:61 "You have heard" = "Hear"

When so adjusted, the character of 3:55–63 as a prolonged plea to God (interspersed, as expected, with elements of complaint) becomes obvious.

As Zion before him, the man here turns to God for help. The character and basic content of the plea are broadly comparable to the petitions that form a standard feature in the individual and communal laments of the Psalms. The "depths of the pit" out of which the man calls on God connect the petition directly to the complaint (3:53–54) and reiterate the utter direness of the man's plight, as he is poised on the very brink of death. The plea for God not to close God's ear (3:56), though not the content of the plea as implied by the presence of quotation marks in the NRSV's translation, specifically seeks remedy from God's obstructionist acts noted earlier (3:8, 44). The request for God to come near when called (3:57) echoes similar language used by Zion (1:21c) to summon God's vengeful action. Here the call is for healing and consolation. The phrase "Do not fear!" means to implicate comfort and confidence, as so often in the Old Testament (Ruth 3:11; Joel 2:21, 22), especially in Second Isaiah (40:9; 41:10, 13, 14; 43:1, 5; 44:2; 54:4). The imagery and language of the next stanza (3:58–60) take on a distinctly legal tenor, recalling 3:34–36. In invoking God as prosecutor, redeemer, judge, and witness, the man seeks legal redress for his unjust treatment. The mention of "taunts" (3:61–63) is intended to incite God to vengeance (cf. Judg. 8:15; Ps. 74:10, 18, 22; Isa. 65:6). The last line of 3:63, "I am the object of their taunt-songs," syntactically recalls the "I am the man who has seen affliction" that began the poem, providing a (penultimate) sense of closure to the poem before it shifts to invective in the final stanza. This syntactic sameness implies thematic sameness, the man's basic situation at the end of the poem is thus no better than at the beginning, just different aspects of his suffering are stressed.

The poem closes in invective against the enemy (3:64–66), recalling 1:21–22 and anticipating 4:21–22. As in 1:22a–b, the idea is that God should deal out retribution in exact proportion to the enemy's crime. The reference to "their hands" alludes to the actions of God's own "hand" at the outset of the poem (3:3) and more generally in Lamentations 2. The precise sense of "anguish of heart" in 3:65 is obscure, though it resonates with the other "heart" language in these poems (1:20b, 22c; 2:18a, 19b; 3:33, 41; 5:17). The Hebrew term translated "curse" can be used synonymously with "taunts" (lit. "reproaches," 3:61; see Jer. 42:18), and thus the poet reinforces his desire for retribution that fits the crime. "Pursue them in anger" recalls the community's similar treatment as relayed in 3:43 and "from under the LORD's heavens" (cf. 2:1b; 3:50), i.e., from everywhere in the world.

Here, then, as in Lamentations 2, the poem ends in speech, in voice regained, language remade, and it is in this linguistic achievement where one finds hope in this poem. Inflected speech stands here as a monument to survival, the voiced hope of pain's obliteration and evacuation. And the man, this "everyman," likewise stands as the paradigmatic survivor, not triumphant but alive.

Unlimited Suffering

LAMENTATIONS 4

In the fourth poem, the formal tensions that build to a climax in Lamentations 3 are consciously relaxed. The alphabetic acrostic once again only constrains the initial line of each stanza, but the stanzas now contain only four lines (or two couplets)—foreshortening the poem by a third. There is also a marked decline in the use of enjambment and the unbalanced qinah meter. This formal diminishment is mirrored by a pronounced fall-off in emotional intensity, effected above all by the less engaged style of third-person reportage that typifies the poem and the lack of other engaging and enlivening voices. As a result, clearly deliberate and carefully thought out (Hillers, 145), there is a palpable "sense of exhaustion and remoteness" about this poem (O'Connor, 1059), as if the depth of anger, unbearable hurt of searing physical pain, and torrent of tears that fired the first three poems at last finally has been consumed, spent. This diminution of emotion and feeling, in other words, colors the poem's tour of the horrifying material and physical conditions of survivors with the kind of mind-numbing trauma that often overwhelms those who suffer in extremity. Here we meet suffering at its most base and debilitating, unadorned by strategies of resistance; here Lamentations comes the closest to realizing the kind of spare and matter-of-fact representation of suffering that exemplifies so much post-Holocaust literature (e.g., Elie Wiesel, Primo Levi), where the horror of previously unimagined atrocities is equaled only by the everydayness of their occurrence.

Structurally, the poem plays a pivotal role in the larger sequence, as it greatly broadens and expands the primarily individual and personal voices of Lamentations 1–3, first, by focusing on various segments of the population, and, second, by finally breaking into the communal voice ("we") that will hold sway throughout all of Lamentations 5, as the use of third-person reportage to call forth voice—a rhetorical gambit otherwise confined to individual poems (esp. Lamentations 1 and 2)— here is grafted onto the larger sequence as a whole. In this a distinctive

129

widening of Lamentations' reach and perspective is perceived, a conscious attempt to democratize its poetics. The poem may be divided loosely by voice, 4:1–16 framed in spare, third-person speech and 4:17–20 realized in the choral ("we") voice of the community. Lamentations 4:21–22 concludes with condemnation of Edom and notice of the cessation of Zion's punishment.

Lamentations 4:1–16
A People's Suffering

The main section of this poem feels scattered and fractured as only the acrostic holds the disparate stanzas together. There is no dominant persona nor the patterned play of pronominal repetition to help structure the section, as so often in the other poems. Yet in a general way the imagery clusters around three topics: the suffering of children (4:2–4), the ravages of famine and hunger (4:5–10), and images of a bloodied and contagion-filled community (esp. 4:13–15). The poem opens with the same exclamatory "How!" found at the outset of Lamentations 1 and 2, strongly linking the three poems within the larger sequence. The stanza itself thematizes in metaphorical and thus open language the city's general state of decline, setting up in the process an implicit contrast with the city's once glorious past. The utter severity of the suffering is powerfully revealed in the image of "gold," usually impervious to tarnishing, turned "dim" and "changed." Hillers's objection that "gold does not tarnish or grow dark in any striking way" is precisely to the point (137): the occurrence of the impossible pointedly underscores the severity of the situation. "Sacred stones" refer most literally and most simply to precious "jewels, gems," implying that what used to hold great value, gold and jewels, now has been rendered worthless. But the reference to "sacred stones" certainly has the metaphorical capacity to refer as well to the now "scattered" "costly stones" (1 Kgs. 5:31; 7:9, 10, 11) originally used to build the temple (so Vg). The term "scattered" itself (lit. "poured out") recalls the fate of the children in 2:12, and thus prefigures the poem's ensuing focus on the fate of the children (4:2–4). Similarly, the phrase "at the head of every street" also recalls the unhappy death of children relayed in 2:19d—"streets" constitutes something of a *leitmotif* in this poem (4:5a, 8a, 14a, 18a).

The next three stanzas (4:2–4) focus on the plight of the children, the epitome of victimization and innocent suffering. As O'Connor notes, this poem's account of the children's suffering is the "most graphic and blistering" of any in Lamentations (1061). The highly meta-phorical language of 4:1 is concretized and focused in 4:2 in the image of the "children of Zion." The repetition of the "how" that opened the poem and use of synonymous terms such as "precious" (// "sacred") and "fine gold" (// "gold") tie the two stanzas together. "Earthen pots" refers to clay vessels, the most common of ancient artifacts, which when bro-ken were simply discarded (Ps. 2:9; Jer. 19:11; 22:28). Indeed, ancient tells are littered with the broken sherds from such vessels. Here, then, is the image of Jerusalem littered with dead bodies of children instead of broken pottery—though the more literal image of corpses lying amidst the scattered sherds of pottery also resonates. The "work of a potter's hands" literally continues the potsherd metaphor. But the phrase, of course, also alludes to God's creative activity—especially the creation of human life—which is often imagined metaphorically in terms of a potter (Gen. 2:7, 8; Jer. 18:1–12). And thus, what the divine potter carefully has crafted—human life—is here broken (Isa. 64:8–12; Job 10:8–12). Personified Zion herself (NRSV's "my people" misses the personification implied in the Hebrew "daughter of my people," cf. 2:11; 3:48; 4:6, 10), whose heroic qualities we have extolled previously, is even driven by suffering's aversiveness to spurn her own children. Her actions are even less humane than those of the cruelest of animals, "jackals" (commonly associated with deserted ruins, e.g., Isa. 13:22; Mic. 1:8) and "ostriches" (cf. Job 39:13–18). Suffering's corrosive cru-elty has reduced her to behaving in a manner not even found among scavengers. The unhappy consequences that such cruelty has for the children is spelled out graphically in the following stanza: the children are dying from hunger and thirst and no one will give them food or drink. The final words in each line of the second couplet assonate and alliterate *(lehem/ lāhem)*, emphasizing that the children receive "noth-ing" instead of the "food" requested.

   Lamentations 4:5–10 shifts away from the tight focus on the fate of children, though continuing the themes of hunger, starvation, and famine begun in 4:4. The severity of the situation is measured in these stanzas in several ways. First, it is so bad that even the wealthy ("deli-cacies" [Gen. 49:20] and "purple" clothing were associated with wealth) are affected, as they are now forced to "cling" (i.e., inhabit, live among, or even perhaps lie dead on) to "ash heaps," which otherwise are asso-ciated with the poor (1 Sam. 2:8). In 5:7 so severe was the shortage of food that even the "princes" (Gen. 49:26; Deut. 33:16) or "Nazirites" (i.e., those who take a vow to abstain from wine, contact with the dead, and cutting their hair) shockingly were affected. Their normally light

131

skin and "ruddy" complexion (signs of health and vigor and even divine favor, 1 Sam. 16:12; 17:42; Song 5:10; Ps. 104:15) is turned black and shriveled by famine. The comparisons to "coral" and "sapphire" are drawn from the realm of the plastic arts where such materials were used in representations of gods and people (cf. Song 5:10–16). In 5:6 yet a third means for measuring the brutality of the situation is offered. Even the punishment meted out to Sodom, a city whose great wickedness is proverbial in the Bible (Gen. 18–19), pales in comparison to that experienced by Jerusalem. Sodom was overthrown instantly, even miraculously ("no hand was laid upon it," cf. Hos. 11:6), while Jerusalem was forced to suffer the prolonged hardship of siege warfare (God "did not withhold his hand from destroying," 2:8b). The language here is textured and allusive. The Hebrew verb translated as "was laid on" has a homograph (if the two verbs are not in fact from the same root) that means "to be in anguish, severe pain [likened often to the pain of childbirth]" (cf. Isa. 26:17, 18; Jer. 4:31; Mic. 4:10)—emphasizing through wordplay the absence of anguish and suffering that otherwise attends physical assault. And the words "overthrown" and "hand" recall God's repeated turning of his hand against the man in 3:3. Lastly, the physical cruelty and harshness of hunger and starvation is such that otherwise "compassionate women" are driven to eat their own children (4:10) and it is preferable to be thrust through with a sword (4:9). In each instance, the poet is attempting to find language that will describe adequately the ravages to the human body and to the human mind resulting from enforced deprivation of food.

With 4:11 the poem turns away from its concentrated focus on famine. In this stanza the Lord once again is identified as the primary cause of Jerusalem's destruction and the people's suffering. God's "anger" and fiery "wrath" also are foregrounded again (cf. 2:3, 5). Hillers rightly calls attention to the hyperbole and symbolism implicit in the stanza's rhetoric—as a city's stone "foundations" hardly can be expected to burn in a literal way (148–49). Still, though figurative, the idea of a city being burnt to its very foundation does resonate quite literally (cf. 2 Kgs. 25:8–9). The dismay expressed in 4:12 at the breaching of Jerusalem's gates alludes to the complex of traditions about Zion that crystallized during the Davidic-Solomonic era and exerted a special influence on certain biblical writings (e.g., Psalms and Isaiah; for details, see Roberts, 93–108). The tradition, commonly referred to as the "Zion tradition," had its conceptual linchpin in the belief that God, conceived as the great warrior-king who was enthroned and thus made present in the temple (Pss. 46:5; 47:2; 48:2; Isa. 6:1), chose Jerusalem as a dwelling place (Pss. 78:68; 132:13). One of the principal implications of this belief was the understanding that Jerusalem and its temple and the hill on which they both stood were all endowed with cosmic potencies befitting the permanent residence of the High God (Ps. 132:8, 13–14), and thus, Zion, the entire city-temple complex, was thought to be impregnable, inviolable (cf. Ps. 48:3–6). Hence, the surprise and unbelief of the "kings of the earth" and "inhabitants of the world" as they learn of Jerusalem's fall.

The next three stanzas are among the most difficult in all of Lamentations. The Hebrew text in places is obscure and scholars are not in agreement as to the overall interpretation of this section of the poem. What may be said most generally is the following. The religious leadership ("prophets" and "priests") comes in for special criticism in 4:13. The stanza as a whole should be linked to what follows as its constituent clauses are dependent on 4:14–15 (lit. "because of" or "on account of") and do not constitute a self-contained statement as suggested in NRSV ("it was"). In 4:14–15 it is the larger community that is here most likely the unspecified entity depicted as wandering blindly and bloodied through the streets. In 4:15 the language and imagery alludes to the treatment of lepers (Lev. 13:45–46). Here, the idea is that Judah as a community has become contaminated (and thus dangerous) and isolated—much like personified Jerusalem in 1:17. In any case, the image of blood and its capacity to defile is prominent in all three stanzas.

The section closes by turning attention back to the Lord and underscoring God's role as the primary agent of destruction. Images of the human and divine "face" are front and center. It is literally "the face of the LORD" (NRSV's "the LORD himself"), which elsewhere turns hostile or threatening (Lev. 20:3, 6; 26:16; Pss. 34:16; 80:16; Ezek. 14:8), that "scattered" the people—very analogous to Enlil's "frown" or "evil look" in the Mesopotamian city laments. In fact, the couplet continues by observing that "he will regard them no more," that is, God withholds the benevolent look (Ezek. 9:9–10) for which these poems are so intent on calling (1:9c, 11c, 20a; 2:20a; 3:59–60; 5:1). In contrast, the "faces of the priests" are no longer literally "lifted up," looked on favorably, "honored" (as in NRSV).

Lamentations 4:17–20
"Our Eyes Failed"

The next three stanzas (4:17–20) are set apart by voice. Here the poem shifts into the first-person plural "we" of the community whose horrible plight has just been graphically depicted. As a result the poem becomes noticeably more intense and dramatic and the poem's community of readers and hearers is written explicitly into the text: "For the first time, the community of survivors tell their experience of the invasion. Retelling is a way of reliving the horror. It makes the invasion present through an understated and impressionistic description that brings the audience into the thick of the attack itself" (O'Connor, 1064). The continuity in general subject matter and the specific mention of "eyes," recalling the "faces" and "regarding" in 4:16, help to smooth this transition in voice. But it is the transition itself that is of crucial importance as the recovery of voice, otherwise realized in strongly personal terms in Lamentations 1–3, is here extended to and predicated of the wider community; the community, at last, is enlisted fully in Lamentations' life-bestowing poetics of voice.

The immediate background throughout this section is the siege of Jerusalem, here relived as if in the words of the community. The identity of the helper in this first couplet of 4:17 is left ambiguous. It could be God (1:7c; cf. Pss. 69:4; 119:82, 123), especially in light of the immediately preceding stanza (4:16), or as made clear in the second couplet, a "nation"—the identity of the latter is left unspecified (Egypt [Jer. 37:5–11] or Edom [4:21–22]?). In either case help was not forthcoming. The feeling of confinement associated with siege warfare is imparted through metaphors of hunting, entrapment, and the chase. Readers feel the pursuit and sense the nearing of the end. The imagery echoes the plight of the "princes" in 1:6 and the man in 3:33 and 35. In 4:20 the phrases "the LORD's anointed" (1 Sam. 24:6, 10), "the breath of our life" (lit. "the breath of our nostrils," cf. *ANET*, 484), and "under his shadow" (Pss. 17:8; 91:1) are all traditional royal epithets, traditional symbols of the hope and trust the people placed in the Davidic king, God's earthly representative (cf. Ps. 89:19–27). But the Davidide, like the temple and the land, has lost his special potency and no longer stands as the guarantor of peace and well-being. To the contrary, the king is imagined here as being entrapped in a "pit" (3:53, 55) like the man in Lamentations 3 and his presence no longer ensures Judah's safety and security "among the nations" (cf. 1:1, 3).

Excursus: **The Choral Lyric**

We have noted the theological importance of Lamentations' poetics of voice, how these poems, individually and collectively, facilitate a recovery of voice that is life giving and life sustaining. But also significant is the quality of the voice that is recovered. In recent generations, lyric poetry has been prized above all as the quintessential literary genre of the individual, that place where one self-consciously turns inward to explore and to reflect on the self in isolation from the outside world and from the larger mass of humanity. Obviously to have such a literary preserve as a safe haven for the construction of self is undeniably valuable. But sometimes we too easily forget that lyric poetry ultimately has its roots in communal experiences, in work, in liturgy and ritual, and in theater. It is this communal dimension of lyric verse that in antiquity, whether in Greece or the Near East, was prized and valued alongside lyric's more individualistic inflections. Indeed, as W. R. Johnson observes, "in ancient formulations of lyric, both solo and choral poetry were equally valid and equally important, each of them necessary to the total shaping of the human personality" (176–77). In our (postmodern Western) culture's general disregard for choral verse, Johnson sees and laments the loss of a potent force for (re)establishing "the great metaphors for *communitas* as the proper and central metaphors for the human condition" (178). It is precisely as a counterweight to the individualism that pervades our culture that Lamentations' thoroughgoing choral sensibilities are well poised to serve the church. For Lamentations ultimately crafts and frames its response to catastrophe in and through a communal idiom.

The poetry itself—in its specifically choral dimensions—as well as the presumed context of its performance affect a patently communitarian ethos. Lamentations' superposing of voice, which at some level always is (implicitly) choric in tenor and pitch but which also gradually becomes more and more explicitly communal as the sequence progresses, compels readers as they reutter these poems to assume a communal identity and persona, to articulate personal hurts and fears in a common voice. This infectious rituality of form is matched by the communal quality of what and how these poems imagine. The suffering of the individual is always linked to the suffering of the larger community, either implicitly as in the communal personae of Zion and the man, or explicitly and associatively as in the many images of individual pain and suffering that reside next to and abut other images and evocations of individual pain. In both ways the possibility for survival imagined within Lamentations is one that can only ultimately happen in the midst and through the agency of Others, of community.

Lamentations' overriding choric sensibility is also implicit in the presumed context of these poems' performance. The constitutive lyric situation of choral poetry is "we and the world" (W. R. Johnson, 177). Martha C. Nussbaum rightly reminds us of the situational significance of the

135

choral lyrics found embedded in Greek tragedies such as *Antigone*. Such poems originally were enacted and performed dramatically, and thus were above all elements in a dramatic performance. "They are performed by a group in word, music, and dance; and they are watched by a group—by an audience that has come together in community and at a religious festival and whose physical placement surrounding the action makes acknowledgment of the presence of the fellow citizens a major and inevitable part of the dramatic event" (Nussbaum, 70). The significance of this performative context should not be overlooked, as Nussbaum further contends:

> For these people experience the complexities of the tragedy while and by being a certain sort of community, not by having each soul go off in isolation from its fellows; by attending to what is common or shared and forming themselves into a common, responsible group, not by reaching for a lonely height of contemplation from which it is a wrenching descent to return to political life. This entire ethical experience, then, stresses the fundamental value of community and friendship; it does not invite or even permit us to seek for the good apart from these.
>
> (70)

If the communal and liturgical setting for Lamentations cannot be known with as great a certainty or with any real specificity of historical detail, the facticity of some such setting nevertheless can be confidently stipulated, and thus, as with the choral lyrics in *Antigone,* the ethical and theological significance of these poems' larger communal setting and experience are just as patent. And if today, by dint of our cultural prizing of literacy, we often necessarily experience Lamentations in a translated mode, as a distinctly bookish, unsung, and undanced kind of choral poetry, it is the liturgical impetus implicit in Lamentations where I find one of these poems' most potentially potent aspects. They provoke us to a renewed appreciation of liturgy as a powerful force for shaping, maintaining, and mending community. Indeed, Soelle observes that liturgy in times past served in just such a way, as an important mechanism for giving voice "to people in their fears and pain," but that now, "in our partially enlightened society," we mostly lack the communal institutions and rituals that previously shielded individuals by providing them with "a language from beyond" and that served to facilitate an acquaintance with others who suffer (Soelle, 72, 70; cf. Billman and Migliore, 122–24). Thus, along with Billman and Migliore in particular, I want to urge the church to explore creative and appropriate ways of carving out liturgical space for the voicing of pain, lament, and complaint, and of reintroducing biblical texts like Lamentations, the psalmic laments, and Job—texts that do not figure prominently in the common cycle of lectionary readings—into the worship life of congregations (cf. Billman and Migliore, 130–34). Human beings are fundamentally communal creatures, and therefore we need to find ways, in idiom and in deed, to nourish and imagine good community, to salve our corporate pain, and to ensure that human hurt never goes unnoticed and unvoiced (cf. Brueggemann, *Old Testament Theology,* 48). The choral dimension that undergirds so much biblical literature, and is especially prominent in Lamentations, reminds us of the importance of community and calls the church back to a renewed awareness of communal responsibility, especially in instances of suffering and oppression.

Lamentations 4:21–22
Revenge and Hope

The poem concludes with alternating expressions of revenge and hope. The initial appeal directed to personified Edom, "Rejoice and be glad," is meant to be sarcastic, as the "cup of wrath" imagery (see Isa. 51:17–22; Jer. 25:15–29; Ezek. 23:30–34; Obad. 16) and the presaging of drunkenness (cf. Jer. 51:7; Hab. 2:15–16) and stripping—here personified Edom is to suffer the same abuse that personified Zion suffered (1:8–10)—clearly show. Edom, Judah's neighbor immediately to the south and east and a traditional foe (Num. 20:14–21), elsewhere in the exilic and post-exilic literature comes in for special comment (Ps. 137:7; Ezek. 35; Obad. 11), apparently because the country failed to come to Judah's aid against Babylon, and indeed they even may have joined in with the Babylonians (esp. Ps. 137:7–9). The brutality of the invective in these last two stanzas should not be sentimentalized or sidestepped. Like blessing the dashing of small children against rocks (Ps. 137:9), the call here for Edom's violation, especially in light of the poet's earlier depictions of Zion's own violation, is ugly and hurtful. Yet, as in 1:21–22 and 3:64–66, the imprecation gives voice to and channels the community's raw rage at suffering's deep hurt such that the fragile flame of life may continue to smolder. The poem's otherwise dominant feel of diminishment is here momentarily checked and held in abeyance.

137

Lamentations 4:22 is frequently understood as pointing toward Jerusalem's ultimate restoration. Commentators agree that the couplet provides one of the more prominent gestures of hope in Lamentations (e.g., Hillers, 152–53). Read straightforwardly, the lines declare that personified Zion's punishment has been completed (NRSV "accomplished") and that God will no longer continue to exile her. Contextually, of course, one can make a strong case for understanding these clauses as wishes instead of declarative sentences—4:21–22, like 1:21–22 and 3:59–66, are formed as imprecations and the use of the precative perfect is well attested in Lamentations—even so, the declarative force of the statements would resonate regardless. This thematic sense of closure—the cessation of punishment—is reinforced structurally. The coincidence of the Hebrew verb *tam,* meaning "to be complete, finished," appearing at the head of the final *(taw)* stanza in the poem cannot be accidental (Job 31:40; Lam. 2:22c; cf. Hillers, 152). Moreover, 4:22a forms the mirror image of 1:3a, again underscoring the strong sense of closure. In the latter, personified Judah is portrayed as going into "exile" *(gālĕtâ)* amid much "suffering" *(mēʿōnî),* while in the former personified Zion's *(bat-ṣiyyôn)* "punishment" *(ʿăwōnēk)* is declared complete and her "exile" *(lĕhaglôtēk)* to be discontinued. Finally, there is a strikingly similar interjection in several of the Mesopotamian city laments ("enough! have mercy!"), which signals the end of destruction and the onset of the restoration. All three strongly evoke in the reader an expectation of closure and its attendant themes. However, instead of the happiness and rejoicing to which the poet sarcastically goads personified Edom (4:21), Lamentations ends with a communal lament that exhibits no explicit signs of restoration, happiness, or the prospect of God's return. To the contrary, the community is pictured as remaining very much in distress and Mount Zion itself is still in ruins with foxes—those prototypical ruin dwellers (Ezek. 13:4; cf. Isa. 13:19–22; Mic. 3:12)—prowling about (5:18). Therefore, the faint hope that these stanzas elicit is short lived, lasting only as long as it takes to start to read the sequence's concluding poem.

In sum, this poem's survey of atrocity, though spare and mostly matter-of-fact in tone, pivotally and crucially extends Lamentations' reach. By dispersing and fracturing the poetry's otherwise dominant inflections of personal voice, the poem gestures to the larger magnitude of the devastation and suffering. The horrors of 586 did not touch only a few, but encompassed a whole community. At the same time, those otherwise more personal embodiments of suffering are herein reinscribed as representative examples of a larger whole. They stand in for the multitude of other individuals whose stories are not told, whose voices are not heard. Finally, and just as significantly, the dispersal of voice enacted over the course of the main body of the poem is by poem's end regathered and recomposed as a collective, strongly implicating a notion of survival that is to be achieved in the coming together of the whole community and in attending to the needs and hurts of others.

A Closing Prayer
LAMENTATIONS 5

The fifth poem in Lamentations constitutes the sequence's concluding movement. The trajectory effected by the poet's manipulation of voice and persona throughout Lamentations constitutes a persistent movement from third-person reportage to direct speech, and from an individual to a communal or choral perspective. The two patterns converge in Lamentations 5 in the choral prayer (several Gk and Lat manuscripts actually label Lamentations 5 as "a prayer") of the community. The intentionality of this trajectory is underscored by the strong sense of closure exhibited in and through this final poem. Ending a lyric sequence poses a difficult problem, above all because its open-ended structure and its sequential movement offers no logical stopping point. Lamentations employs a variety of non-narrative means for marking closure, the two most effective of which involve terminal modification and knowledge of specific literary conventions and genres. As Herrnstein Smith explains, the state of expectation created by the kinds of systematic repetition that pervade Lamentations must be modified so that readers may be prepared for cessation. Modification creates the expectation of nothing, and therefore the audience is satisfied with the failure of continuation (34). Thus, one of the most common and effective ways to conclude a sequence of poems is simply to modify its governing patterns of repetition. In Lamentations 5 the acrostic disappears, except for a correspondence in the poem's number of couplets (22); there is no stanzaic structure; the unbalanced and enjambed lines all but vanish, giving way to the more usual balanced lines of Hebrew poetry with pervasive parallelism; the poem is a third again shorter than Lamentations 4, and thus the two final poems, when taken together, enact (spatially and temporally) a kind of tapering off suggestive of cessation and conclusion; and lastly, there is a transposition into a new mode, as Lamentations 5, in contrast to the other four poems, exhibits the salient features associated with the communal lament (cf. Pss. 44, 60, 74, 79, 80, 83). These modifications in form effectively signal the sequence's impending conclusion. Readers immediately recognize that something new is afoot. And when there is no continuation at the end of Lamentations 5, they are not surprised, since they have been formally prepared for this eventuality. The sense of closure projected by these modifications also strengthens the overall perception of cohesion manifested in the sequence (Grossberg, 99).

The sense of closure in Lamentations is further reinforced through knowledge of its governing literary conventions and genres. Herrnstein Smith writes that "other things being equal, we expect to find what we have found before . . . the reader's sense of finality will be reinforced by the appearance, at the conclusion of a poem, of certain formal and thematic elements which typically appear at the conclusion of poems in that style" (29–30). The frequency with which compositions in the ancient Near East are concluded with prayers and the symbolic significance of the pentad pattern, which is associated with the Pentateuch and especially the various episodes of creation, are two literary conventions that, as symbols of wholeness, help to foster a sense of closure in Lamentations. However, it is attention to the way city laments typically end that brings Lamentations' conclusion more sharply into relief. As noted above, the Mesopotamian city laments usually end by depicting the return of the gods and the ensuing restoration of the city. Thus, the organizing pattern in the Mesopotamian laments is essentially a comic one. The tragedy of the destroyed city is ultimately resolved by embracing the idealized and happy world where everything is restored once again as it was previously—"and they lived happily ever after." In Lamentations the comic turn that should follow 4:22 ("Your punishment is complete, O Zion") never materializes. Here the poet frustrates his audience's expectations, and in doing so radically alters the nature of his composition. What follows in Lamentations 5 is not a description of the hoped for restored city in which God will once again take up residence (see Ezek. 40–47), but yet another rehearsal of Jerusalem's destruction. God, whose absence from Jerusalem is stressed at the beginning of the sequence through the theme of divine abandonment (1:1a) and the image of Zion as a widow (1:1b), remains absent and silent at the sequence's end (5:20, 22). The destroyed and depopulated Jerusalem of the first poem (1:1) remains in ruins with only foxes as inhabitants at the end of the fifth poem (5:18). And the people's suffering, embodied initially by a personified Zion who cannot find any consolation or compassion (1:2, 9, 16, 17, 21), remains unrelieved in Lamentations 5: children are orphaned and women are widowed (5:3), property has been lost (5:2), famine is rampant (5:10), foreign rule is corrupt and oppressive (5:8), young girls are raped (5:11), young boys

141

are enslaved (5:13), and the elderly are disrespected (5:12, 14). Thus, Lamentations ends in tragedy, not comedy; the basic curve of movement manifested in the Mesopotamian city laments takes a tragic swerve in Lamentations 5. For the reader who is still waiting for the comic turn even after 5:22, the silence that follows the last verse brings the poet's point home. There is still no answer from God. God's silence, which eerily suffuses the whole sequence, becomes most conspicuous here at the sequence's end (see below).

Lamentations 5 is structured according to the basic form of the communal lament: address to God (5:1), complaint or description of distress (5:2–18), and appeal for help (5:19–22). The poem receives an added layer of form through the repeated use of the first common plural morpheme (-nû), which occurs 34 times—the exact number of combined occurrences of "we/us/our" in NRSV's translation! Such a profusion of the same pronominal form, of course, helps hold this otherwise strongly paratactic poem together, especially in the long complaint section (5:2–18) which often has the feel of a grocery list as it serially ticks off one aspect of distress after another. However, as already suggested, the play of pronominal form in Lamentations means in its own right as well. In particular, it helps to articulate the sequence's basic curve of movement, as "hes" and "shes" persistently give way to "Is" and "yous" and singular forms meld into their plural counterparts. Both patterns converge in the "we/us/our" of Lamentations 5. Survival is implicated in voice and voice is found in community. "The grammar of survival," as John Felstiner observes (152), "requires pronouns."

Lamentations 5:1
"Remember, O LORD"

The opening address to God recalls in its language ("remember," "look," and "see") the earlier appeals voiced by Zion and the man (1:9c, 11c, 20a; 2:20a; 3:59–61). This kind of lexical echoing is representative of this poem's dense allusive texture. It repeatedly alludes through word, image, and form to all of the earlier poems in the sequence. Therefore, if there is an intentional break in Lamentations 5 with the dominant formal patterns of repetition that marked these earlier poems, it is counterpointed effectively by a myriad of small gestures of coherence tying this poem inextricably to the rest; closure is achieved, but in a way that is fitting and appropriate, that seems to follow naturally and smoothly from the poems that have preceded this one. The phrase "what has befallen us" signifies globally and textually. In the latter case, it encompasses all of the suffering detailed in the previous poems. "Disgrace" sharpens the image, referring literally to "reproach, abuse, shame" as in the "taunts" of the enemy (3:61) and/or in the suffering and humiliation arising from any number of causes (2 Sam. 13:13; Pss. 22:7; 79:4; Isa. 47:3; 54:4; Lam. 3:30). Shame is a dimension of suffering that is often overlooked. But feelings of weakness and helplessness, especially before others, are themselves debilitating and corrosive as they erode the sufferer's sense of dignity. By voicing the community's shame and embarrassment, the poem not only calls attention to this dimension of suffering, but also names and authorizes these feelings, valorizes them alongside the hurt of physical pain, and thus offers gestures of articulation that for those unable to name what they feel inside may be experienced as consoling and liberating. Thus, the last poem opens with yet another call to God to witness Judah's suffering and to note especially the hurt of disgrace.

Lamentations 5:2–18

A Community's Complaint

The next section, the largest of the poem, consists of one long series of complaints detailing the community's general distress. Formed according to the basic dictates of the communal lament, it is noticeably longer than normal for comparable complaint sections in such laments. In this sense, the section is far more reminiscent of both Zion's (1:12–22) and the man's (3:1–18) earlier complaints. And of the two, it is the man's complaint that 5:2–18 most closely resembles: both are approximately the same length, feature lists of complaints, draw on respective psalmic forms and the conventional language of these forms, and impart structure through pronominal repetition.

As there is no obvious way of conveniently mitigating the *ad seriatim* character of this section, we will pursue our exposition in serial fashion, commenting on those aspects of the text that bear exegetical or theological interest as we encounter them. Of course, such listing itself is not without its own rhetorical significance. As complaint is piled upon complaint one gains the impression of a distress that is multiplex and extensive. That is, one effect of such listing is to gesture beyond the individual items actually enumerated to a larger and more

143

encompassing enormity. Thus, while Judah's distress, according to the poem's discourse, includes all the aspects listed here, it is the larger magnitude of the atrocity that is ultimately pointed toward.

The poem's inventory of distress begins rhythmically in the now familiar unbalanced cadence that dominates the other poems. And while this rhythmic glance backward is only momentary (5:2–3, 14), it is effective. The gesture helps tie Lamentations 5 to the preceding poems, and more important, it signifies continuity with the previous descriptions of distress. The first image evoked is a realistic one, that of Judean land and houses commandeered by the occupying forces of a foreign power (5:2). The term "inheritance" refers foremostly to real property, land that may be handed down in patrimony. But the Hebrew term has a more specialized theological meaning that is surely meant to resonate here as well. It refers more specifically to the land that God gave Israel (Deut. 4:38; 25:19; 26:1), and the people themselves are at times even called God's "inheritance" (Deut. 4:20; 9:26, 29). In fact, the term is frequently used in parallel with the word for "portion" (3:24), both generically (Gen. 31:14; Deut. 32:9; Job 31:2) and with more specific reference to the "portion" of the Levites (Num. 18:21; Josh. 18:7) and to the promised land in the conquest narratives (Josh. 19:9; cf. 13:7; 19:51). Thus, the "portion" of the Lord on which the man in Lamentations 3 resolved to hope is shown to be in the hands of foreigners; the land of promise, which symbolized for Judah the special bond they had with their God, is now only a sign of foreign domination. The depth of hurt caused to the Judean psyche by the loss of the land is suggested in the verb "turned over," which alludes quite specifically to the divine beating in 3:3, where God is imagined as turning "his hand,/ again and again, all day long" against the man.

The force of the parallelism in 5:2 ("to strangers"//"to aliens") isolates one of the subthemes that appears throughout the poem's description of distress: the disgrace of foreign occupation. Military defeat necessitated surrender and a pledge of commitment and (treaty) loyalty to the area superpowers (5:6). ("Egypt" and "Assyria" were in political ascendancy just prior to the rise of Babylon under Nebuchadnezzar and symbolize more generally the two traditionally dominant superpowers of the ancient Near East, Egypt to the south and Mesopotamia to the east, and therefore the two are commonly linked, even in later literature, e.g., Isa. 52:4; Zech. 10:10, 11. See Ezra 6:22 for an especially comparable use of "Assyria" as a designation for Persia, i.e., the power in Mesopotamia during that period.) In 5:8 the reference to "slaves" who "rule over us," though a commonplace emphasizing the absence of normalcy and the dire nature of the situation (Prov.

30:21–23; cf. Isa. 3:4; Qoh. 10:6), also likely refers quite literally to the Babylonian officials who were in charge (2 Kgs. 25:24). Basic commodities, such as water, bread, and wood (5:4, 9), are controlled by the occupying forces, and oppression and mistreatment of the native Judean population is normative (5:5, 11–14). When read literally, such a theme resonates well with what must have been the general situation in Palestine, and especially in Jerusalem after the city's fall—and, of course, it also resonates with many historical periods since, including our own.

Lamentations 5:3 focuses projections of vulnerability, especially as embodied in the disintegration of the basic family unit. "Orphans" and "widows" were recognized in the ancient Near East as especially vulnerable groups who required special divine and royal protection (e.g., Ps. 68:6; Isa. 1:23). "Fatherless," as an item adverbial, underscores yet again this vulnerability, but it also may allude secondarily to the absence of God, the father par excellence (see esp. Jer. 31:9 and contrast the plural "our fathers" [NRSV's "our ancestors"] in 5:7—who also "are no more"). The phrasing of "our mothers are like widows" recalls and democratizes the image of mother Zion as widow in 1:1b. This pattern of democratization occurs throughout this section. For example, the lack of "rest" in 5:5 alludes to Zion's similar inability to find "rest" (1:3b) and the community's sickened "heart" (5:17) is specifically taken over from Zion's faint "heart" (1:22c; cf. 1:13c). In 5:11 the confluence of language ("Zion" and "Judah," on the one hand, and "women," "virgins," i.e., nubile young women, and "rape," on the other) recalls the similar fate suffered by personified Zion (esp. 1:8–10). In each of these instances language is used so as to conflate identity, to break down distinctions between Zion's dominant persona and voice and the "we" who voices this final poem. Here we witness the poetry trying to win over readers to its side, trying through its lyric rituality to move readers from their roles as passive observers, watching an "other," to active participants in solidarity with the "other." As Terrence Des Pres notes, all literature of atrocity at one level desires to make the reader complicit so "that inevitably the survivor's scream begins to be the reader's own" (49).

The section features two slightly different notions of sin. In 5:16 we meet a full-throated awareness of sin's origins within the self: "woe to us, for we have sinned!" Lamentations 5:7, by contrast, locates the origin of sin beyond the self—here the idea is that the sin of one generation is visited upon the next generation (cf. Exod. 20:5; the reference to "Egypt" and "Assyria" in 5:6, possibly alluding to the ill-fated foreign policies of the Judean state that precipitated Jerusalem's eventual fall, would color this notion of sin rather specifically with a political tint). As phrased, the latter is at once both a statement of fact and a protest (cf.

145

Jer. 31:29; Ezek. 18:2)—the latter sense arising principally from the explicit presence of the pronoun "we," which adds a disjunctive/contrastive nuance (cf. 3:42), and the use of the polyvalent Hebrew term that can mean both "iniquities" (so NRSV) and "punishments" (the latter sense is to the fore here). Though the language of "sin" here encourages us to hold the two notions together, their distinct local nuances and their detached spatial placement within the poem ultimately resist any attempt to collapse the discordant notes in these two conceptions. The poem's outlook on sin, then, is fundamentally tensive. Sin is experienced *within* and *beyond* us, both mutually implicated but not reducible one to the other. Individual and communal responsibility before God is owned, but the felt reality of sin's perennial "already thereness" is strongly realized and even objected to.

Lamentations 5:11–14 stands out as the only portion of the poem devoid of first-person plural forms. Each couplet focuses on the plight of one segment of the population: women, princes, young men, and elders. The whole is prefaced by reference in 5:10 to the pervasiveness of famine, reminiscent of 4:8. As noted, the fate of the women in 5:11 recalls the similar fate suffered by personified Zion (esp. 1:8–10). The image of princes being hung in 5:12 signifies either execution (e.g., Gen. 40:19; Esth. 2:23)—by hanging or by being impaled on a stake (as, for example, in the Assyrian reliefs depicting the siege of Lachish, *ANEP*, 372, 373)—or exposure of the corpses (after execution) as a means of degradation and for instilling fear in the survivors (e.g., Josh. 8:29; 1 Sam. 31:10). The Hebrew of 5:13 is difficult. As translated in the NRSV, the first line emphasizes shame and belittlement, as grinding was a menial task usually undertaken by women (Exod. 11:5; Job 31:10; Isa. 47:2) and slaves (Judg. 16:21), while the second line focuses on the arduous nature of carrying "loads of wood." Other alternatives also exist. The first line may simply refer to the men's having "to carry or bear" (the usual meaning of the Hebrew verb) the "grind," the product of the grinding, while the second line is frequently emended (e.g., "boys stagger from hard work"). In 5:14, NRSV's "old men" is surely a reference to "the elders" (cf. 5:12), who would gather at the city gate to discuss anything of importance to the life of the community, including adjudicating legal disputes (Deut. 21:19; 22:15). The Hebrew verb used (NRSV "have left," but more literally "to cease") is likely intended to play on the similar looking Hebrew verb "to sit," which is what the elders customarily do at the city gate (Ruth 4:1–4). The plight of each group is reversed from normal experience, symbolizing the general turn in fortune that has overcome the larger community.

This reversal theme continues explicitly in 5:15. The transformation of song and dance into mourning and lamentation is a commonplace in city laments. The specific language used, "the joy of our hearts," alludes to the (personified) city, "the joy of all the earth" (2:15c), whose existence has been brought to an ignominious end. The personified city remains to the fore in the first line of 5:16. Reference to the "crown" falling "from our head" is not simply symbolic language for honor and glory and festivity (Job 19:9; Song 3:11), but a metaphor for the broken and collapsed walls of Jerusalem. The crenelated walls of Palestinian cities were often likened to a great crown that adorns the head of the city. The mural crown is a common motif associated with the personified city in the Old Testament (Isa. 28:1–5; 62:3; Jer. 13:18; Ezek. 16:12). Thus, the image of "fallen" personified Jerusalem inheres in the poet's metaphorical language (cf. Amos 5:2).

The complaint section comes to a close with 5:17–18. The language of 5:17 ("because of this . . . because of these") refers backwards to all of 5:2–16 and not just forwards as implied in the translation of NRSV. It is the general picture of distress and misery evoked in 5:2–16 that sickens the heart and dims the eyes in sadness. The final image of Zion with which the reader is left is that of a ruined city populated only by "jackals" (or "foxes"), the proverbial inhabitants of deserted and ruined cities (Ezek. 13:4; cf. Isa. 34:11–17; Zeph. 2:13–15). Thus, there is a general equivalence in the images of Jerusalem that open and close Lamentations. Both stress aspects of Jerusalem's ruined condition. In 1:1 Jerusalem is abandoned by its human population and by its God, while in 5:18 the city is only fit to be inhabited by jackals and the like. In both, and throughout the sequence as a whole, Jerusalem remains in ruins. There has been no change in Jerusalem's material condition. If anything, the two images considered sequentially, tragically symbolize the city's ongoing misery. Instead of depicting the return of God and the city's human population, as in the Mesopotamian city laments, the sole portrayal of renewed habitation in Jerusalem is that accomplished by animals who themselves symbolize and embody the very antithesis of human habitation and civilization. The city remains in ruins and its eventual rebuilding is nowhere in sight.

Lamentations 5:19–22
Conclusion

The poem concludes by returning to address God directly. The hymnlike 5:19 acknowledges God's eternal dominion ("But you, O LORD, reign forever:/ your throne endures to all generations") and is paralleled elsewhere in the communal laments (e.g., Pss. 10:14–16; 74:12–17; 80:1–3). "However," Westermann rightly observes, "this sentence gives the effect of being a singularly isolated word of praise. It stands in the place customarily occupied by an avowal of confidence—an element noticeably absent here" (212). Later on he elaborates on the nature of this "singularly isolated word of praise":

> [I]t is important to note that this verse is not spoken in straightforward jubilation. One must hear this verse in conjunction with the accusation against God that follows in v. 20. The perpetual enthronement of God in the heavens locates God so far away that God's view from above apparently does not reach all the way down to the level of the human misery that has just been described. The exalted glory in which God sits enthroned, in other words, also places God at an unfathomable distance from the human scene. The survivors have not forgotten to praise God. When they do offer praise, however, a note of bitterness intrudes.
>
> (Westermann, 216)

Here, then, as is common throughout these poems, the poet through juxtaposition—here with the lament commonplace "Why have you forgotten us completely?/ Why have you forsaken us these many days?" (cf. Pss. 22:1; 44:24; 74:1)—effectively undercuts and isolates the hymn of praise. Westermann's view of God's isolation and distance from earthly matters is further supported by the contrast the poet sets up between God's heavenly and perpetual throne and his earthly throne—Jerusalem, "his footstool" (2:1c; cf. 1:10; 2:6a)—which has been demolished and profaned and currently lies in ruins, inhabited only by jackals (cf. 5:18). Here also the image of God literally "sitting enthroned" counterpoints that of personified Zion who opens Lamentations literally "sitting alone" (1:1a), and who in the second poem is "thrown down . . . to the earth" (2:1a). Thus, God is imagined very literally as being spatially separated from and other than God's people.

Lamentations 5:21 contains a short prayer for restoration (Pss. 14:7; 80:19; 126:4; cf. Jer. 48:47), which, in seeking a revival of Judah's relationship with the Lord in all of its material and spiritual dimensions, looks briefly and even hopefully toward the future, a future that will resemble the "days of old," an allusion (with strong closural force, cf. Grossberg, 104) to that time when Jerusalem "was full of people" and Zion a "princess among the provinces" (1:1). And yet the petition's extreme brevity and the "anxious question" that follows in 5:22, which as Westermann notes, "runs contrary to the whole tradition of the concluding verses of the communal lament" (217), work together to counterpoint and erode much of the hopefulness that we might want to read into this verse. The nature of the syntax in 5:22 is disputed. NRSV's "Unless" is rendered better either as "but instead" (so Vg; cf. Num. 24:22; 1 Sam. 21:6; 2 Sam. 13:33), underscoring the Lord's rejection and anger, or even more literally as "for if," in which case the conditional clause's apodosis has been intentionally withheld. But whatever the correct understanding, one can agree with Provan that "it is clear . . . that the poem does not have a confident ending" (134). The obvious pessimism of this verse is recognized in the rabbinic exegetical tradition, where it is customary in biblical books (or chapters) that end on such a sentiment to repeat the penultimate verse in public reading. This practice is routinely carried out with Lamentations 5 and is even reflected in many of the Targum manuscripts, confirming the perception of pessimism and even tragedy here at the poem's end.

But the sobriety of the poem's conclusion, as it names the reality of suffering's still unyielding grip on the community, is lightened and countered ever so slightly but significantly by the naming itself, by the poem's construction of voice. With the conclusion of this poem, Lamentations as a whole ends, as did Lamentations 2 and 3, with voice regained and language remade. What is enacted at the personal level with Zion and the man here is extended and broadened to include the larger community. Voiced hurt already contains the seeds of life revived and resurrected as in the "carpel" or "fruit-leaf" *(Fruchtblatt)* of Celan's poem *Voices*, an image of "a flower's minute ovary-bearing leaf—the nub of life" (Felstiner, 100). And though this "carpel" is "deeply/ nicked" and oozing resin that "won't/ scar over," it retains a "nub of life" nonetheless (Felstiner, 100). And thus Lamentations' closing anxious plaint ("unless you have utterly rejected us/ and are angry with us beyond measure") contains within its very vocality the bequest of life (however "nicked"), an inheritance bestowed ritually, lyrically upon readers each time they encounter and reutter for themselves the words of this poetry, *"Voices* from the nettle path" (Celan as cited in Felstiner, 98).

Excursus: The Silence of God

Poetry often exploits the gaps and spaces between inflections of language, the stretches of silence that circumscribe every word, line, stanza, and poem, and therefore poems may mean even where words and sounds are not. The silence that pervades the gaps and spaces in Lamentations and that seeps in for good after the sequence's final word has been shaped so as to implicate God. It is curious that in a collection of poems centrally concerned with language and the recovery of

149

language, and with voicing and giving voice, the one voice not heard from is the voice of God. This curiosity turns significant when it is further observed that in the Mesopotamian city laments the deity responsible for carrying out a given city's destruction frequently speaks—as, for example, Enlil in "The Lamentation over the Destruction of Sumer and Ur," who toward the end of this lament "speaks a friendly word" (*ANET,* 619), announcing the end of the destructive activity and giving permission for the joyful rebuilding and restoration of Ur. One may surmise by contrast, then, that the suppression of divine speech in Lamentations and the deafening silence that results is intentional and therefore meaningful. The cloud of divine silence that suffuses and counterpoints the eruption of language in Lamentations resonates variously and even contradictorily. First and most negatively, God's silence in circumstances of distress and suffering will always (at some level) be experienced as oppressive by the community of faith, since it implies a refusal to comfort or give aid—and in the case of Lamentations, a refusal even to acknowledge the hurt. Not only does such a refusal seem out of character for the compassionate and faithful God known to other parts of the Bible and professed by Jews and Christians, but there is a very real sense in which radical suffering cannot be overcome except through the help of an "other," one "whose alterity, whose exteriority," as Levinas says, alone "promises salvation" (93). To the extent that God, as the ultimate "other," remains silent and not an active force of merciful care and medication, God becomes folded into the structure of suffering as a part of its malignancy. Though the attribution of even indirect malevolence to God may prove disconcerting for some Christians and Jews, it is an inference that we who stand on the other side of Auschwitz can hardly avoid. One need only recall Celan's epithet for God, "HearestThou" *(Hörstdu),* who "says nothing" and "doesn't answer" and is "not for humans" (from "Conversation in the Mountains" as cited in Felstiner, 143), to feel the stab of God's silence in the midst of atrocity and its aftermath. The Old Testament itself is laced with strands of literature that steadfastly witness the felt hurt of God's silence in times of extreme suffering (e.g., Job, the laments of the Psalter). Indeed, as Soelle reminds us, the malignancy of God's silence is integral to the Christian story. As the Gospels recount it (Matt. 26:36–46; Mark 14:26–31), Jesus in Gethsemane "prayed that he would be spared the agony that lay before him. But to this plea he receives no answer. God is silent, as he has been so often in the history of mankind, and Jesus remains alone with his repeated cry, his fear of death, his insane hope, his threatened life" (79). And then on the cross Jesus echoes the now paradigmatic plaint of God-forsakenness from Psalm 22: "My God,

150

my God, why have you forsaken me?" (Mark 15:34). In its zeal to pro-
claim the good news of the resurrection, Christianity has shown a tendency throughout history to rush too quickly past these moments of
divine abandonment and hiddenness. But it is precisely the "awe-fullness"
and "fearsomeness" of God's hiddenness, David Tracy argues, that postmodern Christianity must squarely face: "It is self-destructively senti-
mental for Christians to allow their understanding of the God who is
Love to be separated from the Hidden God. We must be willing, reli-
giously and theologically, to face the dialectic of the revelation of God's
radical hiddenness as we—and the Bible—experience that hiddenness
in life" (13; cf. 10–11). Tracy concludes that the negativity of God's hiddenness cannot be reconciled theoretically with God's more kindly
aspects. Rather, there is only a pragmatic resolution, as God's hiddenness, however hurtful, "drives the Christian not to further theological
speculation but to the cross" and to "the practice of resistance to evil in
defeat" that it so potently symbolizes "for whatever comfort we may find"
(Tracy, 11–12). The paradox of the cross is that it is at once a symbol of
suffering and abandonment and a symbol of solidarity in suffering and
abandonment.

In Lamentations, the malevolence of God's silence and inattention
is not so much represented or inveighed against, as it is felt, evoked in
the reader, and thus implicitly criticized. For example, every time that
God is beckoned to see, hear, or remember but fails to respond, the
divine silence grows more audible, more suffocating, more oppressive.
Here the mimetic representation of God's silence is thrown into stark
relief by its having been framed by direct discourse: God is spoken to
but does not speak. Another strategy involves the frequent invoking of
a theme, idea, or memory to raise an expectation that is then shown to
be wanting in the present circumstance, and thereby creating frustra-
tion, despair, and oppression in the reader. We have already noted this
at the level of genre, where the expected inclusion of divine speech in
city laments is intentionally flouted. Similarly the fivefold repetition of
the "no comforter" refrain in the first poem resounds against the cultural expectation that family and friends of the bereaved should offer
comfort and consolation, evoking with every successive repetition
greater sympathy and greater anger from the poem's auditors who feel
that the city deserves comfort at such a time. A final example involves
the multiple allusions to the Egyptian captivity in Lamentations 1. As
Brueggemann, for one, well recognizes, the events surrounding the
exodus, in which the "grief and anger experienced, noticed, and voiced   . 151
on earth (in the empire) are received, heard, credited, and taken seri-
ously in heaven (Exod. 2:23–25)," become normative for Israelite and

Judean faith (*Old Testament Theology*, 47). It is precisely the apparent failure of this normative paradigm, God's refusal to hear Judah's cries, to see Judah's hurt, and to bind up Judah's wounds, that Lamentations' allusive language most effectively points up and that in turn evokes feelings of anger, hurt, and disappointment.

From a slightly different perspective, the silence of God in Lamentations might engender more positive associations. Two come immediately to mind. First, silence in its own unique way underscores the corrosive and utterly reprehensible nature of human suffering. As Soelle observes, "Respect for those who suffer *in extremis* imposes silence" (69). Thus, there is a sense in which silence projected metaphysically may aid (though not unproblematically) in the appreciation of extreme experiences of suffering. It also reminds us that however important the recovery of language may be to the ultimate survival of victims of radical suffering, there are times when words should not be forced and silence respected. Second, God's represented refusal to speak has the purely pragmatic effect of creating the necessary space for human speech. The overwhelming importance of human speech in the face of severe suffering cannot be overstated: "the sufferer himself must find a way to express and identify his suffering; it is not sufficient to have someone speak on his behalf. If people cannot speak about their affliction they will be destroyed by it" (Soelle, 76). From the history of atrocity in the last century alone we also learn that silence must ultimately be overcome and speech recovered if only to ensure through telling tales and creating memories that past horrors are not repeated in the future. And paradoxically it is only through speech addressed to God, that "all-encompassing act" of prayer, that the mute and silent God that is sometimes experienced so oppressively can be transcended and the "speaking God of a reality experienced with feeling in pain and happiness" reawakened and reengaged (Soelle, 78; cf. Brueggemann, *Theology*, 375; Levenson, xviii, 127). Thus, God's silence, however hurtful, is not lacking in benefits.

Finally, there is in the silence of God in Lamentations the ever faint reminder of human finitude, the notion that our reasoning and abilities to comprehend, however important, necessary, and worth prizing, are limited and not God's. And therefore pregnant in God's represented silence is a defence of the divine that perhaps the post-destruction community in Palestine and we could not or would not want to comprehend or understand (n.b. the voice from the whirlwind in Job). By saying this I would not be construed as in any way justifying human suffering. To the contrary, I firmly believe with Levinas and in light of abundant scriptural testimony that suffering in another human being, no matter the circumstances and no matter the degree of pain, is utterly abhorrent and forever unjustifiable and that it is our duty whenever confronted by the hurt of another to combat that suffering in every way possible. But I also acknowledge—and it is to this thought that the silence of God in Lamentations provokes me—that the world no matter how it is conceived—naturally, historically, cosmically—is larger than any one person's perspective and that though we can only act in light of what we know, however necessarily partial and limited that may be, we err if we are not at the same time forever mindful of this larger reality, a reality that for present-day Jews and Christians, as for the poet of Lamentations, is given the name of God. There are no more poignant biblical testaments to the human will to live or to the aversiveness of suffering than that found in Lamentations. Neither does Lamentations shy away from indicting God for perceived wrongs committed against Judah. However, Lamentations also never forgets that it is the mystery of God's reality that ultimately shapes, orients, and sustains our own reality, and that whatever the hurt and however brutal the outlook for the present, God must continue to be addressed. For it is in the addressing, no matter how hard the questions, that an orientation toward the future is inscribed and the means for prying open the present with hope and expectation inculcated (cf. Caputo, 178).

In conclusion, the silence of God in Lamentations is hopeful and hurtful, and utterly truthful, especially to the experience of the abyss. But most of all God's silence is that which at once characterizes and provides for the very possibility and meaningfulness of faith. As John D. Caputo notes, "faith is faith in and through and against" God's silence; silence is intrinsic to God's word and God's word ultimately is "always accompanied by silence" (220, 243). Such silence, especially in experiences of extreme suffering—epitomized above all by the events of the cross and the empty tomb, by the long dark night of the Shoah, and by the ongoing scream of silence that is the Palestinian intifada—underscores faith's utter lack of absolute guarantees and its familiar marks of uncertainty and indecision. Faith is faith only if we confess the possibility of faith's error, if the risks to be taken are real, if human input and effort and intellect and interpretation is required and expended. Such faith is unnerving, but it need not lead to the death of faith. Rather, that in faith we necessarily must proceed without the luxury and confidence of knowing the outcome of our investment ahead of time and are finally thrown back on ourselves, on our own finite and imperfect abilities is simply how things are and always have been. And therefore we would do well to follow the example of the Lamentations poet, who confronts God's silence straight on and navigates that silence as best he humanly can, naming the hurt and speaking the truth as he discerns it, drawing on the language and poetics of his day, and working with and molding and sometimes even breaking the literary and religious traditions of his forebears, all in an effort to remain faithful to the God he cannot hear. Lamentations' scream of "Eikhah!" is the voice of faith as it shatters suffering's silence.

BIBLIOGRAPHY

For Further Study

Dobbs-Allsopp, F. W. "Tragedy, Tradition, and Theology in the Book of Lamentations." *Journal for the Study of the Old Testament (JSOT)* 74 (1997): 29–60.

Gottwald, Norman K. *Studies in the Book of Lamentations.* London: SCM, 1954.

————. "Lamentations." In *The HarperCollins Bible Commentary,* edited by James L. Mays et al., 577–82. San Francisco: Harper-SanFrancisco, 2000.

Hillers, Delbert R. *Lamentations.* Anchor Bible 7A. 2d rev. ed. New York: Doubleday, 1992.

Landy, Francis. "Lamentations." In *The Literary Guide to the Bible,* edited by R. Alter and F. Kermode, 329–34. Cambridge, Mass.: Harvard University Press, 1987.

Linafelt, Tod. *Surviving Lamentations.* Chicago: University of Chicago Press, 1999.

O'Connor, Kathleen. "Lamentations." In *The New Interpreter's Bible,* vol. 6, pp. 1011–72. Nashville: Abingdon, 2001.

Provan, Iain W. *Lamentations.* New Century Bible Commentary (NCBC). Grand Rapids: Eerdmans, 1991.

Salters, Robin B. *Jonah and Lamentations.* Old Testament Guides. Sheffield: *JSOT,* 1994.

Westermann, Claus. *Lamentations: Issues and Interpretation.* Minneapolis: Fortress, 1994.

Works Cited

Baird, Marie L. "Emmanuel Levinas and the Problem of Meaningless Suffering: The Holocaust as a Test Case." *Horizons* 26 (1999): 73–84.

Berkovits, Eliezer. *Faith after the Holocaust.* New York: KTAV, 1973.

Billman, Kathleen, and Daniel Migliore. *Rachel's Cry: Prayer of Lament and Rebirth of Hope.* Cleveland: United Church, 1999.

Braiterman, Zachary. *(God) after Auschwitz*. Princeton, N.J.: Princeton University Press, 1998.

Brueggemann, Walter. *Old Testament Theology: Essays on Structure, Themes, and Text*. Edited by P. D. Miller, Jr. Minneapolis: Fortress, 1992.

———. *Theology of the Old Testament*. Minneapolis: Fortress, 1997.

Caputo, John D. *More Radical Hermeneutics*. Bloomington: Indiana University Press, 2000.

Derrida, Jacques. *The Gift of Death*. Translated by D. Willis. Chicago: University of Chicago Press, 1995.

Des Pres, Terrence. *The Survivor: An Anatomy of Life in the Death Camps*. Oxford: Oxford University Press, 1976.

Dobbs-Allsopp, F. W. *Weep, O Daughter of Zion: A Study of the City-Lament Genre in the Hebrew Bible*. Biblica et Orientalia 44. Rome: Editrice Pontifico Istituto Biblico, 1993.

———. "Tragedy, Tradition, and Theology in the Book of Lamentations." *JSOT* 74 (1997): 29–60.

———. "Linguistic Evidence for the Date of Lamentations." *Journal of the Near Eastern Society of Columbia University* 26 (1998): 1–36.

———. "Darwinism, Genre Theory, and City Laments." *Journal of the American Oriental Society* 120/4 (2000), 625–30.

———. "The Enjambing Line in Lamentations: A Taxonomy (Part I)." *Zeitschrift für die Alttestamentliche Wissenschaft (ZAW)* 113/2 (2001): 219–39.

———. "The Effects of Enjambment in Lamentations (Part 2)." *ZAW* 113/5 (2001): 1–16.

———. "Lamentations as a Lyric Sequence." (forthcoming)

———. "The *haggeber* in Lam 3:1." (forthcoming)

Draper, Ronald P. *Lyric Tragedy*. New York: St. Martin's, 1985.

Driver, S. R. *An Introduction to the Literature of the Old Testament*. Cleveland: Meridian Books, 1956.

Farley, Wendy. *Tragic Vision and Divine Compassion: A Contemporary Theodicy*. Louisville, Ky.: Westminster/John Knox, 1990.

Felstiner, John. Paul Celan: *Poet, Survivor, Jew*. New Haven, Conn.: Yale University Press, 1995.

Fowler, Alastair. *Kinds of Literature: An Introduction to the Theory of Genres and Modes*. Cambridge, Mass.: Harvard University Press, 1982.

Geertz, Clifford. *The Interpretation of Cultures*. New York: Basic Books, 1973.

Gordon, Pamela, and Harold C. Washington. "Rape as a Military

156

Metaphor in the Hebrew Bible." In *A Feminist Companion to the Latter Prophets,* edited by A. Brenner, 308–25. Sheffield: Sheffield Academic, 1995.

Gottwald, Norman K. "Lamentations." In *HarperCollins Bible Commentary,* edited by J. L. Mays et al., 646–51. San Francisco: HarperSanFrancisco, 1988.

———. "The Book of Lamentations Reconsidered." In idem, *The Hebrew Bible in Its Social World and in Ours,* 165–73. SBLSymS. Atlanta: Scholars, 1993.

Greenberg, Irving. "Cloud of Smoke, Pillar of Fire: Judaism, Christianity, and Modernity after the Holocaust." In *Auschwitz: Beginning of a New Era,* edited by Eva Fleischner, 7–55. New York: KTAV, 1977.

Greene, Roland. *Post-Petrarchism: Origins and Innovations of the Western Lyric Sequence.* Princeton, N.J.: Princeton University Press, 1991.

Grossberg, Daniel. *Centripetal and Centrifugal Structures in Biblical Poetry.* Society of Biblical Literature Monograph Series 39. Atlanta: Scholars, 1989.

Gwaltney, W. C., Jr. "The Biblical Book of Lamentations in the Context of Near Eastern Lament Literature." In *Scripture in Context II: More Essays on the Comparative Method,* edited by W. W. Hallo, J. C. Moyer, and L. G. Perdue, 191–211. Winona Lake, Ind.: Eisenbrauns, 1983.

Heaney, Seamus. *The Redress of Poetry.* New York: Farrar, Straus & Giroux, 1995.

Hillers, Delbert R. *Lamentations.* Anchor Bible 7A. 2d rev. ed. New York: Doubleday, 1992.

Hirsch, Edward. *How to Read a Poem.* New York: Harcourt Brace & Co., 1999.

Humphreys, W. Lee. *The Tragic Vision and the Hebrew Tradition.* Overtures to Biblical Theology 18. Philadelphia: Fortress, 1985.

Jacobsen, Thorkild. *Treasures of Darkness.* New Haven, Conn.: Yale University Press, 1976.

Johnson, W. R. *The Idea of Lyric.* Berkeley: University of California Press, 1982.

Johnson, W. Stacy. "Rethinking Theology: A Postmodern, Post-Holocaust, Post-Christendom Endeavor." *Interpretation* 55 (2001): 5–18.

Kaiser, Barbara B. "Poet as 'Female Impersonator': The Image of Daughter Zion as Speaker in Biblical Poems of Suffering." *Journal of Religion* 67 (1987): 164–82.

Kearney, Richard. *The Wake of Imagination.* London: Routledge, 1988.

Kinzie, Mary. *A Poet's Guide to Poetry.* Chicago: University of Chicago Press, 1999.

Krieger, Murray. *The Tragic Vision: Variations on a Theme in Literary Interpretation.* Chicago: University of Chicago Press, 1966.

Knox, R. *The Holy Bible.* London: Burns & Oates, 1955.

Landy, Francis. "Lamentations." In *The Literary Guide to the Bible.* Edited by R. Alter and F. Kermode, 329–34. Cambridge, Mass.: Harvard University Press, 1987.

Langer, Lawrence. *The Holocaust and the Literary Imagination.* New Haven, Conn.: Yale University Press, 1975.

Langer, Susanne K. *Feeling and Form: A Theory of Art.* New York: Scribner, 1953.

Levinas, Emmanuel. *Entre nous: On Thinking-of-the-Other.* New York: Columbia University Press, 1998.

Levenson, Jon D. *Creation and the Persistence of Evil.* Princeton, N.J.: Princeton University Press, 1989.

Linafelt, Tod. *Surviving Lamentations.* Chicago: University of Chicago Press, 1999.

Milgrom, Jacob. *Leviticus 1–16.* AB3. New York: Doubleday, 1991.

Miller, Patrick D. *Interpreting the Psalms.* Philadelphia: Fortress, 1986.

Milosz, Czeslaw. *The Witness of Poetry.* Cambridge, Mass.: Harvard University Press, 1983.

Mintz, Alan. "The Rhetoric of Lamentations and the Representation of Catastrophe." *Prooftexts* 2 (1982): 1–17.

Moore, Michael S. "Human Suffering in Lamentations." *Revue Biblique* 90 (1983): 534–55.

Newsom, Carol A. "Response to Norman K. Gottwald, 'Social Class and Ideology in Isaiah 40–55.'" *Semeia* 58 (1992): 73–78.

———. "Job." In *The New Interpreter's Bible,* vol. 4, 319–637. Nashville: Abingdon, 1996.

Nussbaum, Martha C. *The Fragility of Goodness.* Cambridge, Mass.: Cambridge University Press, 1986.

O'Connor, Kathleen. "Lamentations." In *The New Interpreter's Bible,* vol. 6, pp. 1011–72. Nashville: Abingdon, 2001.

Paul, Shalom M. *Amos.* Hermeneia. Minneapolis: Fortress, 1991.

Poirier, Richard. *Poetry and Pragmatism.* Cambridge, Mass.: Harvard University Press, 1992.

Pritchard, James B., ed. *Ancient Near Eastern Texts Relating to the Old Testament* (ANET). 3d ed. Princeton, N.J.: Princeton University Press, 1969.

———. *The Ancient Near East in Pictures Relating to the Old Testament* (ANEP). Princeton, N.J.: Princeton University Press, 1954.

Provan, Iain. *Lamentations.* NCBC. Grand Rapids: Eerdmans, 1991.

Ricoeur, Paul. *The Rule of Metaphor.* Translated by R. Czerny. University of Toronto Romance Series 37. Toronto: University of Toronto Press, 1977.

Roberts, J. J. M. "Zion in the Theology of the Davidic-Solomonic Empire." In *Studies in the Period of David and Solomon,* edited by T. Ishida, 93–108. Winona Lake, Ind.: Eisenbrauns, 1982.

Rosenthal, M. L. and Sally Gall. *The Modern Poetic Sequence.* New York and Oxford: Oxford University Press, 1983.

Scarry, Elaine. *Body in Pain.* New York and Oxford: Oxford University Press, 1985.

Seow, C. L. *Ecclesiastes.* Anchor Bible 18C. New York: Doubleday, 1997.

Shapiro, Alan. *In Praise of the Impure: Poetry and the Ethical Imagination.* Evanston, Ill.: Northwestern University Press, 1993.

Smith, Barbara Herrnstein. *Poetic Closure: A Study of How Poems End.* Chicago: University of Chicago Press, 1968.

Soelle, Dorothee. *Suffering.* Translated by E. Kalin. Philadelphia: Fortress, 1975.

Sommer, Benjamin D. *A Prophet Reads Scripture: Allusion in Isaiah 40–66.* Stanford: Stanford University Press, 1998.

Tracy, David. "The Hidden God: The Divine Other of Liberation." *Cross Currents* 46 (1996): 5–16.

Welch, Sharon D. *Communities of Resistance and Solidarity: A Feminist Theology of Liberation.* Maryknoll, N.Y.: Orbis Books, 1985.

Westermann, Claus. *Lamentations: Issues and Interpretation.* Minneapolis: Fortress, 1994.

Willey, Patricia T. *Remember the Former Things: The Recollection of Previous Texts in Second Isaiah.* Atlanta: Scholars, 1997.

Wyschogrod, Michael. *The Body of Faith: God in the People Israel.* 2d ed. Northvale, N.J.: Aronson, 1996.